APR 83

DAMAGE NOTE: *Scribbles pp. 182*

DATE:_____ BRANCH:_____ STAFF INITIALS:_____

MUSIC ON DEMAND

MUSIC ON DEMAND
Composers and Careers in the Hollywood Film Industry

ROBERT R. FAULKNER

Foreword by Fred Steiner

Transaction Books
New Brunswick (U.S.A.) and London (U.K.)

Library of Congress Catalog Number: 82-2676
ISBN: 0-87855-403-3
Printed in the United States of America

Library of Congress Cataloging in Publication Data

Faulkner, Robert R.
  Music on demand.

  (New observations series)
  Includes index.
  1. Moving pictures and music. 2. Composers—California—
Hollywood. 3. Music trade—California—Hollywood. 4. Moving-
picture industry—California—Hollywood. I. Title.
ML3795.F39   331.7'6178285'0979494   82-2676
ISBN 0-87855-403-3   AACR2

To
Peter H. Rossi
and
Gerald M. Platt
With Gratitude

CONTENTS

LIST OF TABLES AND FIGURES

TABLE

FIGURE

FOREWORD

Motion pictures, as has been frequently noted by writers on that unique twentieth-century medium of popular culture, are an odd mixture of art and business. Cinema is a form which, in its ninety-year history, has at times reached the most sublime heights of artistic achievement, and more often, alas, descended to the lowest depths of crass commercialism. Memoirs of Hollywood screenwriters, directors, actors and actresses, are replete with stories about the difficulties—some quite bizarre—they encountered with insensitive or insecure producers. Many anecdotes in the lore of Tinseltown relate how people on the "artistic" side of filmmaking—contract players, directors, and others—were intimidated or cynically exploited; how entire sequences of films were cut or changed by the front office without the knowledge of their creators—all in the usually vain hope of ensuring box office success.

It should come as no surprise, therefore, that music—which since the inception of movies has been a seemingly indispensable part of their exhibition—has not been immune to conflicts arising between those who want to express themselves artistically and those who merely want to make a profit. Max Steiner, generally acknowledged to be the "father" of Hollywood movie music, was of the opinion that most filmmakers regarded music as a necessary evil, about which they understood all too little. In addition, it was his experience that once a picture was finished, the necessity of adding music to it would often try the producer's patience because it would hinder the preparation of his film for its theatrical release—all of which would lead him to continuously urge the composer on.

Few producers and directors engaged in the filmmaking process are knowledgeable about music, its properties, and the problems involved in its creation—nor can one reasonably expect them to be. Most are not aware of its infinite expressive possibilities, and have only a hazy notion about how it fulfills its functions in cinema. Alfred Newman, another great pioneer of Hollywood music in the grand symphonic style, used to ask his long-time friend and collaborator Ken Darby—"Why is it that our lives as musicians have to be constantly fraught with persuasion, and not-too-friendly persuasion at that?"

1

Putting the problem in question form was Newman's ironic way of expressing his frustration at the position in which he so frequently found himself, in his roles as both composer and music director, engaged in seemingly endless, often fruitless debates with musically ignorant directors or producers, trying to dissuade them from spoiling their pictures with banal, conventional, or ill-chosen approaches to their scores. (Darryl F. Zanuck was an exception, usually giving Newman a free hand.) A typical manifestation of this lack of musical imagination is the tendency of some film directors to associate a situation on the screen with the title of a familiar popular song (a practice already in disrepute in the waning days of the silent film). Many of them would insist on using such pedestrian ideas despite Newman's best efforts to change their minds, despite his long years of experience, and ignoring that he was an acknowledged leader in his field—one who had had many honors bestowed on him for his work.

Another famous film composer, the gifted, original, and outspoken Bernard Herrmann, once forcefully expressed to me his bafflement and impatience with those situations when a filmmaker chooses to ignore the advice of the very composer he has hired—someone who presumably has been carefully selected because of his talent and experience. Herrmann likened such cases to that of a sick man who seeks advice from his physician, but who, when counseled to take a pink pill, perversely takes a green one instead, and thereupon dies.

There is certainly nothing new about composers and other creative people encountering difficulties in their relations with those who purchase their services. Music historians have recorded the troubles that even that transcendental genius Johann Sebastian Bach had with the elders of his church in Arnstadt, who felt that his accompaniments and interludes for the Lutheran chorales were too radical and tended to confuse the choir. For more than four centuries, art historians have been telling and retelling the stories of Michelangelo's tragic and debilitating bickerings with Pope Julius II and his heirs over the planning and execution of the pontiff's sepulcher in Rome, as well as the pathetic tale of the severe economic difficulties under which the great artist labored on his masterpiece, the ceiling of the Sistine Chapel, because the payments he has been promised were not forthcoming.

All of the foregoing, plus countless other anecdotes old and new, amply illustrate the continuing relevancy to the worlds of artistic endeavor of the ancient adage, *Plus ça change, plus c'est la même chose.* Insofar as movie music is concerned, the situation is, at least in one respect, the same as it was in the so-called Golden Age of Film Music—the days of the thirties and forties when pioneers such as Korngold, Newman, and Steiner were laying down what another great name in the profession, Hugo Friedhofer, designated as the ground rules of film composition. That is to say, many who follow this calling still frequently find themselves embroiled in the frustrating and often impossible task of trying to communicate about musical matters with nonmusical directors and producers.

There is one notable difference between then and now which has had a palpable effect on the careers of most of today's screen composers. In the old days, most film studios had music directors, men with varied degrees of musical talent, but who at the very least had sufficient experience and know-how to enable them to discuss scoring problems and approaches with composers on a peer level.

Some were composers themselves (e.g., Newman and Stothart); most of them were studio executives, with sufficient power bestowed on them by the studio bosses so that their decisions were rarely questioned when it came to music making. (It should be remembered at this point that almost all Hollywood movies in those days were produced by studios, major and minor; independent production was negligible until the mid-fifties.) Thus a Forbstein (Warner Brothers), a Newman (Twentieth Century-Fox), or a Stoloff (Columbia) could and would almost invariably assign a composer of his own choice to score a particular film, basing that choice on his own practical knowledge of that composer's style, accomplishments, and what he—rightly or wrongly—considered to be his candidate's unique ability to properly fulfill the musical requirements of that picture. In conformity with the studio's protocol, the picture's director or producer rarely had much say in the matter.

Once an assignment was begun, the composer usually reported only to the music department, which from then on was officially responsible for completion of the scoring. This aspect of the studio system had benefits for all concerned, but especially for the composer. First of all, the music director and his department served as a buffer zone between composer and filmmaker. Thus, an important adjunct of the music director's job was to assuage the fears and insecurity many film directors feel when it comes time to deal with the musical aspects of their creations. He was able to relieve what was to many the difficult and usually baffling task of trying to communicate about arcane musical matters with a *composer*—frequently perceived as an alien, atypical,and mostly unfathomable person who, for all the director knew, was about to do unforeseen and terrible things to his film.

Filmmakers without musical training were ordinarily more comfortable with someone like a music director, someone who (it was supposed) could talk their language. His executive standing would give him a certain credibility in their eyes, offering assurances that, when all was said and done, he was on their side, and implying that he would personally see to it that the score did not ruin the picture. All this, in turn, benefited the composer, who would therefore seldom be burdened with the necessity of spending his precious (and usually insufficient) time and perhaps draining his energy and emotions in such troublesome discourses.

There was yet another advantage for the film composer of those Golden Days, something which could aptly be called on-the-job training. Many of filmdom's most accomplished composers learned the nuts and bolts of their profession from the inside, as customarily anonymous cogs in the wheels of the large, flourishing music departments which were such vital parts of the studio system. They usually worked first as arrangers and orchestrators; then perhaps as members of those two-, three-, or four-man writing teams who pooled their efforts scoring the hundreds of quickie B and C "program" pictures turned out by Hollywood in the days of double features. (Occasionally, in an emergency such as a suddenly advanced release date, this kind of "composing by committee" was utilized for major pictures.) Then, and only then, having displayed talent and having shown satisfactory skill and technical accomplishment, was a composer given his first solo scoring assignment. Among others who started in this manner were such masters of the art as Buttolph, Friedhofer, Mancini, Mockridge, and Raksin.

An invaluable adjunct to this apprenticeship was the opportunity to profit from interaction with a group of talented and industrious colleagues. As Freidhofer and Raksin have noted, musicians of the Golden Days of Film Music were constantly exploring new ideas, developing and perfecting older established techniques, and sharing knowledge with each other. A fledgling composer could benefit immensely, not only from this ongoing communal learning process, but also by seeking practical advice and suggestions from his more experienced coworkers. If he should run into a composing problem or a creative block, or perhaps was unsure about the suitability of his thematic material for a picture, he could always turn to one of them for help.

Of course, the music director himself was also available for consultation, for guidance. and—if need be—to act as a Dutch uncle, to bolster his morale, or to help lift him out of a writing slump. Alfred Newman occasionally went even further; if one of his composers was stumped for a suitable melody in a particularly troublesome score, Newman would sometimes dash off a few bars on some sketch paper, and hand the tune over to the composer, suggesting that he try it out to see if it worked.

Most of the big-name screen composers began their careers in the studio system. In the final analysis, they were able to achieve success because certain studio music directors were astute enough to see their potential, and because, as a rule, those music directors were powerful enough to have their way, to assign whomever they saw fit to score their films, and, in some cases, to sign composers to staff contracts. Indeed, it can be argued (and I for one would agree) that had Alfred Newman not been at the helm of the Twentieth Century-

Fox music department, outstanding composers such as Bernard Herrmann, Alex North, and David Raksin—all of whose music was considered somewhat radical when they started—would never have had such brilliant careers in Hollywood.

However, the Golden Days are gone, and the shape and structure of the old-time studio music department has changed drastically. Following the Supreme Court's *Paramount* decision in 1948, the major film companies began losing power as they were forced to divest themselves of their theatrical exhibition arms. Around the same time, television was beginning to replace the movies as America's favorite leisure activity, creating a progressive drop in box office receipts which the industry has never been able to recoup. With the gradual dissolution of the studio system came severe reductions in overhead and production budgets. Then, following the unsuccessful musicians' strike in 1958, contract orchestras became things of the past, studio music departments were cut back or dismantled, and staff composers, arrangers, and orchestrators were let go.

One after another, most of the old-time music directors retired, resigned, or were discharged. The few who hung on, and the men who came in to replace those who had gone, found their executive powers much curtailed. The functions of studio music directors were eventually reduced to little more than those of a sort of office manager, desk jobs overseeing minimal departments which were mere skeletons of the bustling, thriving musical operations of the Golden Days. At present, I do not know of one studio music department head who has unrestrained authority to make scoring assignments for films or television shows. Indeed, some of them have told me that few of today's breed of independent producers even bother to ask them to recommend composers.

The current predominance of independent filmmakers in the motion picture business has resulted in profound changes in the way composers pursue their careers and learn their craft in Hollywood. No longer can one be selected and boosted by a perceptive and influential studio music director, as were the above mentioned Herrmann, North, and Raksin. No longer can one have a long-term connection with a specific studio, as did, for example, Steiner and Korngold at Warner's, Rózsa at MGM, and Mockridge at Fox. Instead, today's film composers must seek success by trying to ally themselves with independent producers, with all the risks such liaisons entail in a volatile picture and television market.

Rarely can a composer look forward to going off and doing a job with a minimum of outside interference, as so many of his Golden Age predecessors were able to do, secure in the knowledge that an experienced music director, who took responsibility for the final musical product, would interpose himself between composer and producer in the event of a serious conflict of artistic opinion. Instead, today's composer frequently finds himself in direct, one-to-one confrontations with people who, skillful though they may be in other areas of film production, usually have little if any ability to understand the language of music and what it can or should do for their pictures.

Lastly (and most regrettably), the kind of on-the-job training which was so significant in the artistic development of so many prominent screen composers—and therefore in the history of Hollywood's music—is no more. Most of today's novice composers must willy-nilly learn their craft on their own, unsystematically, in bits and pieces. They work mostly in isolation, without guidance, with little chance to experiment, and without the other learning opportunities enjoyed by so many of their predecessors who worked day after day in busy, thriving, and demanding music departments.

Ever since the demise of the studio system, there have been fewer and fewer avenues open to young composers desirous of learning how to write for motion pictures. The present proliferation of university courses in film music, and the few available film-composing manuals can impart little more than the most basic technical information on a subject in which true mastery can be acquired only from hard, day-to-day, practical experience. Furthermore, opportunities to turn to experienced coworkers for advice and guidance are very rare. The members of today's freelance composing community do not interact or associate with each other as formerly. They work independently, at home or in their own studios, and there is little occasion to exchange information or share ideas. Most topflight composers are too busy and their work schedules too irregular to enable them—even if they are so inclined—to spend time imparting knowledge or sharing their musical expertise with young aspiring novices.

How do today's freelance composers cope with these changed and perplexing work conditions? How did they get started on their careers? How do the successful ones manage to remain in the profession? And how does one reach that high, rarefied plateau inhabited by the most active, famous, and highly paid composers—men such as Elmer Bernstein, Jerry Goldsmith, Henry Mancini, John Williams, and a few others?

Before having read *Music on Demand,* I am sure that I, like most people, would have responded to such questions with the usual platitudes about good and bad luck, being in the right place at the right time, knowing the right people, etc. The idea that such phenomena as continuity and success or failure in freelance artistic endeavors could be expressed and explained in a systematic, scientific way would have seemed farfetched indeed. However, that is the very stuff that has aroused the interest and stimulated the labors of a small but growing band of social scientists, including the author of this remarkable book. Readers familiar with Robert Faulkner's previous work already know of his preoccupation with and specialization in sociological studies investigating the roles, behavior, and career patterns of salaried and freelance musicians in our society.

Central to Faulkner's specialization is his interest in *art as work*. In earlier writings he has examined and questioned some commonly held notions about creative artists in commercial work and popular culture: e.g., that their attitudes toward mundane matters such as money, job-seeking, competition, and financial security are or should be different somehow from those of the average worker; that commercial work is or should be disaffecting and undesirable to a real artist; and that creative people who undertake such careers have "sold out" and eventually turn into "frustrated artists."

Faulkner has concluded that such concepts are too simplistic and do not accurately describe the feelings and behavior of artists and artisans working in popular cultures. Instead of relying too much on the existing literature in this relatively unexplored area, he has consulted directly with the subjects themselves. By means of extensive, in-depth interviews with composers and musicians, he has amassed impressive evidence that their attitudes toward their occupations and their visions of their workaday worlds are fundamentally different from those which seem to exist in the public's imagination and in the minds of some social scientists.

To a certain extent, *Music on Demand* continues and expands Robert Faulkner's research in the subject of art as work, but it is much more. In sorting out and studying the seemingly random, unpredictable, loosely organized behavior and career concerns of Hollywood film composers, he clearly demonstrates that freelance operations are far from the catch-as-catch-can, good-luck-vs.-bad-luck, knowing-the-right-people series of happenings that most of us assume.

Notwithstanding its great value as a work of sociology, this book offers the reader far more than descriptions and analyses of the networks and career processes of a group of freelancers. It also gives us rare and fascinating glimpses into the lives and personalities of the subjects themselves (although, for obvious reasons, no names are given). Having been a composer and conductor in films and television for a good many years, it is this personal, intimate aspect of Robert Faulkner's work which I find so valuable.

Others have written about film composers and composing: some writings have biographical and musical data, some describe how composers go about their work, and some have explanations of film music technique. But to date there has been almost nothing which tells us what film composers *feel* about their occupation. No one until Robert Faulkner had explored their aspirations, hopes, and fears, or examined the effects on their creativity of the anxieties, tensions, and economic vs. artistic pressures associated with their ostensibly glamorous and highly paid profession.

Here we find those nearest the craft—the composers themselves—openly and engagingly revealing how they deal with producers, how they struggle to establish and maintain their careers in a milieu dominated primarily by business interests, how they face and come to terms with the sometimes heartbreaking dilemmas spawned by inevitable conflicts between the creative and commercial aspects of their artistic labors, how at least some of them manage to reconcile the ideals fostered within them by long years of preparation and training in one of the fine arts with the often painful realities of the commercial world in which they try to earn their livings—and much more.

Robert Faulkner is well equipped to undertake this sort of double-barreled investigation. In addition to possessing outstanding credentials as a social scientist, he is an accomplished jazz trumpeter, whose greatest pleasures are working with his quintet and playing the "solo chair" in a seventeen-piece jazz band located in the Amherst-Northampton area. He is also an avid collector of recordings of the music of the concert hall and operatic stage. Lastly, he is a film buff who, like me, has genuine admiration and affection for the vintage classics of the Golden Age of Hollywood pictures. It is clear to me that *Music On Demand* will not only be of immense value to sociologists— especially to those interested in studies of groups of freelancers—but that it should be welcomed and read with gratitude by everyone interested in the history, functions, and aesthetics of music for motion pictures—indeed, by anyone who loves the art of music itself.

FRED STEINER
Encino, California

PREFACE

"A study of careers," Everett C. Hughes wrote over forty years ago, "may be expected to reveal the nature and 'working constitution' of a society." I have tried in what follows to reveal the social organization of work in the Hollywood film community by studying one group of creative artists within it. This book is about composers in Hollywood, the work lives they lead, the situations they create, and especially the ways in which they organize their activities and speak about them.

I have three purposes in writing this book: (1) to provide an ethnographic record of the career development of composers working in the film business; (2) to analyze the film industry's social structure by considering the distribution of motion picture and television film projects to personnel, and the transactions between freelancers and filmmakers; and (3) to articulate a perspective on commercial work as subjective experience, as a source of occupational socialization. Trying to grasp the "working constitution" of this industry, I found I needed a combination of approaches. Traditional analysis of social organization had to be developed with and amplified by a more immediate and direct view of the experiences, the personal effects, of such social organization. Neither approach was adequate by itself, because the two are intimately connected, and, finally, that connection itself became a major center of interest. The discussion then deals not only with the relation of the distribution of work to the distribution of resources, but also with the personal experiences and career concerns that inform this particular sort of commercial employment even if they are partly independent of social organizational specifics. I have tried to balance these approaches but always with the aim of understanding the social organization of the entertainment industry as a mode of *acting* in that world rather than as a way of thinking about that world apart from action.

Two fundamentally different conceptions of freelance social organization emerged as I improvised a line of research for myself. The first can be called a distributional approach, the second a transactional or network approach. The first defines freelance structure through the distribution of certain characteristics of film composers and filmmakers, characteristics such as the number of their film credits, Academy Award nominations or Oscars, and the commercial success of their films. Such an approach suggests that small numbers of freelancers capture a disproportionate share of the available film projects and rewards.

The transactional approach looks for complex networks of existing relations. In this formulation the two parties to the work arrangement—the composer seeking the film to score and the filmmaker seeking the composer—are treated as two sides of a complex market. On the employer side of this market, filmmakers have certain resources, options, and preferences. They have definite self-interests and valuable commodities to exchange to protect these interests. They make their choices, trying to secure the services of the composers they want with the resources they have. Money and film projects are filmmakers' most important resources. Money is power and projects are intensely desired opportunities to work; these are the means by which careers are produced as employers make distinctions among individual freelancers. Film assignments provide opportunities for exhibiting the performance capacities of the individual composer. Through work, the freelancer is observed by others exercising capabilities when given specific opportunities. The freelancer thereby accumulates a record of performance. Such a line of activity is a history of the outcomes attributed to an individual's behavior. At the same time, freelancers make distinctions among the industry's jobs and its filmmakers. When jobs occur, highly productive and visible composers are better able to take the initiative not only because of their credible contributions ("track record"), but also because powerful producers perceive them as sources of success for their own projects and seek them out.

Both freelancers and filmmakers will strive to dominate the world in which they work. Comparative advantages and even control over conditions of employment hinge on gaining access to power and publicity. "A better class of product" is what freelancers say. Since for composers this means gaining access to films and their makers as important sources of opportunity and industry legitimacy, they will seek a central position within networks of film producers. And since for the producers this means hiring only the most visible, "hottest," and productive composers in Hollywood as solutions to risk and uncertainty, they will be equally determined to select discriminatingly from within a narrow circle of freelancers. Social network or transactional approaches are principally concerned with discovering the structure of these freelance market relationships and understanding the forces that direct the flow of industry work.

The concept of a freelance career is of major theoretical importance because it promises to join social organizational considerations of phenomenology. On the one hand, careers focus our attention on sequential lines of activity and the accumulation of advantage, privilege, and access to preferred projects and employers. On the other hand, careers make us consider the freelancer's own distinctive outlooks—his estimation of his present position, his past experiences, and his future prospects. This dual outlook on changes in network position and the contingencies upon which success depends provides a frame of reference for studying one group of specialists in the most powerful entertainment industry in society.

I was advised by a number of my social science colleagues to whom I distributed earlier chapters of the manuscript that a distinctive worldview was being advanced and that this ought to be underlined. I have paid attention to their advice and stress that transactions are a core matter and deserve renewed attention in our study of modern industry. I also hope, by exploring issues of productivity, recognition, and rewards in greater detail than conventional status-attainment research commonly employs, to achieve a more plausible understanding of dominance and career success within the professions. There is another perhaps more important theme running alongside these issues of careers and the highly skewed distribution of rewards in the business world. It argues that a useful way of developing theoretical coherence in the sociology of occupations lies in adopting as one's central problem the analysis of the organization of control over work, and the ways in which complex structures of action are built and transformed in response to uncertainty, finite resources, and bounded rationality. Networks of collective action in the business world arise in response to uncertainty in profits, investments, and commitments. The career lines characteristic of commercial work worlds, such as the entertainment and mass culture production industries, take their shape from these structural problems built deeply into the conventions and culture of profit-seeking enterprises.

Most existing business transaction and interlock studies have focused on the descriptive level using elegant mathematical techniques to block off or encircle observed patterns of ties. Few investigators have attempted to theoretically model and explain the market processes through which the interlocks are generated in the first place. Fewer still have interrogated or even casually talked with the real people who populate these networks. The "inner circles"—the productive and visible members of the film community—represent in quintessential form an open system model of social structure: a loosely organized elite of employers and employees operating together to (a) reduce uncertainty, (b) narrow the complexity of their choices, and (c) increase their confidence while boosting their perceived chances of securing control over a turbulent environment. This is the view from the top. Hollywood social structure, I argue, accentuates this matching of complexity reduction and "small numbers."

The clearest indication of success at commercial work is dominance and centrality, but they depend upon a variety of factors—continuity of credits, an absence of employment difficulties, dispersion of business connections among producers, integration into the resource networks of important film-makers, diversification of projects, and power. Although throughout this volume I index success by productivity, Academy recognition, film rentals, and network location, it is this entire package of associated events that is meant by the general term *career development*. Setting off this chain of phenomena is the central career concern of freelancers who have committed their personal talents and energies to "making it" within this work world.

Since I am interested in the process and structure of success, the book begins with an examination of the newcomer's position, the peripheral position from which composers start. The first chapters suggest that working on the periphery is an odd mixture of nearness and remoteness. If we look at freelance interaction as relative proximity, the newcomer is near in that he has contact with many members of his occupation, but remote in that such contact is occasional, incidental, rather than a result of solid ties. This odd mixture makes the newcomer's integration into the company of other composers tentative, precarious; every assignment he gets at this opening stage is crucial to his advancement. Other, more experienced composers are watching, judging, and passing on their evaluations to one another.

In chapter 2 ("Starting Lines") and chapter 3 ("Up from Sprinkler Drain") I show the industry neophyte quickly learning that he operates not only as an entrepreneur with expertise to sell, but also as a social personality, an identity that he wants both colleagues and potential clients to recognize and accept. My aim is not to produce a timeless snapshot of the job vacancies and chains of opportunity, but to detail the contingencies freelancers face early on as they develop a line of freelance activity.

In chapter 4 ("No Musical Revolutions") I show how the freelancer begins to form connections with film and television producers, frequently with the help of his colleagues. With more work, the ways in which things are done become clearer to him, and he is instantly socialized into the conventions and agreements by which commercial work gets done. With more understanding, he begins to focus on finding the most desirable location in the freelance labor market for coming to grips with work problems. As a unit chapters 2 through 4 detail what freelancers consider to be the reality of their career circumstances.

The next three chapters describe the social organization of productivity, recognition, and rewards. Chapter 5 ("A Small Army") focuses on the small number of composers with from two to six credits. It emphasizes the importance of acquiring ties with diverse employers, being associated with visible film productions, and the subjective experience of increasing productivity and risk.

Chapter 6 ("Symbolic Interaction") takes a sharper and more detailed look at the variety of work situations. Composers learn that not every "credit" proceeds smoothly. The producer or director may know little about film scoring in general; understanding scores and what composers do, filmmakers may still not know what they want; knowing what they want, they may not communicate it effectively to the composer; communicating it, they may be unable to adjust to the composer's suggestions about how to go about achieving the effects they both desire. Their dealings are complicated in another way. Composers and filmmakers are linked to one another in an organized dependency relationship, but, the producer and directer may not settle on any one approach to the film; settling on one, they may not find the actual music cues written by the freelancer to their liking; not liking the score, they may throw it out, start over again, fire the composer and hire one of his colleagues. All of this makes communication crucial. Expert and client, composer and filmmaker may not "see" the same film in the same way, so coming to terms is a major accomplishment of film work, an achievement that only underscores the organized "miracle" of successfully making a film—any film—in the first place.

Chapter 7 ("Dual Interests") rounds out this chronicle of professional socialization. It suggests some inner changes that go along with more credits and resources. Given a competitive work milieu, a freelancer becomes entrepreneurial; given the prevailing uncertainty, he becomes circumspect about employers and their changing preferences; given that his efforts are always embedded in the total film project, he becomes adept at putting some emotional distance between himself and his work. He also becomes talented at trading "war stories" with his colleagues. Together they build a culture out of the troubles they share with one another.

The argument to this point focuses on the experiences of those fighting it out in the middle areas just outside the center of the business. In chapter 8 ("Centrality in a Freelance Social Structure") I move to the center of the film industry and describe the structure of networks in the top tiers. We know that those with the greatest dominance and influence ordinarily cooperate with one another to produce a large number of movies. Since business interlocks, which are essentially project-based ties between people, provide the underlying structure of Big Hollywood's action—What is the pattern of these transactions? To answer this question, I look at particular composers, producers, and movies. I show how they are connected and how participants act in relation to one another in the various situations that confront them in their careers.

Chapter 9 ("The Chosen Few") considers the feedback relationship between network location, credits, recognition, and rewards. Everyone tries to reach a position in this industry where he has some direct influence over conditions of work. Becoming selective of one's employers—one's clientele and their film projects—is a major goal for all composers. The dominant composers exercise the most selectivity of all, but selectivity also makes peculiar demands. Interview excerpts with some of Hollywood's leading figures illustrate those demands.

Chapter 10 ("Big Hollywood, Little Hollywood") pulls the argument together. Here I suggest that dominance and influence are unequally distributed even within these inner circles. I suggest the resource alternative theory provides a model not only for the periphery but for the center as well and that such a model explains how industry credits, connections, and rewards inevitably focus certain projects on certain subsets of freelancers, resulting in a cumulative advantage at the center and a poverty of credits on the periphery. Information from the fields of freelance directing, screenwriting, and cinematography is briefly introduced to amplify the essential point that freelance social organization can best be viewed as the purposeful action of many freelancers and filmmakers seeking together to realize their own self-interests.

Although many people were interviewed for this book, I would like to cite in particular those who gave extremely generously of their time to talk about the industry, their work, and their careers. For such insights as I may have developed I am particularly grateful to Jeff Alexander, John Cacavas, Pete Carpenter, Richard Clements, Alexander Courage, Dick DeBenedictis, Frank DeVol, Allyn Ferguson, Jerry Fielding, Gerald Fried, Ernest Gold, Billy Goldenberg, David Grusin, Jim Helms, Lee Holdridge, Elliot Kaplan, Fred Karger, Ken Lauber, John Mandel, Richard Markowitz, Vic Mizzy, David Raksin, Ruby Raksin, George Roumanis, Leonard Rosenman, Lawrence Rosenthal, Walter Scharf, Albert Sendrey, Richard Sherman, Robert Sherman, Duane Tatro, John Williams, and Patrick Williams.

One of the most gratifying aspects of doing this kind of social research is the opportunity to know many people who are first-class human beings as well as contributors to the making of today's music for the screen. There are five composers whose cooperation went well beyond anything I might have reasonably expected. Fred Steiner has been a friend and mentor over these years. Lyn Murray, Fred Karlin, Jim DiPasquale, and David Shire provided many different kinds of guidance and support. They offered wise counsel when I was entranced with counting credits and connections; they provided access to their colleagues when my own efforts failed; and they helped me gain a perspective I might otherwise have lacked. Agents Al Bart and Marc Newman endured many requests and put up with a variety of questions, the answers to which must have seemed obvious. Irwin Kostner at Universal took the time to show me around and kindly offered to open the complete television scoring schedules of MCA-TV. John Elizalde at Quinn Martin Productions gave generously of his time, patiently explaining steps in the sponsorship and screening process that had eluded me. Verna Ramsey and Bonnie Rothblatt, librarians at The Academy of Motion Picture Arts and Sciences, provided the necessary historical materials on producers and directors. In short, my debt to the members of Hollywood's film community is enormous.

However invaluable and indispensable, the field work experience alone was insufficient for the simultaneously personal and structural perspective I wanted. Data from extensive tape-recorded interviews had to be supplemented with information about every composer who worked on a Hollywood film. The notion of career as a succession of assignments or "work points" was the strategic link between the structural features of the freelance labor market and the attainments of individuals in the film industry. Every film reviewed in *Daily Variety* became a "work point." We compiled a substantial file of over a thousand films and their participants. Such quantitative data was necessary for inferring the structure of connections and for generating working hypotheses about the networks of collective action in Hollywood, and led me to a major finding of the sharp division of Hollywood into those who worked on a recurrent basis and those who did not. Yet major and minor contributors could only be understood accurately as parts of the same work community. So-called hard quantitative data and soft qualitative data can work hand in hand to build theory and advance the narrative; each approach can enrich and validate the other.

An acknowledgement of gratitude is due those who contributed to the collection and organization of these quantitative methods. To my friends in the Social and Demographic Research Institute, I can only put in print what I hope they already know of my deep appreciation. Dee Weber-Burdin, Jerry Wilcox, Richard Morse, Anne Shlay, Cindy Coffman, Jeanne Reinle, and Laura Martin put up with my improvisation and impatience. Paul Weiss and Lisa Sushelsky facilitated my work with industry sources such as *Weekly Variety*. They helped develop detailed files on seventeen years of film credits for producers, directors, screenwriters, and cinematographers. Their good will, humor, and detached concern sustained me during the project. Tricia Schroeder read and gently but firmly criticized numerous drafts of the manuscript, often seeing more clearly than I what I was struggling to say. Sally Ives provided a keen editorial eye and invaluable typing assistance. The Center for Creative Leadership in Greensboro, North Carolina, developed several of the figures that appear in this volume; work at the center's Innovations in Methodology Conference (August 25-27, 1981) was supported by the Office of Naval Research and the National Institute of Education.

My work has been improved in particular by the comments and support of Harrison White, Ronald Breiger, John VanMaanen, Karl Weick, Anselm Strauss, Paul DiMaggio, Anthony Harris, Andy Anderson, Peter Park, John Hewitt, Malcolm Spector, David Riesman, Patrick McNamara, Gary Edgerton, John Loy, Dorothy Mariner, Mary Ellen Kranz, and Jake Epstein. With all this help, the volume ought to be a strong portrait of career development and social organization; to the extent that it is not, I am to blame.

F. Scott Fitzgerald once commented about Hollywood: "People in the East pretend to be interested in how pictures are made, but if you actually tell them anything, you find they are only interested in Colbert's clothes or Gable's private life. They never see the ventriloquist for the doll. Even the intellectuals, who ought to know better, like to hear about the pretensions, extravagances, and vulgarities—tell them pictures have a private grammar, like politics or automobile production or society, and watch the blank look come into their faces."

Howard S. Becker, Gerald Platt, and Peter H. Rossi always saw the ventriloquist for the doll and insisted that movie making had a private grammar as well as a publicly accessible production process. My indebtedness to Becker's work on art worlds should be evident throughout. His writings suggest that freelance social organization ought to be viewed as a network of cooperative activity, an insight that transformed my conception of the nature of data collection and the analysis of how pictures are made. Gerald Platt was in on the project from the very beginning; he knew that the film industry talked of movies as "product" and insisted that I examine the "machine" that made popular culture. For arousing in recent years an interest in social organization and community decision making among elites and for arousing in me the desire to link the two in a meaningful way, I am especially thankful to my colleague and friend, Peter H. Rossi.

For her constant understanding and encouragement during our Hollywood and Amherst years together, I am most grateful to Monica, the only person with whom I will ever be able to share the experiences of the Pico Lanai, the El Cerrito Apartments, the Serrano, between Sunset and Hollywood Boulevards, and Moss Lane.

ACKNOWLEDGMENTS

The author is grateful to the following corporations and individuals for permission to quote material as noted below.

The American Film Institute for materials from their Dialogue on Film series. Reprinted with permission from the I issue of *American Film* magazine, © 1975 and 1976. Material from "The Man Who Paid His Dues," by Bernard Drew is reprinted with permission from the III issue of *American Film* magazine, © 1978, The American Film Institute, J. F. Kennedy Center, Washington, D.C. 20566.

The American Sociological Association for material from "Art as Collective Action" by Howard S. Becker, *American Sociological Review* 39 (December 1974): 767-76. © 1975 American Sociological Association.

Marshall Berges for excerpts from "Carol and Jerry Goldsmith," quoted in *Los Angeles Times Home Magazine* (September 19, 1976), reprinted by permission of the author. © 1976 by Marshall Berges. And for excerpts from "Julie and Roger Corman," quoted in *Los Angeles Times Home Magazine* (October 22, 1978), reprinted by permission of the author. © 1978 by Marshall Berges.

The Daily News for material from "For Jerry Goldsmith, Scoring Is Everything," by William Carlton (July 10, 1979). © 1979 New York News Inc. Reprinted by permission.

Daily Variety for material from "Elite Cadre of H'W'D' Stuntmen Get the Bulk of Pic, TV Work," by Will Tusher (May 24, 1979). Reprinted by permission of Daily Variety Ltd. and Mr. Tusher.

Down Beat for material from "Henry Mancini: Sounds in The Dark," by Chuck Berg (December 7, 1978). Reprinted with permission of *Down Beat*, 1978.

The Film Society of Lincoln Center for material by Robert Aldrich, "I Can't Get Jimmy Carter to See My Movie" in *Film Comment* (March-April 1977). © 1977 by the Film Society of Lincoln Center. All rights reserved. Reprinted by permission of *Film Comment*.

1.
CREDITS AND CAREERS
An Introduction

*You can take Hollywood for granted like I did, or you can dismiss it with the
contempt we reserve for what we don't understand. It can be understood too,
but only dimly and in flashes.*
> —Cecelia Brady in F. Scott Fitzgerald's *The Last Tycoon*

*He had written . . . five novels and was the hottest thing in Hollywood and
New York. It is not remarkable to be the hottest thing in either city—the hottest
kid changes for each winter season.*
> —Lillian Hellman writing of Dashiell Hammett

No one hums the cinematography to the last Bertolucci movie.
> —David Shire, freelance composer

You either have credits, or you don't have credits.
> —F. Scott Fitzgerald on Hollywood, 1937

This study began as little more than an investigation of the dilemmas and
contradictions of commercial work in the motion picture and television film
industry. I was interested in the work roles of composers in this mass culture
industry, a business loosely organized along craft lines where the conflicts
between professionals in the technical area and entrepreneurs in the business-
managerial sector were ongoing. I assumed that, as with other professions,
there was a more or less coherent set of common values and assumptions
embodied in this work community. I also assumed that networks of social
relations organized and differentiated freelance labor. I suspected that freelancers depended on their connections to filmmakers and, additionally, that
they experienced problems in their art and craft to the degree that their
clients—employers of expertise and controllers of projects—failed to exhibit
in reality the ideal held by composers.

I kept track of the projects that tied composers and filmmakers together; I
interviewed dozens of major film composers, and started to discover recurrent

patterns of accommodative adjustments between employees and employers. Gradually, curiosity about the larger social organization of freelance activity, particularly the networks of collective action and the careers of its participants, become dominant. Why did so few have their names on so many films? Was there a pattern in the ties or business interlocks between composers and filmmakers? Was the occupational structure a relatively fluid one, and how many people in Hollywood experience anything resembling an unfolding sequence of feature film assignments? If credits were so crucial, as everyone was telling me—How were they distributed? What was the relationship between productivity, recognition, and rewards?

These were by no means the only worthwhile issues that might have been raised but I thought they were of fundamental importance and had not been given the serious attention they deserved. Since the details of career development, especially the ways in which career lines took their shape from the exigencies peculiar to the making of movies, were understood "only dimly and in flashes," I tried to find out more about them. And since, as I soon discovered, these things had not yet been clarified in any comprehensive fashion, either by film critics or observers of the Hollywood scene, or even by social scientists writing on the entertainment industries, I decided that there was a need for a more substantial description and analysis of social organization and career development in today's film business than had yet been presented in print.

In the seventies there was an enormous outpouring of film criticism and writing, analyzing and explaining the careers of major film directors, top screenwriters, big-name cinematographers, highly successful producers and, of course, actresses and actors in this industry. This literature was useful for an anecdotal portrait of one part of Hollywood. But critics and other observers gave only a partial picture of the organization of credits and connections, and those who occasionally addressed these issues never found the appropriate sources and methods. Their sights were typically fixed on the major deals, the top-grossing films, and the most visible contributors. They produced perceptive studies of the careers of leading Hollywood figures, but tended to neglect underlying social processes. So in addition to the information about the celebrities at the center of the business, I needed to know about the condition and experiences of the minor contributors on the periphery, including the interdependencies between freelancers and filmmakers across various levels of productivity.

It appeared to me that Scott Fitzgerald's and Lillian Hellman's comments were indeed typical of the views held by many in the film business today, by the successful and the unsuccessful alike. Their phrases suggested that getting credits and acquiring visible credentials and work experiences is the only way to survive in the industry. Thus, I started to turn attention toward the macroorganizational level, toward a collection of information about who gets what films, who is recurrently cooperating with whom on these projects, with what commercial success, and whether the composer, screenwriter, director, or cinematographer experienced anything resembling an unfolding sequence of projects within a given period. I began to develop data files of all films and their personnel, an activity that made me an avid reader of *Daily Variety* and *The Hollywood Reporter*. I also began to speculate about who was currently in or out of favor with shifting climates of Hollywood opinion.

Scholarship from the social science disciplines, sociology in particular, should and did cut through to some essentials of industry organization, but conventional sociological definitions of "occupational mobility," "status attainment," or "work careers" appeared to lead to conventional analysis of work systems. The literature was largely directed toward the origins and destination of samples or cohorts of members of the labor force.[1] The literature ignored a crucial dimension of social organizations: the degree to which productions can be a joint effort between employers and employees, and the resultant networks of collective action. It was unclear from scholarship on mobility that business transactions, the basic stuff of industry, are sets of activities and relations in a market, and that multiple transactions over time join sellers of skill, talent, and expertise to buyers and their projects. Although there was extensive literature on occupational and industrial macrostructures and on how to define and conceptualize occupational career, there were few notions available to link the two issues coherently, focusing on an industry as a network of transactions.[2]

Continuing interviews suggested that the freelance Hollywood scene is a bunch of tangible film composers, with various track records and accomplishments, attracting to themselves and their work a population of buyers. Each film project is a separate piece of business whose ultimate purpose is profit from sale to a mass market of audiences. The internal market of business transactions, linking freelancers and filmmakers, is more important to me. This internal labor market is the primary mechanism for organizing the factors of production and decisions of freelancers and filmmakers as economic agents. The film industry is not a static structure, but rather a shifting set of business transactions constituted for the film project and dissolved after completion of the work. It was a business subject to high rates of reconstruction; highly sensitive to the sucess of individual film projects and their makers; a business in which highly expensive entertainment commodities were produced and sent out into a volatile market of potential audiences; a business in which there was much confusion about cause—the unique film production—and effect—its commercial success or failure; a business in which freelance specialists had to be part artists, part technicians, part diplomats, and part dramatic actors or actresses in selling themselves to nervous and powerful filmmakers.

At best, the film business as "an industry" was a nominal kind of classification, a misguided summary of a loosely organized, but nevertheless related, set of persons including producers, directors, screenwriters, cinematographers, electricians, production designers, art directors, unit production managers, film editors, music editors, stunt coordinators, composers, performing musicians, animators, distributors, exhibitors, and others. The single film project was the point at which all these craftsmen, technicians, and businessmen got their act together, as it were. There were major film companies in this "industry." But these film companies today are basically corporations that finance and distribute motion pictures. There was once a time when they actually made all the pictures as well, and sometimes still do. But more the rule now is for a company—United Artists, Universal, Columbia, Warner Brothers, Twentieth Century-Fox—to work on a contract-by-contract basis with smaller producing outfits and individual producers for films it distributes. The company charges for financing and providing facilities and services. Without this "distribution deal," filmmakers would be at a loss for widespread dissemination of their projects.

The position of the composer resembles more closely the freelance professional's than the salaried employee's. His work and career are organized along craft rather than bureaucratic lines.[3] He competes in a marketplace for projects and in a network for access to the owners and controllers of those projects. It was immediately apparent that access breeds success, so there is continual pressure toward monopolization of work. There is a restless seeking of access to the material means for exercising one's expertise and craft. Composers showed deep interest in how to become recognized and visible to potential employers because of the pressure to push one's image and credentials deeper into the industry's culture. Projects are the material means for making these social announcements about one's ability and identity. Here are their expressed career concerns as gathered from extensive interviews.

First, there is general agreement that the industry is competitive. Everyone talks about who is getting what, who is working with whom and with what effect. The competition is naked and frequently raw, and a composer must accept the fact that his assignments define his place or position in the division of labor. Frequent expressions of frustration and annoyance over delayed inclusion into the busy center of work and pressing concern about getting onto the right freelance "plateau" or into the right "league," as members call it, all point to the subjective effects of work allocation.

Second, assignments are valued by the extent to which they expand connections and increase visibility. A composer wants film and television assignments which will enlarge his share of responsibility, and so his chances for association with a successful film project or television series, and then, more money, business ties, and credits.

Third, there is the common sentiment that one must grow professionally, move toward increasing expertise. Self-interest centers on whether freelance assignments enlarge or contract chances for personal development in a given direction, for experienced selves, and for becoming more skilled as a composer. There are frequent expressions about being "locked" into an unchallenging television series, not "getting the better films in town," or "losing touch" with the talents that brought one into the business in the first place.

The situation is even more complicated for first-timers because employers see them as high risks and high risks, say many producers, are harder to take these days. With a sketchy or unproven track record with, say, a single credited project, many composers have limited access to more assignments. Such composers, and there are many, do not represent anything like "a discovery" to filmmakers, but rather a liability: their industry output has been tested and, to date, they are found comparatively wanting.

Finally, a concern with career development is sometimes seen as merely avoiding many of the negative and degrading features of film work. A composer can suddenly find himself engaged in lines of business ties to producers and projects requiring the adoption of skills and attitudes that constitute a liability for moving onward and upward. It is well recognized that in work worlds the occupancy of some assignments results in overspecialization or continually working within the same narrow genre, writing the same cues over and over again. Moreover, one becomes publicly known by others as the composer who writes those cues over and over, and the negative label has consequences as potential employers may turn to other, more attractive, candidates. Thus the acquisition of some credits and connections may not open up access to important points of industry activity. A career line may then become narrowed by specialization and damaged by the typecasting and negative reactions of others who have the resources to make their judgments felt as a force directed toward composers.

Additionally, freelancing is a dynamic activity and creates risks for everyone involved. There is no such thing as a sure-fire hit. The basic ingredients that make a box-office sensation are poorly understood, if at all. Consequently, there is continual pressure for freelancers and filmmakers alike to handle uncertainties surrounding credits, connections, and industry identities. The expressed concerns are about building ties with various filmmakers, recurrent "bread and butter" accounts with one or two producers on whom they depend for work. Freelancing demands many nonrecurrent or one-shot connections with producers. A "spreading of accounts" is a way of hedging bets. "A name" is a way of gaining favor and visibility in the wider circles of the business, of expanding a composer's credibility to multiple filmmakers.

A composer's position in the market affects his perception of the problems. Those with sagging productivity lines complain about filmmakers chasing after fads and fashions in hiring composers. They grumble about how employers "don't need us, but we need them." Busy freelancers are concerned about better work, more pretigious assignments where their musical talents could be utilized. They want the freedom to turn down undesirable projects and producers and complain about working too much. Such are their elegant dilemmas. Productivity is not without its advantages, in both material and artistic terms.

"The Industry" as a Loose Aggregate of Business Units

After two summers of field work and fifty interviews with film composers at different stages of their careers, I was intrigued by the shifts and turns among these freelancers, their colleagues, and employers. I was still interested in the personal and professional dilemmas of commercial work, but curiosity about job distribution, the sharpness of the division of labor into major and minor contributors drew me toward a different perspective. Why were productivity, recognition, and rewards so closely linked?

If I was to study the film industry as a segmented organization of activity, I had to develop my own means to do it because neither film writing nor sociology had done so. I needed a perspective which would permit me to understand each segment individually, each segment's relation to the networks of collective action, and the organization of work as a whole. In other words, the means for studying Hollywood had to be receptive to the multiplicity of effort in the film business and the unifying organization. Each film project involved producers, directors, a composer selected by these filmmakers, numerous support personnel, and a Hollywood distribution company to release the film; each project was a complicated and separate business in itself. The film's review in one of the film industry's trade papers, such as *Daily Variety* or *The Hollywood Reporter* was something of an event, if not for the entire industry, certainly for the people who contributed to making the movie. This suggested another baseline for the case study of composers in the 1970s and 1980s: film credits as "events," a source of information that could complement the interviewing of informants and respondents. Extensive records could be compiled using every film reviewed in *Variety* complete with credits for producer, director, screenwriter, cinematographer, and film composer. Information on films and film personnel were cross-referenced and supplemented for 1964–80 from *Halliwell's Film Guide: A Survey of 8,000 English-Language Movies; Screen Achievement Records Bulletin,* compiled by the Academy of Motion Picture Arts and Sciences; *International Motion Picture Almanac,* 1965–79; and for 1960 to 1970 films, *The American Film Institute Catalog of Motion Pictures.* In this way the volume of work could be charted on a year-to-year basis. Connections between producers and/or directors and support personnel could be located. A means could be devised from these data for inferring the structure of work relationships, and perhaps the causes of that structure could be seen more clearly. From the standpoint of the individual freelancer, each project as an event constituted the point through which lines of activity joined. The connecting lines could be called a career. The trade papers provided linkages between credits and the careers of Hollywood's freelancers.

The flow of film assignments into the ranks of composers can be seen in Table 1.1 This is a year-by-year breakdown of projects and personnel. The aggregated number of projects has fluctuated between 90 and 155 films over the past sixteen years, with a moderate increase in films scored during the 1977–78 to 1979–80 production seasons. (For my purposes, a production release season begins in October, calendar year, and ends in September of the subsequent year. For 1977–78, the season started October 1, 1977 and continued until September 30, 1978.) The number of composers with film credits has also fluctuated. Freelancers scoring films reached a low of 58 on 90 projects in 1965–66 and a high of over 100 during two seasons in the early 1970s. Ninety freelancers scored 145 film projects in 1978–79. There are more jobs than freelancers indicating the direction of selection procedures. This confirmed what the informant interviews already suggested: a small number of composers appeared to dominate the business. They also appeared to be tied by work transactions to the most productive film producers in Hollywood.

It was difficult not to become something of a credit buff, and the obsession grew for "hard data"—as massive files such as these are called in social science circles. I found that most people who work in feature films work very little and that a small number of visible freelancers are responsible for composing far more than their proportionate share of scores for Hollywood's films. Ten percent of the population is responsible for one of every two industry projects, and only a small percent of the composers in Hollywood consists of highly productive, central figures. A few names have enormous credit lists; a great many names have only one, two, or three credits. A "J shaped curve" shows the distribution of freelancer composers and their film credits.

Few composers could boast a more impressive list of credits over the twelve years than John Williams, Jerry Goldsmith, Lalo Schifrin, Jerry Fielding, John Mandel, Elmer Bernstein, Leonard Rosenman, Michel Legrand, and others. These composers were often recurrently tied to Hollywood's major film producers and directors. The credit list for producers also revealed a "hollow curve" pattern, with relatively few capturing the large share of the market. The *pattern* of credits and connections suggested that half of Hollywood's film participants work on a one-shot basis, while the central figures

TABLE 1.1

Feature Films Scored and Number of Freelance Composers Working by Year

Year	Films Scored	Freelancers
1964–65	108	66
1965–66	90	58
1966–67	100	60
1967–68	112	76
1968–69	91	65
1969–70	129	93
1970–71	129	97
1971–72	129	105
1972–73	132	103
1973–74	124	84
1974–75	92	65
1975–76	119	82
1976–77	125	93
1977–78	133	89
1978–79	145	90
1979–80	155	105

Source: Weekly Variety, October 1964 to September 1973; Variety Anniversary Issues, Volumes 41 to 47, from October 1973 to September 1980.

are more or less tightly coupled on a recurrent basis. There appeared to be a complex weave of talents, personalities, connections, and career continuity for a chosen few in the 1970s and early 1980s. The year-by-year market flow of assignments seemed to move toward less than 10 percent of all the people with credits. Thirteen people, for instance, scored 17 or more projects between 1964 and 1976. Twenty-seven composers in the "cut" just below the highly active top tier scored between 7 and 16 film projects. The forty, taken together, were in what I called the two top productivity tiers. They captured nearly one out of two films scored by composers in the film industry. These data are shown in Table 1.2, a summary table listing the composite transactions of composers and film producers by productivity categories—a crude but conservative estimate of who works with whom. Surrounding these major contributors were hundreds of freelancers with fewer credits. As can be seen in Figure 1.1 and Table 1.2, the 150 in Tier 3 (with 2 to 6 film credits) scored 477 of the 1,355 films between 1964 and 1976. On the periphery were 252 freelancers with only one credit during these years. The credit list was heavily skewed; the "big names" dominated the scene. The "little guys" on the periphery failed to score the second film that would join two credit points to form a line of activity.

The quantitative data on credits by freelancers uncovered a deeply etched pattern of inequality, but the meaning to freelancers remained unclear. The qualitative interview data, on the other hand, uncovered the meaning of career lines, but the macroorganizational patterns remained unclear. The "hollow curve" indicated that something was going on, but not what that something was as experienced by freelancers. The obvious implication was to work from both kinds of data, blending methodologies so as to compensate for the weaknesses of each and thereby extend the insights of each. In the summer of 1977 I had compiled a complete filmography for everyone who had scored a project in Hollywood from 1964 to 1977. I returned to Los Angeles and arranged interviews with people at various "points" on the skewed distribution of credits. A revitalized wave of interviews took place. Armed with the freelancer's history of credits and producer/director ties by specific films, I interviewed in a manner resembling what is known as "focused interviewing." In general the following principles were followed: (1) interviews moved, by film credit, from abstract to concrete; (2) the interviewer's treatment of the respondent, again by credit and tied to the abstract-concrete dimension, moved from nondirective to directive; (3) every effort was made to elicit details on what happened over the course of the job—from initial sessions with the filmmakers to the eventual commercial outcomes of the project; and (4) every effort was made to vary technique to fit the personality of the respondent. The constant pattern of moving from credit point to credit point, from abstract to concrete on each point, and from nondirective to

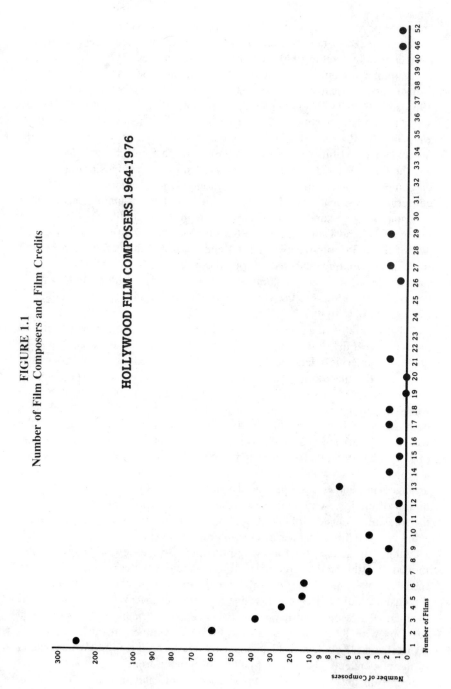

FIGURE 1.1
Number of Film Composers and Film Credits

HOLLYWOOD FILM COMPOSERS 1964-1976

TABLE 1.2

Composite Transactions: Four Tiers of Composers Hired by Filmmakers, 1974 to 1976

| | Freelance Composers[a] | | | | |
	Tier 1	Tier 2	Tier 3	Tier 4	N (Film Projects)
Producers[b]					
Tier A	32% (156)	30% (144)	28% (134)	10% (49)	(483)*
Tier B	29% (68)	19% (48)	42% (104)	12% (29)	(249)
Tier C	26% (70)	16% (42)	35% (93)	23% (61)	(266)
Tier D	14% (50)	13% (48)	41% (146)	32% (113)	(357)
	(344)	(282)	(477)	(252)	(1355 films)

[a] Tier 1, 17 or more films scored; Tier 2, 7 to 16 credits; Tier 3, 2 to 6 credits; Tier 4, one credit.

[b] Tier A, 5 or more films produced/directed; Tier B, 3 or 4 films; Tier C, 2 films; Tier D, one credit. Listed as "producer-director," "executive producer," or "producer" of a U.S. released film reviewed in Variety, 1964 to 1976. Multiple producer "teams" are counted as one "producer."

*The rows total 100 percent.

directive, was necessary to focus on the issues of career concerns, work satisfaction, and the tensions of commercial work. In dealing with important areas of connections to employers I wanted to hear opinions and attitudes, not as separate, atomized, bits of data, but in the hope of establishing a range of perspectives in which opinions about employers and agents, as well as expressions of self-interest, could be seen in a broad emotional and social setting.

Interviews combined with credits by composers suggested that recurrent coalitions of economic and artistic interest often formed among particular composers and film producers, and that the highly active freelancers in the top tiers worked with a variety of the best and most productive filmmakers

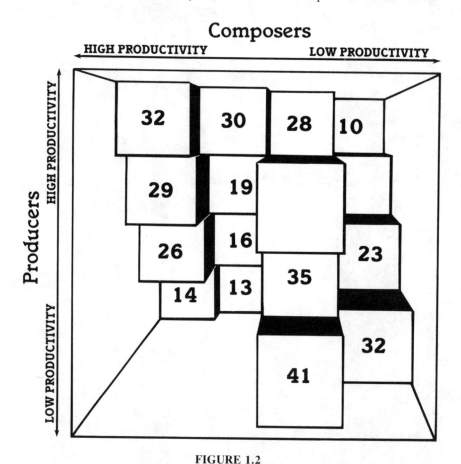

FIGURE 1.2
Composite Transactions: Which Tiers of Film Producers Are Coupled with Which Tiers of Film Composers? 1964 to 1976

on diverse kinds of projects. Diversification and depth of connections obviously counted. Moreover, networks of active filmmakers and freelancers were formed through these *recurrent transactions*. This meant that networks of composite transactions were literally packed with projects (credit points or social nodes) recurrently joining sets of employers to sets of employees. The most active film producers selected the services of the few most active composers, as shown in the upper left-hand corner of Table 1.2. With few exceptions, it appeared that a *core personnel* in filmmaking and film scoring were linked through recurrent business transactions. On the outside of this cluster the periphery was similarly linked so that producers with a single credit in the twelve years were typically linked to film composers either through the same nonrecurrent credit point or with composers who scored from two to six feature movies.

The relationship between productivity and recognition, and film rentals is striking. High contributors among composers dominated the Academy Awards, both in nominations and Oscars, and their projects are often box-office winners. Their kudos means something in Hollywood, and everyone knows it.[4] A highly productive 10 percent captured a disproportionate share of industry nominations and Oscars (see Table 1.3). There appear to be levels upon levels in the top tiers. The productive 13 in Tier 1—those with 17 or more film credits between 1964 and 1976—have a total academy recognition in nominations and Oscars combined that far outdistances the other tiers.

To a remarkable extent, considering the diverse quality of commercial films, *productivity is in unabashed alliance with success*. As noted earlier, 50 percent of composers who have a credit "event" at all experience only the single "point" in their years in Hollywood. As shown in Table 1.3, less than 10 percent of composers are responsible for over 45 percent of all films scored, and only 3 percent of the freelancers are highly productive contributors with extensive career lines and successful films to their credit. Film producers, screenwriters, cinematographers, and directors follow a similar pattern of productivity and recognition. This suggests that a single business transaction— a film reviewed in *Daily* or *Weekly Variety*—could be treated as a proxy for a point in a specialist's career line. There was an objective way of distinguishing between the major and minor contributors in Hollywood. Productivity, recognition, and economic rewards divided the industry into an active core of personnel surrounded by a semiperiphery (or middle area) of only moderately active freelancers, in turn surrounded by a periphery packed with freelancers who had only worked on one film.

The industry was segmented into center and periphery according to commercial payoffs. Each year *Variety* publishes a list of all-time box-office champions in terms of rental fees, not box-office grosses. The rental fee is the money the theater exhibitor pays the distribution company to show the

TABLE 1.3
Freelance Composers, Four Tiers and Selected Outcomes: 1964-65 to 1975-76

Tier	Size	Film Projects		Film Scores		Film Rentals (in millions) means/(sum)	Total Academy Recognition (12 years) (mean)
		Nominated	Oscars	Nominated	Oscars		
1	13	13	3	23	6	$123.72 ($1608.41)	3.46
2	27	8	2	21	5	$ 45.98 ($1241.42)	1.33
3	150	17	4	18	4	$ 11.61 ($1754.24)	.29
4	252	3	1	4	1	$ 1.28 ($323.18)	.04

F values with (3, 438) d.f., for all columns, $p = < .01$.

feature film. The box-office gross is the cash the moviegoer pays the theater to see the movie. An example will help establish the dollar volume involved. When they made *Star Wars* producer Gary Kurtz and writer-director George Lucas were worried whether it was possible to do all they wanted on a budget of only $8 million. The final direct cost turned out to be somewhere around $10.5 million, which proved to be one of the great bargains in today's cinema. When these filmmakers looked over the books a few years after release, the film had earned about $165 million in rentals in the United States and Canada and more than $70 million abroad. Since rentals paid to distributors generally run a little over half the box-office gross, customers had paid something in the order of half a billion dollars to see *Star Wars*.

A basic formula for movie profits is that a film must recoup two-and-a-half to three times the negative costs, depending on the margin of profit demand. Because of advertising, print, and distribution costs, the film must bring in several times its cost. *Close Encounters of the Third Kind* cost around $19 million—which meant that with advertising and other postproduction expenses the film had to bring Columbia, the distributors, $51 million in rentals simply to break even. This meant it had to be one of the fifteen or twenty biggest Hollywood productions ever. It was. At one point it was bringing in $1 million each day to the distributors, just as *Star Wars* did for Twentieth Century-Fox.

The ultimate hope in the film industry, assuming the picture moves successfully through the stages of filming, scoring, recording, and distribution and release, is that there is going to be a gross. There is only sometimes a net. Most films are not spectacular performers at the film rental level. A project that brings in $10 million from rentals may leave a dwindling profit for investors to divide up. A relatively inexpensive film can cost, say, $4 to $8 million to make with another $5.5 million for promotion and advertising. Warner Brothers put up less than $3 million to film *Oh, God!* and then spent more than twice as much on prints and ads. And the big cut, off the top, is the 30 percent or so the distributor—a major studio organization—takes of every dollar that comes from the theaters.

In short, getting a film made and released involves high costs and risks. With so much at stake, this industry belongs to those with continuity in the market, recurrent work, some successes here and there, and connections. Filmmakers usually work for the studios as independents, with contracts that provide for production fees as well as financing, distribution, and profits, and the people capable of putting such contacts together are almost invariably veterans—producers, directors, editors—or agents who have been putting together and selling packages in Hollywood for years. The same names appear again and again on the credits as the major studios and distribution organizations invest in people and their projects. The bulk of independent production financed outside the distribution-studio segment comes from a handful of large companies making five to ten pictures a year, who have solid bank credit lines, and still distribute through the majors: Dino De Laurentiis' Production, Roger Corman's New World Films, and Joseph E. Levine, to name a few.

The main point is that the top tiers of active freelancers across many specialities are not only the recipients of industry and colleague recognition, but are also associated with money-making ventures. That association is crucial for career development. Over and over, freelancers stressed the payoffs that come with successful films.

My new interest in the structure of the industry expanded the cast of characters. By the end of a third summer of field work I had interviewed seventy composers. I talked with twenty of the forty most active film scorers. The interviews lasted between ninety minutes and four hours. Some people saw me three or four times. Twenty-five interviews were completed with composers having 2–6 credits over 1964–1976. Fifteen interviews were with men on the periphery, either on their way in or out. The remaining talks were with freelancers working mainly in television, people rising through the ranks of an important segment of the business. I was lucky enough to obtain information on every television episode and television film ever scored at Universal-MCA, the biggest television production studio in Hollywood, and these documents, combined with interviews with the major television freelancers, gave me a detailed picture of television as a port of entry into the business-art of movies, the crucial role of colleague sponsorship, and the ways in which chains of concrete tasks were delegated. In the 1970s, composers called Universal-MCA "a training ground"; it was an organization of labor and social connections in which many of Hollywood's leading freelance figures broke in, a place where industry hopefuls began to accumulate credits and recognition.

These multiple sources of data collection began to suggest a composite picture of the relation of the demands for certain skills and talent in a labor market, the work processes that provide candidates with credentials, and the subjective experience of moving through these processes. All of these are most evident in the transactions between major filmmakers and the most active film composers in the work community.

Centrality became a major theme. Once I had shown productivity tiers from television and the periphery, through the 2–6-credit middle areas, to the most productive and visible segment of the business, I could confidently assume a certain set of circumstances for a freelancer in a central position: (a) the person is carrying on a particular kind of activity and/or maintaining a certain level of productivity; (b) the person is tied into the web of industry information, gossip, and communication; (c) the person is linked to social networks of highly visible employers; and (d) his centrality and his successful contributions to Hollywood's film projects make him a freelancer who is highly valued and sought after.

Looking at the film business as a collection of transactions, attributes, and choices among alternatives adds nuances to the description of business worlds. I show that commercial films are put together as *combinations of personages* with performance profiles. This approach to collective action focuses on the ways freelancers respond to their work world and the ways in which they try to gain individual rewards contingent on the actions of others. Walton Hamilton and his associates argued over forty years ago:

> In a literal sense, there is no such thing as an industry. Instead, there is only a host of individuals . . . engaged in a varied assortment of personal activities—the digging of coal, the smelting of ore, the advancement of personal fortunes. . . . They are human beings who engage in human activities. . . . It is amid this babble of tongues, this confusion of purposes, this drama of divergent dramas that industry is to be found . . . . Yet industry is a name for what is at best a loose aggregate of business units engaged in . . . producing a single commodity. . . . An industry is like an individual . . . it has a character, a structure, a system of habits of its own.[5]

This paragraph has a striking quality and fidelity characteristic of some of microsociology's best metaphors. That it was written by economists interested in price theory should renew sociologists' efforts toward an ethnography of social structure, encouraging us to view work organizations as the real transactions linking people to one another in numerous ways. For my own purposes, the paragraph lays bare the "divergent dramas" of loosely linked business units and redirects analysis toward how freelancers and filmmakers react together to "habits" or cultural conventions of their own making and in so doing bring to life (a) social networks of cooperative activity and (b) marketable commodities of commerce. The most attractive feature of this approach is its applicability to testing in the field. Because the film business continually produces accessible and accurate information on concrete business events, we can study persistent structures of named freelancers and film producers and generalize about the social structure within which the "advancement of personal fortunes" unfolds.[6]

Extensive data on credits, connections, and career attributes are complementary to two other approaches to the ethnography of Hollywood's film industry that I use for this study: (1) an approach that develops inferences about productivity and recognition on the basis of intensive analysis of a few "crucial" cases, and therefore carries little information about the proportion of the freelance population that follows any particular pattern; and (2) a sociopsychological approach that generalizes about social structure on the basis of self-reports of articulate individuals, and thereby carries virtually no information about what people actually do to "own" a line of work about which they then have something to say. Each approach has strengths and weaknesses; each can enrich and validate the other. My record is full of cross-references. It carries information about exceptions to its own generalizations—unlike some studies of industry which for decades have been comfortably abstract or, more precisely, conveniently shielded from falsification by multiple indicators and diverse methods. A multimethod model for inferring the structure and social psychology of career development can enliven now fashionable terms such as business interlock, network, and intragenerational mobility with a substance and meaning which more closely corresponds with what we observe in organized commercial worlds.[7]

Each Credit Is a Separate Business Project

From concept to screen, there are several basic work stages of filmmaking: raising the money, preproduction (writing the screenplay, getting the actors, director, and personnel), shooting the picture within a reasonable cost (production), scoring and dubbing in the final sound tracks and other completion work (postproduction), and distribution and exhibition. Since all the major distributors function as both producers and distributors, they usually become deeply involved in the financing, production, and sale of the producer's project to exhibitors. Unless the producers take a renegade route, the filmmaker is likely to deal ultimately with one of the Big Six distributors—Columbia, Paramount, Twentieth Century-Fox, United Artists, Universal, or Warner Bros.[8]

A freelance composer typically enters this work drama during postproduction; he is ordinarily one of the last specialists to contribute to the creative side of the film.[9] In the old days of dominant studios and booming production, composers were on staff, available for the projects that flowed in one long chain from studio into the studio-owned theater circuit, with revenues from previous films generally paying to produce new ones. Producers, directors, writers, actors, ushers, and cashiers were all salaried employees, hired hands, who kept the operation moving.

Today, the composer takes work on a project-by-project basis, hired by the filmmaker. Studio executives may participate in the decision to hire a particular composer, cinematographer, art director, film editor, or other specialist, but ordinarily the final decision concerning personnel is in the hands of the film producer. Most producers realize how important a score is to the final project. They, too, attend the Hollywood parties where many talk about the contributions such and such a composer made to so and so's film, or they consider the successes of films such as *Rocky, Star Wars, Breaking Away, The Amityville Horror, The Electric Horseman,* and others to appreciate the work of composers such as Bill Conti, John Williams, Patrick Williams, Lalo Schifrin, Dave Grusin. They may even be touched by the original songs for films such as *Norma Rae,* with David Shire's music and lyric by Norman Gimbel, or Henry Mancini's music and Robert Wells's lyric for *It's Easy to Say,* the song from Blake Edwards's success *10.* Back at the office producers and executives can simply pick up the list of Academy Award nominations and top film rental champions and their personnel.

Contracting for a composer's services starts with the employer's decision of whether to have a custom-made original score for the film, an adaptation score, a song score, or some unique combination. Top filmmakers can hardly afford the risk of hiring an unknown film composer for a highly expensive venture. The big-budget film needs proven ingredients, and that narrows the range of candidates. Although some filmmakers also realize the benefits of tapping an unknown composer with talent, one who may be hired for an inexpensive fee, this practice is typically engaged in primarily by smaller, weaker, and more poorly capitalized film productions.

Contracting with freelancers and their agents makes the filmmaker, and in part the whole business enterprise, dependent on these specialists; this dependence breeds nervousness and a search for signals that will assure the producer that he or she will be taken good care of by the composer. When he develops a music budget, the filmmaker considers which composers would be desirable as participants, valuable as contributors, and even exploitable for their cachet value. He develops a list of freelancers and then contacts their agents. Agents now serve to articulate the business-art interests of the two parties, filmmaker and freelancer, and try to work out a balance of the following ingredients: (1) the composer's current career status and that of the filmmakers and their projects; (2) the money the composer "deserves" as against the fee the producer is talking about; (3) mutual compatibility of freelancer and filmmaker; (4) whether the business deal will benefit the agent; and (5) whether the most preferred people are available to score the job in the first place.

The range of candidates is narrowed. Ordinarily one freelance composer is picked. He then meets the filmmakers and looks at a version of the film, a product that lacks only the final music score and some sound effects not included in the filming. As they look at the film in continuity, reel after reel, they talk about what the screen action, characterization, and story are developing. The composer tries to figure out how this producer works, what kind of film project this is likely to turn into, and what kind of artistic contribution he can make. In a tentative, complicated, and guarded exchange of ideas, the composer tries to "read" his client(s). The tensions of dealing with business and art simultaneously are particularly severe in these encounters. Each party knows, and knows the other knows, that they are dependent on one another, and such knowledge produces strategic interaction in which each hopes to accomplish certain objectives by maneuvering the other to define the situation in a certain way and to act accordingly. Filmmakers test the composer, get interpretations of the film's scenes, and see whether the freelancer is flexible, compatible, and motivated to comply with their standards. Composers similarly have to involve themselves in a presentation of self, which involves actively announcing their ability to perform contradictory tasks, in order to get the film project. Any attempt to fight the contradictions of commercial work—part commerce and part art and craft—results in another colleague getting the assignment, credit "point," and work connection. It is a tough tradeoff, and even under the best of circumstances composers and producers find it difficult to develop a form of communication adequate to the tensions between remunerative and musical rewards. Under the burden of tiny budgets, composers find their musical resources severely limited, which creates incompatible demands and severe conflicts. On big-budget projects filmmakers may demand contradictory things from the composer, so the "agreements" reached are always subject to redefinition; decisions about a particular use of music are tampered with by the producer and/or director, or perhaps the producer and director cannot decide what they want, or, having decided, cannot explain it to the freelancer. Under these conditions, and given the difficulties involved in talking about drama and music simultaneously, the instincts for compromise and goodwill that characterize the early meetings between the parties can be quickly exhausted.

If the partners decide they can cooperate, the business contract is worked out with the composer's agent. The terms include details concerning the fee for service, the amount of music to be written for the film, as well as the following: time allotted for composing the score, for orchestration and copying, and for recording the cues in the studio. Once this agreement is satisfactorily arranged, additional sessions are set up and the work begins.

The "spotting sessions" start. Spotting is the process of deciding specifically where the music will start and end within the film. The producer and/or director, music editor, and composer gather in a screening room. The composer offers suggestions about style, concept, orchestration, and generally how the music will advance the dramatic action. The film is ordinarily broken down into reels of about ten minutes each; each reel is viewed and discussed separately in many cases. Decisions are jointly made and the music editor writes all the general information about each "cue"—the place and piece of music—in the spotting notes—which tell where the music begins, ends, the overall time, and other pertinent facts about the matching of screen action and musical score. Each cue is timed, and, at the end of these sessions, overall timing is calculated to see how much music the project will now require. When things work smoothly, composers and filmmakers, along with their support personnel, have reached a clear agreement on the tasks to be done.

Assuming all editing on the film is completed—and it is, ordinarily, by the time the spotting begins—the film is then given to the duplicating department which makes multiple copies of the entire picture, reel by reel. These are inexpensive work prints, usually in black and white, which are then distributed to all the departments of the production studio working on the project—sound effects, editing, music, and so forth. Each department has a copy of the entire project (called a ''dupe'') which it uses in completing its tasks on the film.

The next work stage for the composer is writing the music. He works with the assistance of a music editor whose job is to prepare a detailed discription of the individual scenes for which music is needed. The editor develops a complete set of cue sheets by going through the entire film—reel by reel—and making very careful and exact notes on each piece of the film that is to have music. The spotting indicated generalities about each cue in the spotting notes, but now the music editor notes the timing, usually to a tenth of a second, and writes down every detail, nuance, and camera angle he thinks is important to the composer. Meanwhile the composer is in his private studio thinking about his approach to the film and working out the main title, themes, motifs, end title, and the other large-scale pieces in the project.

The detailed timings arrive by messenger at the composer's work site and with piano, timings, metronome, and stop watch, the composer goes to work. Composition proceeds with attention to the thematic material, harmony, orchestration, instrumental texture, stylistic idiom; musical rhythm, pace, and time must complement and augment the particular scenes. Some composers prefer to have very sparse timings and find too much detail distracting.

Composer Jerry Goldsmith's score for *Alien* (1979) took four months to complete. ''I tried to write primordial sound,'' he told William Carlton of *Daily News*, ''we used conch shells, a diggery do (a two-note bamboo instrument), an ugly Baroque horn called a serpent that emits a baritone sound, and also a sort of chinese oboe with an awful noise that cuts right through an 80-piece orchestra. Then we electronically processed the music to make it sound even stranger.''[10]

Goldsmith, a fifty-year-old Los Angeles-born screen composer, is one of the most productive on the Hollywood scene. In the top tier, he has scored over eighty films in his career, and has won an Oscar for his music for *The Omen*. Ten of his other films have been nominated for the Academy Award. The *Alien* soundtrack was his thirty-seventh score released on record. Veteran of several horror films, he said that this project was one of the most difficult.

"When you have good human relationships between people," he said, "music can function best, because it's an emotional element and not a sound effect or a description of a painting on the wall. Whatever the emotion may be—love, hate, fear, warmth, humor—music can intensify it on the screen. It helps us to see the unseen."

Alien presented challenges because there was no final cut to work with and so no continuity in the scenes, and because of the dramatic emphasis in the film. "The human relationships were the least important part of the picture . . . you're basically dealing with effects and heightening suspense. Another problem was the special effects. I usually work with a final cut. I have to have the visuals in front of me. Because of the special effects in *Alien* I couldn't get the film in a straight sequence; all I could get were scenes preceded or followed by special effects."

Whether the composer works with detailed timings, a copy of the final cut, or a combination of the two, the piano, timings, metronome, and a stop watch are essential tools. The reel footage and length of the film sequences for which he is to compose have been closely calculated by the music editor down to a tenth of a second. The film action, dialogue, special effects, and action breakdowns are timed precisely.[11]

Once a screen episode has been selected for scoring, there are several ways of exactly synchronizing film and music. The scene is a haunted hotel, let us say, and the particular film sequence calls for exactly 60 seconds of absolutely terrifying music to buttress every horrible second on screen. The composer and filmmakers know that this scene is crucial; they also know that a cacophony of screeching violins, electronically amplified tubas, and, say, "an ugly Baroque serpent horn" are likely to combine to heighten a sense of helplessness and anxiety that will drag the audience into one big, screaming climax—at precisely 55 seconds into the cue. Thirty bars of music at two bars a second will exactly fit this individual cue. The composer works through a number of conceptions and finally settles on an idea that works—"a solution." The tempo creates the movement; it is designed to convey the hysterical urge of the sequence and the actors toward the hotel's main room, where horror awaits. He sets the metronome at 120, or 120 beats per minute. In 4/4 time (four beats per measure, a quarter note receiving one beat), this would then equal two beats per second, or four increasingly resounding beats every two seconds. This is the tempo that will do it, and the tuba will carry some of the beats bringing the characters closer and closer to their fate. For the good composer, even within these fine tolerances of timing, there is scope to develop his own style, for within this 60-second 4/4 pace, he can compose a small but wild and vivid fantasia for strings.

The film reel moves at 24 frames per second, so in this episode 48 frames pass through the projector during each 4/4 bar of shrieking sound. The bars of music and the film footage are thus matched precisely. This matching process is important when visual cues or "punches" or "streamers" are imprinted onto the work print's reel for the composer to work from and for the orchestra conductor to follow during recording.[12]

This combination of screen action, compositional solution, and technical matching is only the beginning. The composer writes perhaps three of four minutes of music a day until the entire score is finished. Then the music editor and staff further coordinate film reel and the completed cues for the film score. They often work out an even more elaborate timetable for the individual music segments, film breakdowns, and footage. They mark out and then imprint onto the reel what they call "timing markers"—visual cues for the composer and conductor to follow. When the time for recording comes, the conductor will direct not only from the score, but also from the film reel projected on a screen in back of the orchestra, a screen which dominates the recording stage. The editors may imprint visual markers directly onto this reel. When shown through the projector or on the sound recording stage screen, they become timing signposts. These markers can be placed, of course, with a great deal of accuracy since the film moves through the projector at 24 frames per second. Each frame has four square holes that fit into the sprockets (or teeth) of the wheel rims on the camera and projection apparatus. With the aid of a small projection machine which can be run at various speeds and stopped at any time, reel time and measures of music (and even beats per second) can be calculated.

What the composer has written to stopwatch and metronome (to serial time and musical time) the editing department further synchronizes with the film celluloid (filming time and actual footage). Editor and staff prepare those frames which are crucial for the conductor to attend to, such as the following: (1) preparatory measures and rhythm so the conductor and freelance orchestra will know the metronomic pacing of the music; (2) downbeats of measures so that the pace will not speed ahead of or fall behind the desired tempo like the final measures or 5 seconds before the conclusion of the hotel scene cue noted above, allowing the composer-conductor to anticipate exactly where dynamics, phrasing, and his violins and tubas appear both in the score and on the screen; and (3) cues for the end of an individual cue so that the conductor can anticipate the fades or cutting of a film sequence and thus coordinate exactly the musician's performance to those cues.

Several related techniques are used to achieve a tight synchronization of music and film during recording. One is the use of "streamers." Following the composer's metronome markings, music editors determine which frames begin exactly on the beat. A white diagonal stripe is then imprinted onto the frame where the beat occurs and then onto several frames preceding this point frame. When run through the projector on the recording sound stage, they will appear on the projection screen in back of the musicians, producing, by persistence of vision, a solid white band. Thus if the music cue is written in 4/4, a streamer will appear on the beat of each quarter note. The stripes will move from left to right across the screen. Editors can imprint various cues on the reel similar to the white stripes. Sometimes streamers are employed to set the tempo of the music cue or to signal the end of a sequence. Flashing dots are used by some to indicate the downbeat of every two or three measures, giving the conductor another set of signposts to assure synchronization of score to fit, as he conducts the orchestra. Music editors set these specific markings onto the celluloid reel and also note them on the conductor's score.

Another technique is aural rather than visual. It is used in conjunction with these other sets of timing markers, but here the performing musicians are directly involved. Electrical impulses or "clicks" are transmitted to earphones worn by members of the orchestra, ordinarily those with the most exposed and rhythmically important instrumental parts. Music editors set these impulses onto a sound track after determining the precise tempo at which the score must be played to match the frames; just like a metronome, a hard, metallic syncopation accents metric time. The composer will write his film music using a book of charts that indicates metronome tempos and seconds correlated. This insures that the music will fall in the right place at the right time, as long as the musicians are wearing headphones which give them the same tempo in which the composer wrote the cue. Sometimes, the composer will decide to begin with clicks and then at a certain point into the music will have the clicks turned off and conduct the remainder of the cue to stopwatch with the aid of streamers or dots. The reverse is also possible; our composer of the hotel horror sequence started with free timing and then switched to click track in order to accent exactly the *sfz* cluster in the strings that brings the cue called "Hotel Scream: M-237" to a nail-biting climax. (M-237 means Music Cue, reel 2, Cue: #37.)

While composing the music for the film the composer *may* show the producer and/or director the themes and musical motifs he is developing. The reactions he gets are in many cases very important, for now both freelancer and filmmakers have something specific on which to focus their attention. In the inital discussion and spotting sessions they talked about an idea or concept. Now, part of the film's score, or at least some of the most important features of it, can be heard and discussed. Revisions may be requested. Some filmmakers contribute useful ideas along the way. The composer may try to incorporate these suggestions into the work in progress with a minimum of rewriting, editing, and trouble. Thus, the composer has a chance to check his ideas and specific music with the filmmaker. This may give assurance to both filmmaker and freelancer; both may return to their individual tasks with renewed security and confidence.

While composing and orchestrating, the composer works under extraordinary time pressure, and, though he will always make a more or less comprehensive "sketch" of which orchestral instruments are to play what features of the score, at times he may leave the job of actually writing out the full orchestral score to an orchestrator. Of course, sometimes, depending on the composer and the film project, the composition and orchestration will not be divided processes at all; the composer may write the music directly onto a full score for the entire orchestra without making a sketch at all.

The completed scores are turned over to copyists who begin writing parts for each musician of the orchestra. In the meantime, the freelancer is working with the music editor, telling him how he has broken down each cue, where he wants additional dots, streamers, and clicks to be laid into the film reel and marked on the conductor's score. In the meantime, the composer puts together the orchestra to record this music. Here he works with Hollywood music contractors; both have definite preferences for the freelance musicians they want to hire for the recording session. Composers frequently write a total film score, or individual cues, with particular freelance musicians in mind.

The composer ordinarily conducts the orchestra. Filmmakers attend the session to make sure the score fits properly and fulfills the intended functions, and, if necessary, to suggest how the music may be changed on the spot to make a scene work better. The music editor assists the conductor and keeps a detailed account of what is being recorded and the number of recording "takes"; he also works with a music supervisor in the engineer's booth who makes sure the music is properly performed and balanced when it is recorded.

After the score is recorded, "dubbing sessions" begin in which all the sound elements of the project are combined into one composite sound track. Music, dialogue, sound effects, and loops (additional dialogue recorded after the project has been filmed) are integrated for total effect. Reel by reel the film is run over and over on the screen while all the elements are mixed and balanced against each other by engineers called "sound mixers." Each of the separate tracks is then recorded onto one master track which becomes the final soundtrack of the picture. From the freelancer's standpoint, a successful dubbing session is one in which his recently composed and recorded music remains intact and audible. His favorite theme for the leading character is not buried under dialaogue, the timbre and range of his woodwinds do not conflict with dialogue, and the balance of strings, brass, percussion, and sound effects on the film's main title and end title is crisp and effective.

But any number of things can go wrong. The dubbing sessions are the first time that all the elements are being heard and seen together; changes may be necessary to improve the relationship between dialogue, music, and sound effects. The producer, for example, may decide that the "Hotel Scream" cue in reel number 2 is conveying too much information too soon, and that the volume of the 60-second cue ought to be reduced. Moreover, the director adds, the movie's most frightening scene is just terrific as it is and does not need that much musical emphasis anyway. Outnumbered and under pressure, the composer gives in. Considerable stretches of his meticulously crafted M-237 are "pulled down" by the mixer; the cue is now nearly lost under sound effects, except for a musical accent or punch at the important 55-second point. Or, the composer's beautiful trumpet line in the first reel, his favorite cue and favorite performance by a musician, is similarly dropped from forte to pianissimo on the soundtrack because the director vigorously insists on emphasizing a crucial piece of dialogue between the highly paid stars. The singer in the main title, who sounded so fantastic in an earlier recording session, now sounds "thin," and the composer's subtle scoring for soprano, strings, and trumpet is overwhelmed by the opening visuals. After some negotiation and muted, but controlled, conflict over intentions and purposes between filmmakers and film composer, the singer's entire track is eliminated and the trumpet track is pulled forward into audible foreground. Situations like these can and do occur, often. In these dubbing sessions, freelancers begin to understand the collaborative nature of filmmaking. Where the composer was a hero and champion during the recording of the music, in these sessions he often watches his music and himself change to accommodate more powerful interests. It is here that parts of Hollywood are understood not so dimly but in flashes.

Finally, when the filmmakers, composer, and sound editors eventually settle on the composite sound track, the "answer print" is prepared for screening. In this final screening, "last chance" decisions are quickly made about the overall quality of the work to date. They may consider some reediting and rerecording, but if everything seems satisfactory on this film production that is now running costs into the multimillion dollar area, the film is sent back to the lab where multiple prints are made. The film is now ready for commercial distribution.

The composer has worked months on his contribution and weeks in collaboration with editors, mixers, filmmakers, orchestrators, musicians, contractors, and numerous production personnel. Ever since the completed music score for the film left his study, matters have been moving slowly out of his hands. Cooperation has meant dealing with others whose self-interests, perspectives, knowledge of cinema, and awareness of music's functions differ from his own. Negotiation among these outlooks constitutes a major part of his commercial work life. The entire experience constitutes one credit, one point in an unfolding sequence of assignments, challenges, and compromises. Once the film is distributed, he becomes vulnerable to the reactions of an even wider audience of industry personnel—filmmakers he does not even know personally, composer colleagues, and, most impersonally but most importantly, the audience that pays to see the film in which his music is embedded. He knows that many "civilians" do not even realize that a score is written for the film; he also knows that "insiders" of his own industry are not likely to examine his contribution for its own merit but rather in relationship to the picture's success or failure. Such knowledge is sobering.

He hopes for good reviews and favorable reactions to his music. If cooperation has been smooth he hopes to work again with these filmmakers. For now, he tries to put to rest these uncertainties. His immediate concern is getting the next assignment, a chance to go through the entire process again.

Notes

1. This literature is large and controversial. See specially Peter M. Blau and Otis Dudley Duncan, *The American Occupational Structure* (New York: Wiley, 1967); Otis Dudley Duncan, David L. Featherman, and Beverly Duncan, *Socioeconomic Background and Achievement* (New York: Free Press, 1972); Alan C. Kerckhoff, "The Status Attainment Process: Socialization or Allocation?" *Social Forces* 55 (1976): 368–91; Patrick M. Horan, "Is Status Attainment Research Atheoretical?" *American Sociological Review* 43 (1978): 534–41.
2. The literature on occupations and society has been summarized in the following texts: Richard H. Hall, *Occupations and the Social Structure* (Englewood Cliffs, NJ: Prentice-Hall, 1969, 2nd Ed.); George Ritzer, *Working: Conflict and Change* (Englewood Cliffs, NJ: Prentice-Hall, 1972, 2nd Ed.); Paul D. Montagna, *Occupations and Society* (New York: Wiley, 1977).
3. Arthur L. Stinchcombe, "Bureaucratic and Craft Administration of Production: A Comparative Study," *Administrative Science Quarterly* 4 (1959): 168–87; Paul M. Hirsch, "Processing Fads and Fashions: An Organization-Set Analysis of Cultural Industry Systems," *American Journal of Sociology* 77 (1972): 639–59.
4. Unlike most of the other categories in the Academy of Motion Picture Arts and Sciences—editing, acting, directing, etc.—the creators themselves rather than academy members must make the first move in the Oscar race for the music awards. They do this by filing an official submission form with the academy. In general, the procedure is for members of the various branches of the academy to choose nominees by voting from a reminder list to all eligible people. Depending on the branch, either a preliminary list of ten nominees or the final five nominees are decided from that initial balloting.

    And so with the awards for best original score, best original song score and its adaptation, or the nominations for best adaptation score. Like some of the academy's twelve branches (music, actors, directors, cinematographers, sound, writers, art directors, editors, producers, short films, executives, and public relations), the music branch also uses a reminder list of eligible films. The branch depends on the freelancers to "certify that . . . the work is an outstanding achievement worthy of consideration for nomination for an Academy Award," to use the wording in the academy's rulebook. It is therefore not necessary for the writer or adaptor of the music to be an academy member, either. A member of the music branch may recommend that a work not his or her own be considered for an Oscar, but the creator still is obligated to fill out the appropriate forms.

The function of this branch, like the function of all academy branches, is to honor achievement through the awards. It is separate from the guilds like the American Federation of Musicians, American Guild of Authors and Composers, American Guild of Musical Artists, American Guild of Variety Artists, Composers and Lyricists Guild of America. The requirements for getting into the segment are these: a candidate must have three theatrical film credits that, in the opinion of the executive committee of the branch, have achieved a level of distinction. It also takes two sponsors. At times, a composer may have fewer than three film credits, but the work is deemed so much of a contribution or so significant that admittance is granted anyway. There are over 200 members of the music branch governed by a 26-member executive committee. In short, the composers and song writers themselves retain control over who moves into consideration and who is selected from among the talent contributing scores to Hollywood films.

5. Walton Hamilton et al., *Price and Price Policies* (New York: McGraw-Hill, 1938). See also Norman K. Denzin, "Notes on the Criminogenic Hypothesis: A Case Study of the American Liquor Industry," *American Sociological Review* 42 (1977): 905–20.

6. Sociologist Harrison C. White has suggested that we view the existence of a particular market of activities as problematic, asking if concrete "bunches of producers and buyers can get an act together." I am taking the leads of Hamilton and White and saying that putting on a "joint performance" is literally the issue for internal labor markets organized along craft modes of production. Harrison C. White, "Markets as Social Structures." Plenary Session: Theory and Research, American Sociological Association Meetings, Boston, 1979.

7. The idea of social organization I will utilize here is in Harold Garfinkel, "Some Sociological Concepts and Methods for Psychiatrists," *Psychiatric Research Reports* 6 (1956): 181–95: "The term 'an organization' is an abbreviation of the full term 'an organization of social action.' The term 'organization' does not itself designate a palpable phenomenon. It refers instead to a related set of *ideas* that a sociologist invokes to aid him in collecting his thoughts about the ways in which patterns of social actions are related. His statements about social organization describe the *territory* within which the actions occur; the *number* of persons who occupy that territory; the characteristics of these *persons*, like age, sex, biographies, occupation, annual income, and character structure. He tells how these persons are *socially related* to each other, for he talks of husbands and wives, of bridge partners, of cops and robbers. He describes their *activities*, and the ways they achieve social *access* to each other. And like a grand theme either explicitly announced or implicitly assumed, he describes the *rules* that specify for the actor the use of the area, the numbers of persons who should be in it, the nature of activity, purpose, and feeling allowed, the approved and disapproved means of entrance and exit from affiliative relationships with the persons there."

8. Thomas Guback, "Theatrical Film." In *Who Owns the Media? Concentration of Ownership in the Mass Communications Industry*, ed. Benjamin M. Compaine (New York: Harmony, 1979); *Analysis and Conclusions of the Washington Task Force on the Motion Picture Industry* (Washington, D.C.: Government Printing Office, 1978); Axel Madsen, *The New Hollywood: American Movies in the 70s* (New York: Crowell, 1975). See also *Daily Variety*, 46th Anniversary Issue (October 30, 1979).

9. For the aesthetic of film music see Hanns Eisler, *Composing for the Films* (New York: Oxford University Press, 1947); Frank Skinner, *Underscore* (New York:

Criterion Music Corporation, 1960). There are also several sources which provide valuable biographic and interview material on the best-known screen composers. Tony Thomas, *Music for the Movies* (New York: A. S. Barnes, 1973); Irwin Bazelon, *Knowing the Score: Notes on Film Music* (New York: Van Nostrand Reinhold, 1975); Mark Evans, *Soundtrack: The Music of the Movies* (New York: Hopkinson & Blake, 1975); Clifford McCarty, *Film Composers in America: A Checklist of Their Work* (New York: Da Capo, 1972; repr. of 1953 ed. with minor corr.).

10. William Carlton, "For Jerry Goldsmith, Scoring Is Everything," *Daily News* (July 10, 1979).

11. If film composing is an art, it is not an art like sculpture or even painting where one can make almost anything out of the raw materials. Rather, it is work very much like architecture in which it is possible to show disciplined creativity by producing elegant and efficient work while shaping raw materials characterized by finite budgets, limited time, accepted customs by which things are done, client or employer ideas and preferences for what is needed, and business reasons for reducing complexity. On synchronizing music to picture see Earle Hagen's *Scoring for Films* (New York: Wehman, 1972); Roy M. Prendergast, *Film Music: A Neglected Art* (New York: Norton, 1977).

12. For the activities between contractors, composers, and the performing musicians in Hollywood see Robert R. Faulkner, *Hollywood Studio Musicians: Their Work and Careers in the Recording Industry* (Chicago: Aldine-Atherton, 1971).

2.
STARTING LINES
Entry Points and the Web of
Colleague Affiliations

*At the start I faced the big problem we all face: you can't work in this town
because you lack experience, and you can't get the experience unless you get
the work.*

—Freelancer with two film credits

He who does not have a dog to hunt with—must use a cat.

—Brazilian proverb

Conventional indications of career development such as promotion, increases in responsibility, and changes in skill, status, or salary do not apply
easily to freelancing. There is no stable hierarchy and therefore no clearly
marked line of career progression. Even the work itself is unstable and un-
connected since filmmakers and composers come together for one project and
then move on to another project with different partners; each project is a
separate business. How does one examine such a field?

The problem is not one of ethnography or of listening to our respondents
more closely and organizing their work biographies more exactly. Freelancers
are unusually artful in their quotable and anecdotal reconstruction of their
pasts, but such reconstruction usually reflects a rather banal "I did it my
way" individualism unrevealing of anything beyond the individual. Nor is
the problem one of making up more precise definitions of our subject matter.
We have had quite enough of those. Their very number is a symptom of our
malaise in ordering observations about work and early career development in
the film industry.

It is legitimate and academically fashionable to look for correlates to "success"—the forces that shaped a current level of status attainment. Most of
our social science studies do just that by interrelating the origins and traits
of people and their social and occupational rank at the time of the study.
These correlations then become the highlighted conclusions. Such findings

are not very enlightening, not only because they formulate mobility as governed primarily by the qualities of the candidate, but also because they glide past that which we most want to know: What complex of directed actions, shared cultural experiences, and market relationships finally brings together the available people and available jobs? Every film is the result of such a matching process, and from the perspective of any one person working on it, can be seen as a point in a line of activity composed of several or many such points. We need to see how those points occur and, if possible, where they lead.

At any given moment, this occupation contains people at different stages of their careers.[1] Some have already "made it," at least for the time being; others are on their way up into the top echelons; some are stuck in the middle ranks; still others are getting their "first shots." Of the 125 feature films scored from October 1976 to September 1977, 22 were scored by the busiest composers in town, those with considerable track records and access to the heftiest assignments with the heaviest filmmakers. Twenty-five films were done by composers with recognizable names for equally recognizable producers. Thirty-four films were written by those with steady, moderately productive credits. Forty-four were scored by newcomers with no previous feature credits.

For some of the newcomers, this first film is the reward of years of dues-paying and climbing up through the ranks of television. They may have started by helping colleagues in a jam, moved to doing episodes here and there, landed their own television series, then a movie for television or a television pilot, then, with growing reputation and visibility in the business, they received their big break into a full-length feature.

But for others this one film will be the beginning and the end of their Hollywood careers, if we can call them that. Typically, their previous credits are slim and their connections in the business limited. While their work in the record business, commercial jingles jungle, jazz world, rock and disco business, off-Broadway, even the academic groves may be impressive, they are unable to sustain a line of work in the film industry. Such brief careers are not the exception but the rule in Hollywood. Of the 442 composers on 1,355 U.S. films produced, released, and reviewed from 1964 to 1975, 57 percent (252) have only *one film credit*.

These composers discovered that, though work in Hollywood is accessible, continuity of work may not be. They are usually tied to film producers who are themselves trying to get a start—almost 70 percent (174 composers) worked with producers who had only one or two films to their credit over the same twelve-year period. These similarities in rank, measured by number of films, suggest that like hires like. Low-volume buyers hired low-volume sellers (composers) for their, typically, low-budget features.

If there is one thing harder to acquire in the film business than a start, it is "legs"—professional durability, the talent to keep on running. Of the 228 composers who scored films from 1964 to 1969, 58 percent (132) failed to continue their string into the seventies; 71 percent (92) of these 132 composers worked on only one film. Does this pattern hold for the seventies? Only 96 of the 310 freelancers credited with films released between 1970–71 and 1975–76 have credits going back more than six years, which means that a full 69 percent (214) of the 310 working in the seventies were brand new to the industry. One veteran composer with several nominations and two Oscars summed up this perspective when he said: "The greatest award in Hollywood is to be asked back again." Those who are not, and there are plenty, only confirm the gloomy wisdom of this town's tragedian, Scott Fitzgerald—"there are no second acts to American lives."

Ports of Entry: A Focus on Universal Television

Given the high casualty rate among composers working in features, there must be other points of entry, other ways of making and sustaining connections, and other strategies for building a reputation and a string of work. There are. The main area, though not the only one, in which the novice freelancer acquires experience and makes connections is in television. In the mid-sixties and seventies the principal centers of activity have been Universal, Quinn Martin Productions, MGM Television, Paramount, Screen Gems, Lorimar, Spelling/Goldberg Productions, MTM Enterprises, and Warner Brothers Television.

Half the composers who have respectable strings in features now either came up through television or started out with one feature and then "dropped back" into episodic or series television. The powerhouse of the industry is Universal television. MCA (Universal) is the twenty-sixth largest industrial company in California, the largest television production company in Hollywood, and the major employer of freelance composers, performing musicians, copyists, contractors, sound mixers, music editors, recording engineers, and other related music staff.

Over half of the inner circle of composers in the early 1970s—the top 7 percent who did 35 percent of the feature film work—got their starts by working at Universal. David Grusin, Quincy Jones, Lalo Schifrin, John Williams, and others are Universal alumni who came up the ranks, some under the tutelage of Stan Wilson, who for years was the head of the music department.

At the height of one television season in the early 1970s *Daily Variety* reported 30 composers at work on various Universal television and film projects. A total of 1,874 performing musicians, at an average of 75 per day, were hired by the studio during one five-week period. Henry Mancini, David Grusin, and John Barry were scoring feature films in those weeks, while on the television side, Mancini was writing the theme music for the "NBC Mystery Movie," Elmer Bernstein was doing the main title for "Owen Marshall, Counselor at Law," Alex North was scoring "The Man and the City," Lalo Schifrin was working on a project called "Partners," and Patrick Williams and Robert Prince were scoring television movies under the banner of "World Premieres" and "ABC Weekend Movie."

Other freelancers were scoring main titles and episodes for continuing television series: Quincy Jones on "Ironside," John Lewis on "Night Gallery," Nelson Riddle on "The D.A.," Fred Steiner on "O'Hara, U.S. Treasury," and Frank Comstock on "Adam-12."

A larger number of freelancers worked on an array of projects such as television movies, main titles for continuing series, and the follow-up week-to-week episodes for those series. David Grusin divided his efforts on features and the main title for the popular "The Bold Ones" plus an "ABC Weekend Movie" and "World Premiere." Jerry Fielding was writing the theme music and episodes for "McMillan and Wife." Lyn Murray was working on a couple of television movies as well as weekly episodes for "Owen Marshall" and "The Bold Ones." Billy Goldenberg, who was much in demand at Universal in these years, was assigned the mystery series "Columbo," "Alias Smith and Jones," and a ninety-minute television movie. His colleague David Shire was writing the theme music for "McCloud," doing episodes for a series called "Sarge," and also landing a "World Premiere" television movie. Leonard Rosenman composed the main title and all the episodes for the long-lived series "Marcus Welby," in addition to scoring a ninety-minute television show.

Other composers at Universal were working mostly in week-to-week segments or episodes for series that had already been kicked off by their colleagues. The late and very gifted Oliver Nelson was contributing to episodes for "Ironside," for which his colleague Quincy Jones had earlier written the main title; he also scored weekly segments for many other series, including the popular "Night Gallery." John Tartaglia, Richard Hazard, J. J. Johnson, and Marvin Hamlisch were all working primarily on series episodes such as "The Bold Ones," "Partners," "Alias Smith and Jones," and "Owen Marshall," with little crossover into television movies or writing their own series.

This dense thicket of specific assignments can be trimmed by looking at the kinds of jobs there are in television and who does them. Distinctions can be drawn by whether the composers are working on *newly created projects,* whether they are *added on to continuing projects,* or whether they are doing a *combination* of originals and add-ons. Ordinarily, newly created jobs such as 90- to 120-minute television pilots, movies for television, and new series are the most desirable, for the composer has a chance to develop the musical approach, style, and overall idiom from scratch. Newly created television projects also offer top money; two-hour pilots can now carry budgets of up to a million dollars and sometimes more. At typical composers' fees of $5,000 for a two-hour film, $3,500 for a 90-minute production, and $1,500 for a one-hour show, the money up front is attractive. It is all the more attractive if a freelancer can put together a string of these in one season. If a series is successful and pulls a long run in syndication, like "Star Trek," "Kojak," or "Mission: Impossible," a composer's ASCAP or BMI income (for the theme music and weekly episodes) can be substantial and long-lived.

Newly created series not only offer good money for those who first score them, but also open up opportunities for others. A "name" composer with a hefty track record is a valuable resource for television producers and directors, since he boosts the whole image of the project. Bargaining because of his reputation and proven worth, he can work out a deal where he writes only the music for the television pilot and a few of the opening segments. He will establish the style and conventions of the series—themes, motifs, orchestration, which characters get emphasis in the music—and then, having developed the approach, turn over the weekly work to someone else. A composer with clout can demand an "automatic out," meaning that he will agree to get the series going, but can be released from obligations if a "better project" (a television movie or feature film assignment) occurs. But who will carry on his ideas?

A leading composer can recommend a favored colleague. This is a kind of inheritance. In order to protect his own position, the lead man will make sure the colleague knows his stuff, understands the project, and recognizes his obligation to the producers. Perhaps the two composers have worked together before; maybe the producer even knows and trusts the colleague now being brought in. All this is done to provide continuity and smooth transition from the crucial opening segments of a series into the week-by-week routine. If the series does well and if the producer is happy with the replacement's music, the add-on will find himself with a home, at least for that season. The next year, however, it is a new ball game, and the newcomer must again compete with his peers and colleagues. His survival depends on whether he has proved himself on the series and on the reputation he acquires among colleagues and producers.

Openings occur then because the headline composer is in demand and wants to move on to better assignments. They also occur because of day-to-day production pressures. The television scoring season is going full tilt from September until early January. Series composers find themselves hemmed in with too little time and too much music to write. Episodes to be scored start arriving late from the editors; the producer and director decide the dailies are awful, recut many scenes, call the composer and ask him to rescore some of the work he has already done; work piles up, pressure mounts, good will evaporates.

Pressed by these exigencies, the freelancer does what he can in a craftsmanlike and professional way, but as deadlines tighten around him, he turns to his network of colleagues. In Hollywood, there are many, many helping arrangements running the full spectrum from parasitic exploitation to mutual colleagueship. Whatever the form, the problem is to find someone who will competently and quickly turn out the two, three, or four minutes of music needed by the deadline. A composer can seldom, if ever, risk going into a recording session with cues left unwritten, though some do—either because their perfectionism has kept them from meeting the deadline, because they were unable to quickly find suitable colleagues to help them, or because they are confident that the performing musicians will pull them through. When composers do get help, they create short-term opportunities for those they turn to, opportunities not only for work experience but also for connections.

The productivity of Universal television makes this studio an excellent place to study the distribution of composers among the available projects. A total of forty freelance composers worked at this studio in the 1971 production season, for example. Fifteen composers with long trackrecords in the business worked exclusively on new projects. They scored 16 movies for television and series pilots, doing 31 percent of the newly created work. They were not the most active, however. A highly productive core of eleven freelancers did 69 percent (35) of the 51 newly created projects and worked on 50 percent of the 122 individual television episodes. By contrast, the top fifteen did a total of only 19 series episodes, suggesting that they scored the main titles and first weekly series episodes and then moved on to other projects.

Fourteen of the forty composers were on the perimeter of all this action. They scored a total of only 41 episodes and did not work on any newly created projects. One in three were newcomers to Hollywood with no prior industry credits, and the others' experience varied. Some had slipped back from the middle ranks of film work in the 1960s; others, who had recently climbed up the ladder from episodic television work into more and better assignments, returned to Universal for a brief assignment on a television episode, while others helped out an overworked colleague on a segment or two.

Three out of four freelancers who were doing only episodic "add-on" work at Universal from 1970 to 1975 still have no feature film credits. By contrast, over 60 percent of those who had scored 7 or more television movies, series, or pilots scored anywhere from 2 to 24 films in those six years. This suggests that jobs added on to existing series are filled by industry newcomers, involve the most routinized and ready-made assignments in the industry, and are filled through a chain of recommendations. A composer on a project needs help and passes work on to those at the periphery; through colleague referral, newcomers are matched to routinized and low-risk work.

The direction of referral is always from center to periphery. The two core groups—Universal's fifteen top composers and eleven busy freelancers—pass work out to others. Such referral or sponsorship certainly helps the rookies in their search for experience, but it is a slow way to get work. Only two peripheral composers scored more than six shows in 1971, for example. Half did only *one* segment. This suggests the slowness and caution with which newcomers are worked into the division of labor at one studio.

The caution of referral is related to the calculus of risk in commercial work. A core colleague who wants to bring in a recruit can reduce his own risks by giving the protégé routinized and ready-made assignments. The more clearly defined the tasks, the easier it is to socialize a neophyte into the assumptions of commercial work, the ins and outs of studio politics, the technical demands of scoring for small orchestras and a three-inch television speaker, and the ways in which colleagues have to help one another. The matching of rookie to routine work serves a number of purposes. First, it reduces the amount of time a sponsor has to spend coaching the neophyte. Second, it assures that continuity will be built into the score for the ongoing series. Third, this work gives the incoming rookie time to become known as a potential colleague, personality, and genuine composer. And last, it reduces the fear of other freelancers that the newcomer may be moving along too fast and, more important, that he may be encroaching on their own share of available work.

A start on the perimeter is no guarantee of inclusion into the center of available work or of a smooth, uniform climb to better assignments. Three years later only *four* of the fourteen who were added on in 1971 became members of the *new* core group doing large shares of newly created projects and series. They replaced a couple of composers who moved onward and upward into film work and more exclusive television. Two rookies in the industry in the early seventies shot past their colleague competitors and by the mid-seventies were in demand by many feature film producers in Hollywood. A composer interviewed when he started to work at Universal and then five years later when he had, as he put it, "graduated," described the situation this way:

> To get the work and the experience, you need an "in," so you can show people you know your craft, won't screw up their project, and won't embarrass the guy who's helping you. I don't know any composer who wants to spend his whole life in television, and especially doing just episodes—week-in and week-out. Everybody has the same set of things they want to get going. They want to write music that they get

a certain amount of satisfaction from, and that pays well, and that leads to better work, and that feels like they're not swinging a toothpick when they should be swinging a 32-ounce bat. We want to be challenged to our full capabilities. There's a serious game to be played here. There's a lot of politics and hopefully if you stay in there long enough you will get those things going that you want to get going. That's the way it looks from this angle.

The angle, of course, is stratificatory. What he talks most forcibly about is work and connections, and what it says about them is that they are crucial. Getting known, developing a reputation, securing ties with others, and moving ahead are all crucial and all related.

Sponsorship as a Matching Process

Coming into the business, the newcomer must get his bearings. He must learn who is in favor and who is not, who is willing to help him and who is not, and who can be trusted and who must be tactfully avoided. He finds a sluggish market for his skills; the avenues to full expression and quick visibility are blocked, and he often has to do what others want him to do against his own resistance. If he came into the business at Universal in 1975 he would see eight to ten freelancers who, it seemed, were doing everything in sight. That studio had again emerged as the king of television production with twenty television movies, pilots, and specials, and twenty series. The number of episodes rose from 122 in 1971 to 215 in 1975, an increase of 77 percent. "The Six Million Dollar Man," "Kojak," "Marcus Welby," "Baretta," "Rockford Files," and "Emergency," all kept lead writers and many newcomers like himself busy. As in the early 1970s there were forty freelancers working, but a smaller core group of eight to ten were scoring more than 70 percent of the newly created projects and 60 percent of all the episodes. When he got work it was because these freelancers passed their work out to freelancers like himself.

In some cases the newcomer was asked to "ghost" for another composer, to do the work through usually without official credit. Often the man who gave him the job was not interested in recommending him to another producer or director. In other instances, he might be eased into a project as another colleague supervised him, showed him the conventions and routines of the show, and then mentioned the quality of his writing to the producer of the series. In some cases he received official cue sheet credit for his work. In other work he might function simply as a hired hand, "helping" someone, doing the job, getting the credit, but without active recommendation from the person he "helped."

Few newcomers complain about these arrangements since it is not wise, after all, to get a reputation as a troublemaker. He is told everyone has to learn his craft, undergo hardship, and generally "pay his dues." He does not understand how things are done at the studio, and the only people who can teach him are concerned about getting assignments for themselves. As a seller in the marketplace of talent, he sees that he does not have much to offer the buyers. Producers do not know who he is, already have their choices of composers, and are not willing to give him a chance to work.

Often the beginner's response to these situations is to look elsewhere for a job, like another television studio or a potential filmmaker who has a low-budget project in the works. But since he is unknown and inexperienced this is also difficult. Some pack their bags and leave almost immediately, but if the rookie decides to stay, he must learn to make sense of what is happening to him and others. If he wishes to continue, he has to learn how to improve his market position and his visibility in the eyes of others. Since each work assignment can be conceived of as a separate business, he faces a changed situation with different colleagues, cues, and important others each time he goes to work. What does not change is the importance of having good information and contacts.

Coalitions among composers are formed for specific work projects and are short-lived ties which involve an exchange of jobs, favors, and friendship. But they can be easily jeopardized by (1) shrinkage in the volume of work available, (2) movement of the mentor or "senior partner" into feature films and away from television, (3) reluctance of the television producer to go along with the arrangement, and in some cases (4) rivalry between mentor and newcomer. Some more established composers, fearing the competition, are not interested in passing work out to those on the edge of the business.

Freelancing tends to be a combination of occupational individualism and colleagial solidarity, a combination which is most visible in the complex system of sponsorship. A sponsor is a freelancer who assumes responsibility for a newcomer and, by carefully following the etiquette and politics of moving a new person in, presents the candidate for approval or confirmation by significant others.[2] The sponsor makes himself responsible for teaching the newcomer "the ropes" and overseeing his welfare as he is moved into work openings where he can learn more about commercial routines, potential colleagues, and all the important others who contribute to work. The sponsor implicitly promises his colleagues that the rookie will not be allowed to "muscle in" on their own work, assuring them that the limits within which a candidate is judged will not be unfairly widened. After all, work and potential competitors come and go, but collegial relationships must be maintained.

The sponsor's motives are partly altruistic; there is satisfaction in teaching what one knows and giving a newcomer the chance to break into the business. There are also strong interpersonal ties between composers, strong preferences for being in the company of colleagues who share your own values and tastes. In addition work pressures make it absolutely essential that a busy composer find someone he can depend on. If other, more established composers are busy, he naturally turns to those who are not as busy. All these motives and practical solutions exist in a context. Whether one recruits friends, allies, helpers, or ghosts depends on the volume and allocation of jobs.

Everyone has something at stake in the system of sponsorship. The sponsoring freelancer runs the risk of offending his colleagues and perhaps disappointing the producer or director with his choice of an extra add-on. The protégé faces real trials and crucial evaluations of his work. And those in the core and at the periphery must confront the painful possibility that the potential successor may be more of a composer and industry hustler than they are.

Work is passed along with deliberate care. The patterns and linkages of this system of sponsorship remind us of the center/periphery structure of Hollywood. Clearly a segment of the industry is deeply dependent on colleagues for survival. Imagine that composer A does the main title of a television series and then passes the episodes to B, who then scores a couple of episodes and passes assignments on to C, who gets D to help him on one television assignment. Here we have a linkage of three. If A had done alone the entire show the linkage would be zero. Not surprisingly, freelancers take considerable interest in these linkages, in when they are coming into a project, at the start, middle, or end. They also watch who has worked before them on the project, for this is often an indication of where they are vis-à-vis colleague competitors. The number of links give a rough estimate of job allocation and the number of opportunities or openings at one studio over a period of time.

From 1972 to 1976, links of zero—meaning that the freelancer wrote the main title and themes for the series and then did all the weekly shows— accounted for 44 percent of the credits on television series. The lead composer had one associate in 32 percent of the projects, three associates in only 10 percent of the projects, and four or more in 14 percent of the projects (N = 73 series). Different kinds of processes are involved with different kinds of linkages. A sponsor's efforts are directed at moving a newcomer closer to the point of job origin. Those with long links to work in this labor market, those most *distant* from the core of activity, receive the least desirable jobs. Those *closer* to the center are more likely to get satisfying work. A 32-year-old composer moving from the fringe to the center of television work talked about the steps in passage from merely helping colleagues to becoming a lead writer.

In '71 I'd been doing orchestration for some composers when they got
into trouble, but the break was a shot at [a prime-time television series].
The guy on it at the time was very busy and he asked me if I'd like to
do an episode, the whole thing. I'd never done a complete episode—
little things, orchestration, arranging, some series of cues, that's it. This
was a heavy show, lots of music. So I went to the factory. He had set
it up for me. They put me into a projection room and I'm sitting there
and the man in the projection booth says, "Are you ready to run?" I
said, "I don't know. Isn't somebody supposed to be in here with me?"
He says, "I don't know. I'm going to run it anyhow." He pushes the
button and I'm in there a whole hour all by myself getting wrapped up
in the thing—it was a fairly complete cut—then I walked out to the
secretary's desk and asked her if someone wasn't supposed to be with
me. She said, "No. Here are your cue sheets. Go home and write the
music."

The cue sheets told him where to start and stop and the individual cues, and
the assignment was fairly routine, but it did not seem routine at the moment.

I went home, cried, stomped my feet, cursed, walked up and down and
didn't sleep that night. I finally figured that I had seven days left and
couldn't afford to do this. I had to put something on paper. And I put
the first note on paper and the second note and the ones that went along
with them, and before I knew it I was finished. I had no idea who was
to conduct the music or anything, so I brought my baton to the recording
session. My friend walked in and started giving his downbeat; then he
looked over at me and said, "It's good." The people in the music
department then grabbed me and rushed me upstairs to the projection
booth again and said, "This is *next week's* show." "But my music is
recording downstairs," I said. They told me there was no time for that;
the composer liked the music. "Here's next week—do it." And that's
how I got started.

The cue sheets indicated how long the specific cues were to run and the
range of stylistic possibilities were narrowed for him, but despite such protection his inexperience led to a mistake on his second effort. "I had a fight
sequence and I overwrote. I must have had nine symphonies playing at once
in that episode. The producer of the show got mad, and my friend was
embarrassed. With all of this happening so soon after the first things I had
written for the show, they didn't want me back."

He had not yet learned that some of the most effective musical and dramatic
meanings can be expressed with the least opulent musical resources. An
experienced composer knows that you do not draw attention away from a
chase scene with a symphony. During his third week in exile, his sponsor

again prevailed with the studio brass and the producer of the series and got him another chance. He did three more episodes, and by the end of the season had reestablished a good working relation with his colleague-sponsor, received his first television credits, and made some new connections with television producers he had met during his stay. He also met more composers, a couple of whom chuckled over his mistake in the second session. "It happens to all of us," one said later. "You pour everything you've got into that first assignment and that may be exactly what they *don't* want. They don't want *everything*. They want music that is right for the episode. They don't want any surprises, not in the middle of the season when the show's more or less locked in, you have to understand the game," he noted icily. "The important thing is to get invited back."

Toward the end of our composer's first year in the business a television producer at another busy studio got wind of the composer's talent for scoring— as the producer put it, "Jolly, happy music"; he had become known as someone with a flair for "the light stuff." He was quickly hired to work on a children's series after his commitment to the first series ran out. Looking back on those days, he remembered the pride and excitement. "It was so magnificent. Here I was developing contacts with producers and respect from my colleagues." But he also acknowledged his inexperience. "I was making some terrible goofs and doing some terrible things but learning as I went along, like we all have to."

Another turning point. His original sponsor was in trouble and needed help.

> One of his series at the studio was in trouble. He wanted me and had cleared it, so nobody's toes were getting stepped on over there, but he hadn't talked to the producer about me, so it was tricky business for both of us. So I went over to the studio and stood over his shoulder while watching the movie with him. As we walked out into the parking lot, he gave me the cue sheets and said, "I'll see you in two weeks at the recording session." He gave me a tape of the music he had used on the first show and handed me some of his sketches. "Use as much material as you can." I did. Probably 90 percent of it was his material since the sketches were pretty complete. In that situation you develop ideas but the sketches contain the basic material you work with. Here you're working with someone else and *their* material, the sound *they've* worked out for the show. You still have to write the music, but there are givens. So I went to work and two weeks later he had me there at the recording session. I've worked for some guys who wouldn't let you near their recording session if you wrote their music. They want you to ghost; they pay you for your work, but they get the credit on the sheet. I've always had the greatest respect for that man [his sponsor] and he really proved himself that day in that session. The producer ran

up and said to him, "This music is the greatest, it's even better than the first show we did." And my friend turned around and said, "I didn't write it—he wrote it," pointing at me.

Freelancers who cooperate repeatedly rely on ways of doing things. In the above case, certain aesthetic decisions have been made by the one composer for the other. The project they are working on together is a sequel to one that already achieved some success. The producer of both projects has certain expectations about what he wants for his project. Given the success of the first, it is clear he wants music in the same style, he has talked this over with the lead composer and they have agreed to do things in much the same way as before. The new composer being added on to the second project sees the materials he has to work with—the dramatic action in the form of a film, and the blueprint for the film score in the form of compositional sketches. He follows both. Note that the lead composer on the project had not told the producer ahead of time that he had someone else working with him on the score for the film. But he graciously gave credit where it was due. By contrast, some composers are reluctant to bring their "helpers" along to the recording session. As the newcomer noted, such gracious acknowledgement cannot be assumed, and when it is not freely offered there is little the newcomer can do. Though a producer may not be able to tell the difference between a composer's and his ghost's work, performing musicians usually can. The composer/conductor, being unfamiliar with his counterpart's cues, may have some trouble conducting his way through them, but he is willing to take this risk because he realizes his first obligation is to bring the entire scoring project in on time. And he can be assured that alert musicians will live up to the most universal maxim of colleague obligation and keep what they know to themselves.

Take the case of the following freelancer. In 1973, he was just starting out doing television episodes at one of the top studios. He had ghosted for two core writers and was becoming connected with one associate in particular. The protégé saw himself spending at least two, but not more than four years getting the experience he needed to graduate into feature films. He had a degree from one of the universities in the Los Angeles area, had done some arranging for big bands and rock groups, was interested in the film business and decided to give it a chance.

I understood the process [talking about the techniques of composition and film scoring], but there's no substitute for experience, for coming face to face with reluctance or unwillingness of the people who hire you, even some other composers. You pay your dues, I was willing to do that. I started by ghosting for someone who shall remain nameless.

The style was set from the previous session, and I was familiar with the routine so it was not that difficult to copy. I met B [a busy core composer] one day and we had the same copyist and the same contractor at that time. The copyist mentioned to him what was happening with my ghosting, the no credit for the work, and B thought it was disgraceful. He said he'd like to do something and so he went to the studio. I don't know what he said to the head of the music department, but I assume it was, "There's someone I'd like you to hear." In this way he's been very important in getting many of us into the business, helping us become known. [He moved into B's work as an add-on for one of his television series.] I did a couple of cues for him, a detective show, and I guess for all intents and purposes it was proved to the powers that be—whoever they are—that I knew how to write. All of this is happening now when, in effect, I'd been writing, ghosting, on one of their shows at [the studio] for a year previous to that. Apparently all went well. The producers saw that I could hold a baton, and I knew where the screen was, what the orchestra was, and so forth, and that I could bring the show in on time. A couple of days later I was given an episode of a big show to work on, and so I started to work for the producer of that show, a very talented guy. Some good composers have worked for him, some of the top guys. [He named five core freelancers at the studio in the early 1970s, two of whom had moved into the top level of features. Work led to work.] I then did two pilots for him, one or two movies of the week, and then I did the whole series that next year. I was learning a lot about producers because I hadn't been allowed to see one producer for a year when I was ghosting—the whole show was a big thrill for me. He's helped a lot of us, I've been fortunate. There were about six composers and myself at one point. We were putting out seventeen, eighteen shows a week. Those of us who were working there, if we happened to look like we had nothing under our arms, we would get another show, as well as the one we were doing during the week. Many times I did a mystery show, which was a light one, maybe ten to twelve minutes of music, and at the same time I was doing that I had a movie-of-the-week pilot, then a series episode and then another episode. It was a great training ground for all of us, and for me it was a place to learn, especially by making mistakes.

Until 1976 the following freelancer was a writer of commercial jingles with some record work thrown in. A chance meeting with a young filmmaker his own age led to work on one of the man's first films. This brought him to Hollywood. The film was a big flop and was pulled off the market after a few weeks. Through the help of a composer friend, someone moving up the ranks of television, he landed a job as utility writer at one of the busiest television studios. He encountered the usual difficulties breaking in: "It's that insidious thing, they won't take a chance on you until you have some credits, until you have something to show, but how do you get the credits if no one takes a chance on you? That's why the tie to him was a key in getting me out here. He was in a strong *position* to do something." The sponsor was in the center of work at Universal televison studio; he was very favored by some active television producers, and could recommend his choices to them with some security that his newcomers would be added on to the series. Even such sponsorship does not guarantee steady movement toward the center of the business. Patience, work, and luck are also all necessary to develop a large enough circuit of contacts.

Despite the fact that all the series he had worked on had been cancelled, he did not intend to leave the studio, not yet. His connections with two producers were getting better. He talked about a circuit of ties.

> To me you get on a sort of circuit. The longer you're in the business, the more friends you have who recommend you for jobs. It's getting those first jobs that is hard, getting the producer to take a chance on you is almost impossible. I'm grateful to him for being my champion. Now I can also recommend people when I can, and they recommend me. You don't always get the job, but, well, there are a bunch of us here in town who are now just beyond getting started and coming up in television, and we know people and people know us, everybody knows everybody.

Not exactly. Getting known is first, then staying known by working is next. In the case above, B recommended C to the producers he was working with, and that got C started. It took C three years to move from the periphery to the core of work at the studio; then C took D from the world of records and jingles into his own referral network. After passing his first trials under the wing of C, D began moving deeper into the circuit of recommendations and referrals. He started to "stockpile" his contacts. Here's how he sees this chain of events working for him.

> He [C] started taking me around the studio. I watched a lot of people work for two or three months. We went all over town watching various people work, I saw a lot of my idols. There's so-and-so, and there's so-and-so. Meanwhile I was still doing some commercials and I'd fly back to New York for something, go back to Chicago, and still do a few things out here. Then I did a picture with C. He was in some trouble at the time, having some emotional problems and a hard time writing. He had taken too much work and one of his films had just gotten creamed in the New York papers. Usually reviewers don't single out the music, but in this case they were very critical of it. And C, who's supersensitive, was just devastated; he was literally crying for days. Anyway, he called

me and said, "Listen, you're brand-new in town and I can't finish this picture. Why don't you come help me on it?" He said it would give me a chance to get my feet wet at the studio. "You'll get me out of a scrape. I'll feel like it's a friend of mine working with me and I won't have to work with someone that I don't really know." So I did it. I wrote about thirty-six minutes and had my baptism under fire. It turned out well and so I was waiting for my next shot. You know, I was saying, "Okay, you guys, here I am, I'm ready."

He was ready, but others were not. In a case like this potential employers might say, "Yes, D's indeed ready," or "Maybe he's pretty good," or "No, he's still too green and untested," or "He helped C last week, but we don't know what C did and what D did." The placements and typecasts of others are consequential, especially at this starting line of work. Presumably, the job seeker is searching for openings in the set of all jobs which he might potentially be invited to fill. The controllers of jobs—colleagues, potential clients, and the people in charge of handing out assignments at television studios—are searching for the talent that is willing and able to fill the jobs they have to offer. Since hungry freelancers are trying to advance claims about themselves, they are always on the market. Since employers are trying to get the best talent possible and reduce their own risks, they are reluctant to give a new, untested freelancer the job. They hire those they know. Breaking this cycle is difficult, but it is possible. Here is the continuing saga.

It turned out that the head of music at the studio was sick the entire time I was working on the stage with C's project and so he didn't see anything. And he is not one that can recognize talent when he sees it. He only knows from what people tell him. So nothing happened. I had three other calls. Three composers. Every one of them wanted me to do ghost jobs. They'd heard I'd done this work for C and people were talking and they said it was good. So they wanted me to ghost. I said no. I have seen what can happen if you begin as a ghost out here. A friend of mine who's a very good writer started that way and he never got a shot because they always thought of him as a ghost.

His friend and mentor continued to act on his behalf when special opportunities arose over the next year. As of the mid-seventies, he was still waiting for his first feature film, but in the meantime his work with C on a series at another studio connected him to two television producers and possible future work.

He [C] got a call to do a pilot; he couldn't do it because he was too busy. By this time he was doing everything. So he recommended me and recommended me very highly. He worked with this particular producer the previous season on [a successful television show] and was obviously the first pick. When C said I was good, the guy believed him. So this producer called me and asked me to come in for a talk. [Notice the move of D to P is not the result of direct application for a job. Rather, P's interest is the result of information *and* assurance supplied by a composer whom he has worked with.] I asked P if I should bring any tapes of my music. He said he didn't want to hear any music. "How about film?" "No, " he boomed back—and here I've been running around town to everyone and this guy doesn't even want to see any tapes. [They met and enjoyed one another's company.] I went in and he asked me what kinds of scores I liked, what kinds of movies. He's asking me, "Where's your head at?" We talked, and at the end of half an hour he threw me the script. "Let's do it," he said.

They did the pilot. It sold as a series and the series ran nine shows before being taken off the air because of mediocre ratings. He met with the producer often and worked well with him, and the latter indicated that he would like to work with the composer again, soon. The producer's own work was expanding, and he was scheduled to develop three more shows in the upcoming production season. Composer D, however, was still not the first choice of this producer; sponsor C still had the inside track for all this filmmaker's work. "But," D said, "I now have a friend in this guy and I know we'll work together again. I'm not his favorite, that's C and [another freelancer moving into very exclusive television work and features]; but I'm next in line, and when they graduate or are too busy, then I'll be there."

There is reason to suspect that producers prefer short referral chains just like this. They do not have unlimited time to spend on composers, who, after all, are only one part of their project and one small chunk of their budget. If they cannot sign the man they want, they use personal contacts to learn about others in the market. Some producers rely exclusively on the judgment of the head of music at a studio. Others turn for information to composers they know and have worked with. The television producer and/or director can either go on a long, extensive search for composers, casting a wide net in the hope of finding just the man he thinks he needs, or he can look over those recommended by people he trusts. As D's case illustrates, this puts an established composer in a very strong position to recommend a protégé to a producer. Then the producer wants to know the following: Who is this new guy being touted? Can we talk? Is he to be trusted with my project? Was C's pitch credible?

Sponsors understand this pressure from producers and realize their own reputations are on the line. One of the core composers at Universal television in the mid-1970s said that it is often a good idea to intentionally collect job information about ongoing projects and the working style of certain producers. Such information is useful when he is called on to help employers (filmmakers in television and features) and freelancers match up, and provides some protection against the risks of engaging in such matching.

> I wrote the theme and early episodes of a series this year, and turned down some of the other episodes because I had other assignments. I did not recommend a replacement because the producer had the people he had confidence in. I didn't feel that I should step in and tell him who to use. When you recommend, you've got to be careful. In all fairness, you can't drop a new composer on a producer for an episode. He's relying on your instincts, and he doesn't want to be burned at the recording session with a lousy score.

For the inexperienced composer, a recording session can be terrifying.

> You're up there on the stage conducting your music, desperately wanting to please the producer and the director, and trying to watch the screen, the score, the timing, and the musicians all at the same time. And then there's this row of people in the back of the session with white shirts and ties, and they're watching you. It's just like a Fellini movie. So, let's face it, when you're recommending someone, you've got to know what they can *do*; you have to talk to the producer about it; and you have to make sure things go smoothly.

Several themes are important here and can now be emphasized; they appear with regularity among those moving from the periphery of work into the center of activity in television and films, and especially among those who have enjoyed a continuity of credits and connections at the core of television work. First, one dimension in which commercialism works is the amalgam of buying and selling talent. Composers learn that producers and directors come to them as they would to a commodity to match their product. Who gets matched to what projects depends on a lot of things—what the one colleague thinks the project needs, whether he can "sell," in a very real sense, the television filmmaker on the choice for add-on or replacement, the sponsor's own clout, and the risks involved.

Things can go more smoothly when the replacement is eased in where the show's episodes are fully routinized, packed with conventions, and the musical approach can be fully seen by those who look and listen. The sponsor's job here is to pass the episode(s) to the aspirant, and to make sure the newcomer *understands* the requirements. He will also try to prepare him for the "Fellini" episodes that are likely to occur.

All this can be done most easily and with the least wear and tear on everyone when the project is episodic television. It is more difficult in feature films where the producers and directors are very reluctant to hand their project over to an unknown, or to somebody without a calculable track record of credits, or someone whose musical approach may be totally unexpected, unconventional, and full of risk. This is not to say that these matchings of newcomer to new producer do not occur. They do, with regularity; these are the ways in which career lines extend into feature films, as we shall see. But it should be no surprise that these jobs are usually low-budget productions with highly conventionalized characters, routinized story lines that move totally within the appropriate genre, and call for what might be labeled "predictable musical effects." These projects, to put it unkindly, are the feature film equivalent to television sit-coms and cop shows. They are the kind of films you watch in a movie theater and come to anticipate a commercial break.

Second, much of what happens in early career to these composers resembles Beckett's *Waiting for Godot*, rather than *8 1/2* or *La Dolce Vita*. Freelancers undergo a slow process of matching, and a sluggish process of prolonged apprenticeship. They have to be prepared to expect long delays before being rewarded for their dues-paying and loyalty to such a system. Careers are not made overnight. They are slow cumulations of credits. The rewards of moving into more and better work appear attractive enough to keep the fledgling freelancer from jumping ship and abandoning his aspirations. It seems that in Hollywood the more dues a freelancer has to pay, the more valuable work is when one gets it. To work, and keep on working, is the reward.

Third, and related, sponsorship is only as good as the number of jobs available in a freelance system. It is also only good as long as the "inner fraternity" of composers at, for instance, Universal television, is *willing* to do something for someone else. Because of their central location in the division of labor, they can match more effectively men to jobs and jobs to men than a more formal intermediary, because of their personal knowledge of the people and work involved. This does not guarantee that this linkage will automatically occur. Thus, the caution on the part of the "inner fraternity" creates the waiting and extended apprenticeship for those trying to break into the business. One of the top composers on the inside had this to say about sponsorship:

> I get to the point where I need help, we all do; but that *kind* of help as far as I'm concerned is not just that easy to come by. There are a lot of talented people around, but you almost have to take someone and train him because the experienced guys are busy. If you want to find someone who is talented but doesn't have the credit or the experience, you've committed yourself to spending a lot of time. If you're going to vouch for somebody, you'd better look over his shoulder at his music before you bring it to the recording session. But if you're going to have

to look over the music and make changes in it and have to do this and that—by the time you get through, you may as well write it yourself. [The sponsor will tend to turn to favored others to protect himself.] You get somebody with whom you *know* you don't have to do all that work.

Thus who he helps and on what kinds of projects are interdependent. As the sponsor moves from series work to more and more feature films, his chances for bringing in replacements to series obviously decline. But the chances for passing on a recommendation to a film producer increase, and he will not recommend just anyone. He is most likely to recommend someone close to the core of work, someone near the "inner fraternity," because he understands that film producers and directors have their own ideas about what and who they want.

I'm in a position now that if I see something I don't like, rather than simply just leave the room and have the producer go his own way, I'll suggest somebody for the project. I won't suggest somebody who is at the same point in his career as I am, but somebody who's proven himself on episodes and who needs the credit and needs experience on some of the heavier things. I may have to do a little con job on the producer, and a lot depends on how fixed his ideas are.

Summary

This system of sponsorship involves a great deal of time and considerable risk for the sponsor; it puts a great deal of pressure on the newcomer. It remains a vital part of the industry because, despite such disadvantages, it ultimately works to everyone's profit. The matching of freelancer to job through the process of referral and sponsorship (1) puts the newcomer or protégé into direct contact with potential clients, (2) gives him a chance to work with an experienced freelancer and increases his chances of becoming visible to others, (3) boosts his performance royalties with ASCAP and BMI, and (4) moves him into position for more and better work. Depending essentially on other freelancers for his referrals, the composer on the periphery is sensitive to the demands of his colleague. He will soon find that as he moves closer to the source of work—those who make and produce television or film projects—he will be more and more constrained by the wishes and preferences of his clients.

From the viewpoint of the sponsor who is himself moving up the ladder the sponsorship system (1) opens up opportunities for potential colleague "allies" who can be trusted and depended on, (2) signals to others that they are willing to put themselves on the line for a *specific* freelancer, (3) increases their own span of credits in both television and feature film work, and (4) provides the particular work setting with a crop of fresh, preselected, and colleague-coached candidates.

Notes

1. The idea of "career" has been and remains nothing more than a sensitizing concept in which to place observations and inferences about people moving through processes. More invoked than investigated by social scientists, the notion has never really graduated into a concept. For an important and justly influential exception, see the work of Howard S. Becker and Anselm L. Strauss, "Careers, Personality, and Adult Socialization." In H. S. Becker, *Sociological Work: Method and Substance* (Chicago: Aldine, 1970). See also Barney G. Glaser (ed.), *Organizational Careers: A Sourcebook for Theory* (Chicago: Aldine, 1968); John Van Maanen (ed.), *Organizational Careers: Some New Perspectives* (New York: Wiley, 1977).
2. *Sponsorship* is derived from the Latin *spondere* meaning "to promise," or "to act as guarantor." It is a social process which consists of one party taking actions that will shift the circumstances of another party, such as directly intervening in the means by which credits, connections, and career lines become distributed in a craft system. At this stage of the freelancer's career, to draw a line, one needs only two points; but of all the stages of commercial work, the most difficult to accomplish is the early unfolding of a *sequence* of work points. On sponsorship in the business of medicine see the pioneering work of Oswald Hall, "The Stages of a Medical Career," *American Journal of Sociology* 53 (1947): 317–36. On the politics of reputation, competence, and connections, see Robert R. Faulkner, *Hollywood Studio Musicians* (Chicago: Aldine-Atherton, 1971). For the commercial scene in Nashville, and a very similar model of sponsorship, see Richard A. Peterson and Howard G. White, "The Simplex Located in Art Worlds," *Urban Life* 7 (1979): 411–39.

3.
UP FROM SPRINKLER DRAIN

We have seen composers hurry and be hurried about in a competitive struggle for advantage and advancement. As they move toward the center of work they begin to see the complexity and risk tied to such advancement. During any one week in Hollywood there are composers winning and losing on a tiny scale. There are muted jealousies as some are pushed out of the way by others. There are not-so-disguised gloatings as a freelancer gets the job he has been looking for and gets access to powerful and productive television filmmakers. Many do not openly acknowledge the competition, and there is no official scorecard. Everyone seriously in the running, however, considers his competitive position and experiences either sieges of resentment or surges of euphoria depending on his particular balance of expectation and achievement.

Newcomers tend to assume that the tension and risk are part of the dues any beginner owes. Only gradually do they realize that the tension is inherent to the work arrangements, to the matching between freelance and available scoring assignments. Tension is constant as the composer moves from the periphery to the center of work, but the elements of the tension change, so the composer whose career is established while still young, experiences different anxieties than the newcomer does. A composer who has his initial credits and enough contacts to ensure continued work must start to consider the nature and effects of the work he will do in the future. He is presented with a perplexing set of opposing tendencies: (1) increasing volume of jobs—but rising expectations about the quality of work he should be permitted in the marketplace of talent; (2) increasing access to television producers—but the danger of narrowing the network of potential work ties to small and closed circles of producers and directors; (3) increasing visibility of his work—but the risk of becoming typecast as "just another television writer"; and (4) increasing income—but the hazard of making commitments that he can maintain only by continuing to work at the high volume level which exists only in television. A profession is a state of mind as well as a job, and as these tensions define the state of mind of the young freelancers they help us define the profession.

Breaking Away: The Importance of Overlapping Work

Both the competition and the tensions would be more manageable if talent were the sole criterion of judgment. The following story illustrates how luck and financial pressure (elements which in proper combination produce ''Hollywood success'') complicate the issues. A young freelancer who studied at a major conservatory in the East worked for a film director and producer in New York on a couple of ''arty-farty'' films in the 1960s and moved to Los Angeles when the producer moved. After scoring a low-budget melodrama, the producer ''went quiet,'' meaning he had trouble finding a ''property'' that could be promoted into a feature film or trouble getting money for such a project. The composer too went quiet, having nothing to work on with the producer. He did know some other composers starting out on the fringe of television work and they showed him how to start making the rounds of MGM, Columbia TV, Universal, Quinn Martin Productions, and others. After a year in episodic television, a friend of his New York producer heard about him and hired him to score a pilot at Universal. When the pilot was bought by the network, the composer became one of the forty freelancers working at the studio in 1971. Because of the status of the series, he was assigned his own office, a 26-by-18-foot wood-paneled office in the music building. Next door was a smaller office housing another composer who had just scored a pilot which had also been purchased by the network. Here is what happened.

> We started on two television shows with two new composers. My office was rather large, with wood paneling—but his office didn't even have his name on the door. It had a sign on the door that said, ''Sprinkler Drain''—inside were the sprinkler hose and the drain. So for six months or so *I* had the wood-paneled office. Then my show folded and *he* moved into the panelled office. He's been there ever since—very successful. His show was a hit and from that assignment he got a big-budget film and a lot of other things. This is not to say his music for the TV show was not as good as the music I did for my show, but it turned out to be music for an enormously successful show—it's still going strong—and *that's* the kind of thing Hollywood understands.

A chronic feature of freelance work is the indifference or ignorance of the client about the music in the project. Producers look at a project in terms of commercial success and rarely have the ability or interest to separate the success or failure of the music from the project as a whole. If a project fails, the composer, no matter how good his music is, fails with it. The only defense is to diversify work; the more work one has, the easier it is to spread the risks of one or two projects falling through. Said one composer:

> I'm in a different place now than I was three years ago. I'm no longer a new face in town. It doesn't do me much good any more to send tapes and go and talk to people. They all know me. If and when I can be of service to them, they'll call. I have some pretty good people, some contacts who will, I hope, come into their own and start producing films, TV projects, whatever. I just wish I was working more right now. I did an excellent score for a movie of the week, but whoever heard of it? It may play a few theaters in Europe. I may do a lot of minutes of music, wall-to-wall, but it's one thing—only one thing. A couple of shows fell through last season that I was on; one of them was my show and the other I was helping someone else out. Both were cancelled.

Freelancers have little control over these factors. The rejection of television pilots and series is seen for what it is—a painful but "normal" kind of trouble. The speed and frequency with which networks change their programming contributes to the uncertainty of the composer's experience. Changing styles in shows also have consequences. In 1977, for instance, there was a marked change in emphasis from police and private-eye shows to situation comedies. The latter call for a main title, frequently a song, short cues to move from one screen action to another, and preparations for commercials. Compare the music for "Welcome Back, Kotter," "Barney Miller," or "Mary Tyler Moore" to the music for "Starsky and Hutch," "Kojak," "Charlie's Angels," or "Switch" in terms of length, development of motifs, and size of orchestra.

"You're gambling all the time," one freelancer with work on one of the adventure detective shows noted. "There are no guarantees," he insisted, glaring at me as if I assumed there *were* absolute guarantees in freelancing. "You're in a market, and people who don't understand that don't understand this business." This freelancer had a combination of energy, anger, shrewdness, and talkativeness that was as alarming as it was refreshing. He had been in the business longer than some of his television colleagues. While he did not have many film credits, his latest film was stunning. As he talked, it became clear that he disliked a lot of what he had to do and many of the producers he had to deal with. He had walked out on some, he said, and I had no reason to doubt him. He was the kind of man who could say to a producer, "I'm sorry, but I'm not right for your project" and mean, "Your film stinks." What he did like was the money. I also think he liked fighting against the odds and coming out on top.

I'm a percentage player. The scuffling for jobs never stops around here. It changes levels, that's all. Styles change. Producers change. Guys [composers] change. Henry Mancini didn't know that Blake Edwards would be his big break with *Peter Gunn*—there are others like this, all the time. The fact is that I never had a Blake Edwards, I've had fringe-area people, you know, they've said, "I want this guy" or "Here's a guy with a couple of successful shows [on television], let's get him." The fact is that certain people—producers—control the work in this town. It's that simple. The people who control the work give you the opportunity and it's the same as it is in any marketplace—you're dependent on them. They *own* the product. The question is, when do they start asking for *you?*

In this composer's opinion the answer to that question was entirely a matter of financial success, and the emphasis on money disgusted him. "An old friend of mine once said that whatever happens in this town it's better to be a shit in a hit than hit in a shit—that's really the truth. Producers base opinions solely in terms of financial success because they have no other measure. They don't understand your performance and your musical contribution. They're only interested in the rating, was it successful or not, did it sell, and was it a hit?" Results—in this case of the audience delivered to the advertisers and hence the network's profit—are what count. While freelancers are frank about all this, most are not as blunt as this man.

The next composer was comparatively successful with seven recent film credits, a string of television sit-coms, and two other shows still in syndication, but remembered vividly the difficulty of getting started. "If I had known more about the realities, about how difficult it would be for me to break in and get something going, I would have approached it in a much more tentative way," said the freelancer. He had written and produced a couple of top-selling records in the late sixties, moved his family to Los Angeles when he signed to do a film, and then had to figure out what to do next.

"I was lucky," he said. "There were a few people here, just a few, who were willing to recommend me and a few who were willing to take a chance on somebody new. That kept me going and gave me a lot of experience." He moved through Universal and was very familiar with both the Sprinkler Drain and the wood-paneled office next door. "I know that place," he smiled. "I got to do a lot of different kinds of shows there, a cop show this week, and episode of a western that week, episodic TV—we all go through it. The studio was doing eighteen hours a week, so you met the guys and were put in contact with producers. They would try to get you, especially if you were connected with a successful show. They talk among themselves."

One producer moved to another studio to develop a new show and took this composer along, a move that was important because he had started feeling hemmed-in working exclusively at Universal—a feeling that others also share. "That show was my show and I stayed on it for a few steady seasons. The association [with the producer] was instrumental in bringing me some recognition, now that I look back on it though I didn't realize it at the time. Then I got a call from the people at another studio and I did the pilot and you know the rest."

The rest was that this pilot was a comedy series that turned into one of the biggest hits in television, but the composer was reluctant to see it as the single pivotal point of his career.

> Careers are not made with any one thing. It's a cumulative effect. You're gambling all the time: will this series make it, what about this pilot, maybe this will take off, you see? Nobody knows whether it's going to make it or not. You just work for this musical director at that studio, this colleague at this time, this producer on this project, and then they learn over time that they can depend on you. You show them you know what you're doing and you take your craft seriously. All this has a building effect to it [only gradually are connections and thus careers established]. No matter *where* you are in this business, it operates on word of mouth [he paused for a few seconds and corrected himself]. Let me say that it works by word of mouth until you're at a level where because of your credentials *everyone* knows who you are. I mean Henry Mancini does't need any word of mouth; Jerry Goldsmith and Johnny Williams don't need any word of mouth. But even those guys came through television at one time. So at one time in all our careers a lot depends on producers talking to one another, "This composer is really good, he's got it." That's because when you're at a point where you're not known, your name is not substantial enough where they can just say the name and everybody says, "Of course, he did such-and-such."

He returned to his own circumstances noting how even good connections are not enough to guarantee consistent work. "Last year I did five pilots—one sold. I figure I'm lucky with at least one. I could have gone 0 for 5." Even if a pilot sells the network may cancel it soon. Describing the history of one of his most successful series: "That show was a stiff the first year, they were going to drop the show, it wasn't a hit at all. It was struggling along and in the summer, in the reruns, they kept it on and that actually made the show. When it came back on in the fall it became a top twenty show. But out of the box it was a loser." The year before, one of his series almost survived the season cut—almost. "I really thought that show was going to make it. I would have bet a hundred dollars that the series would do well in the ratings. I felt that if the network would just give it one more year, it would have found its audience. They cancelled it. So you make your bets and you win and lose. The main thing is to keep getting the chance to work both in television and films. Hopefully you break out and become valuable to people working in both [television and feature film work].''

Rates of participation in films by television work at Universal are shown in Table 3.1. Freelancers are at different points in their career lines and at different locations in their overlapping participation in television and films. There are composers who are working in both areas, as shown in the lower right-hand corner of the table. They are small in number. Sixteen percent (18) of the 112 are called upon again and again to score the more important and high-budgeted television projects while also enjoying connections and visibility in the market beyond the gates of this studio. They are selective about their television work, and they are tied to producers and directors who work on the studio's movie of the week, network pilots, and specials.

On the periphery of both television and film scoring assignments are those who work almost exclusively in episodic television. As shown in the upper left-hand corner of Table 3.1, a few may have a single film credit in the five years. Most do not. There are colleagues who are a step ahead of these freelancers. The proportions of composers with 2–6 television credits with 2–5, and 6–24, feature film credits are 23 percent and 9 percent, respectively. These freelancers are presumably a group in transition, beyond merely "breaking in" but far from the centrality and success of continuous film work. Their concern is with "breaking out" of the work that several years ago they were eager to get. They want to move up in the division of freelance assignments, but oppotunity is limited and chancy. Moreover, their better track record and network connections should give them a competitive edge over other, newer, unknown freelancers when seeking to secure assignments with producers and directors. They now hope to mobilize more filmmakers and directors to back their candidacy for preferred television and film assignments than would other, less connected and less visible freelance composers.

There is an emotional logic in the freelancer's career experience but also a painful irony. The credits and visibility he has gained raise his expectations, so, despite his achievements, he is still hungry for more and better jobs. The irony is that as soon as he breaks out of the Sprinkler Drain he begins to feel hemmed-in by the limited opportunities for feature film work. The situation changes but the patterns of rising expectations, inner tension, and competition remain.

The Value of Diverse Connections as "Accounts"

Recognition and resources are crucial, but a freelancer must be careful about how he becomes known and how he becomes connected to his employers. It appears that social networks as indexed by involvement in overlapping television and feature film productions contribute to career continuity.

TABLE 3.1
Film Credits (1970–75) by Television Work at Universal

| Television Work[a] | Feature Film Credits | | | | | Composers[b] |
	None	1	2–5	6–24		N
Episodes only	74%	15%	11%	--	100%	(27)
1	70%	22%	8%	--	100%	(36)
2–6	58%	10%	23%	9%	100%	(31)
7 or more	17%	17%	33%	33%	100%	(18)
						(112)

[a]Includes TV pilots, Movies of the Week, television Movie Premiers, Specials, and TV productions where the freelance composer is listed as the writer of the main title and theme.

[b]Freelancers with one or more film credits during this period constitute 35 percent (46) of the 310 composers working in films.

If social network factors do play a major role in Hollywood as expected, several subjective career concerns are anticipated. First, a freelancer can lose ground by being known only to a narrow circle of colleagues and clients, being known only as someone who works mainly in television or for a particular group of television producers or directors, someone "tied to" a particular studio. Each of these appraisals by others can restrain a composer's freedom and opportunity to move onward and upward. They can become mobility traps.

Gaining recognition and gradually working into the organization of work at one major television studio was fine for the following freelancer, for a while. He was actively sponsored by one of the "inner fraternity" at the studio in the late sixties, worked on many of his sponsor's television series, and had earned his stripes by the early 1970s. He had worked on and off in Sprinkler Drain when he first started out, but was now accustomed to better facilities. Like three out of four respondents, he strongly emphasized the importance of connections, but then noted the importance of the *context* or *place* of those connections. In my second interview with him, in 1975, he talked about the competition, the pace of career movement, and spreading his work ties among television and film producers.

> There are a number of things you gradually learn. It doesn't all come to you at once, but in bits and pieces—like what to take and what to turn down. When I first started out, I would take any job, but you read the trade papers, see where guys are, who they're working with, the guys who started working about the same time you did, and you get a sense for whether you're moving fast or slow. Like right now I'm starting to turn down jobs that two years ago I would have died to do. Then you see others who would never, absolutely never, take a television series. They just want to do the main title and this is where I'm moving now. And if I move into that level of work, fine.
>
> Producers see what you can do. Right now I'm working on a project with a producer at the studio. I've made a number of close associations at the studio over the past few years. But I'm starting to see the value in moving. You have to spread yourself around. My efforts now are in the direction of becoming known at other places, becoming known by other people in movie-movies, features. Not all film work is as comfortable as the work with some of the producers and directors I've known at this studio, but my agent and I agree. He doesn't want me to work *only* there. I've done a lot of work there, but now it's a good policy to become known at other places. [He talked about some of the risks in staying:] Suppose the head of music at the studio drops dead tomorrow of a heart attack. What if he's one of the only people in town who knows my work? You don't want to have all your eggs in one

basket. Certainly there's more safety in getting known at a number of places. Also if you're tied to one place you've got to take only what they are doing. Suppose you get a great picture for someone who's working somewhere else? You have to turn it down and lose the possible relationship with the producer or the director.

Spreading accounts is a career strategy designed to weaken the hold of ties and involvements at one work site and to expand them at other places. I talked to this composer's agent a year later and he agreed about the risks of staying tied to a particular work setting. He represents over sixty composers and several of his clients had come to the big fork in the road. One road leads out of the comfortable place where a composer has made his start; the other follows the set course and keeps the composer in the routine he has established.

> If you just work in one place, people think you're almost *exclusive there* and they then *forget about you*. If producers know that you're doing all these things at one studio, after a while they just stop calling you. In the beginning they call and you keep saying, "I'm sorry, but he's doing this at X and he's doing that at X studio." They'll say, "Well, that's the point, he's doing everything at X." So it's important to a fellow's career to spread himself around town, to work in as many places as possible, to work with as many people as possible. In the beginning, when a guy's starting out and has little experience out here, he should have a base of operations because that gives you the place to start. But at some point you've got to get going at some other places. You spread your accounts, but carefully. You follow—hopefully—the good projects.

The freelancer can only follow the projects he is asked to do. The more work, the more choices. If a composer is doing a lot of work at Universal, for example, and a producer wants him for a job at Burbank at the same time, the man has to weigh certain costs and gains. If the second assignment is no better than the first, then our composer is probably wise to stay where he is. Thus "spreading accounts" always has to pay attention to the work attached to the account, the kind of project tied to the client. Moreover, there is always a certain amount of loyalty involved to the "home" studio, the place a composer got his first foothold in the business. There are choices to be made and the choice to move is only sensible if it leads toward, as one composer put it, "something really important with prestige, something that gives the composer an opportunity to make a musical contribution—not just another shoot 'em up, a cop show or something routine like that. A great show, well, of course a composer's going to take that rather than the other."

These sentiments are representative of the perspective from which freelancers view career progress. Close work relations are a main source of social support for freelancers, but since close relations tend to be confined to small and closed social circles, they can impede the social integration of the man on the move toward a wide network of clients and projects.[1] Moreover, excessive dependence on a small number of producers can jeopardize a career. Some composers have allied themselves closely with a producer who seemed to be rising toward feature work. Many such composers hoping to coattail their way into feature work have been disappointed by the producer's lack of loyalty. A producer has to pay attention to his own new social circle and its demands. He may feel obliged to hire composers with "names" and "better track records once he has a film which involves a lot of money and prestige," as one recently disappointed composer expressed it.

Though staying in one place too long can limit a composer's horizons, spreading accounts is a complicated and tricky strategy. A freelancer must not develop a reputation which will cause clients to reject his candidacy for a job out of hand. To the extent that a composer gives off signals about what he's doing, where, with whom, and for how long, staying in place for too long can start to rule out occupancy of desired jobs. Producers and directors stop calling. The solution to shrinking circles is by no means simple. It involves doing the work one is getting at the studio, while giving off signals of availability to potential clients. Some fast footwork is often required, such as: (1) continuing to do the original project but also taking the second one and then staggering the two assignments back to back; (2) bringing another freelancer in to "help" or "ghost" on the first project while writing the music for the second one; (3) trying to hold off a final "no" to the new client until the first commitment is successfully completed thereby buying some time; or (4) accepting the second assignment but then farming it out to someone else. There are risks all the way down the line. If a freelancer takes on too much work in hopes of spreading his accounts, he may get into writing ruts and go stale. Also, clients justifiably feel entitled to the services of the man they have hired and paid for. Thus farming out a score is always a risk, because if the composer is "discovered" or the music is lousy, the relationship will sour and future work and connections will be jeopardized.

Early Credits, Early Castings

Composers, like actors, directors, even producers and film cutters, are "typed" throughout their careers. One freelancer was known in Hollywood circles as a great "western" writer because he had scored several successful television series dealing with gunfighters, mavericks, and horses. He had trouble kicking the label for years. Another did a lot of television work for a studio specializing in ocean exploration and sea sagas, and was known as a great "underwater" writer. Still another was known for his situation-comedy scores and complained that no one was calling him to work on anything else. A composer with a hit series which used a small combo with rhythm section and bongos—a choice dictated by the small budget—got tagged as a "slick jazz writer." His real métier was avant-garde, classical composition.

Getting typed or placed in a pigeonhole is a distinctly mixed blessing to early careers. It's good, because at least people make a link between the composer, his score, and the project he scored it for. It's bad, because producers and directors tend to confuse what a composer *does* with what he *can* do. The freelancer on the move wants to announce something about himself in order to expand his range of choices: "Here I am, I'm working, I've got experience, I've got some credits, I can provide you with what you want, I can talk with you and we can arrive at the score that will be just right for your project." The problem, of course, is getting someone to listen to all of this. Producers listen to other producers, not composers, and a producer's appraisal is more likely to be something like, "Yeah, he writes greater underwater stuff—and he's cheap."

The successful freelancers learn quickly. Here is a young composer who has just broken out of television and is on the move. He was part cynical intellectual and part romantic, torn between what he would ideally like to do as a film scorer and what he had to do in order make a go of it. He was inured to the insult typecasting implies, tough in his evaluations of other colleagues, and realistic about what it might take to break through the reservations of producers.

> I'm getting quite an education. I know what I can do and I want to get the chance to do it. Like anywhere in the entertainment business there are people who get typecast. In television there are composers who have done *so much* of it that they've fallen into a formula in what they've done. They've scored one show or one type of show for many years. Filmmakers say, "Oh, that's a television actor," "That's a television composer"—meaning that they really don't expect to get fresh enough solution out of them, so filmmakers tend not to choose them to work on a feature. And of some people it is true, and of some people it isn't true. Let's face it, to make a living some people have to do lots and lots of television and maybe they're very capable of doing a terrific film score, but they never have the opportunity, they're just pigeonholed as a television composer—period.

He saw some of these people around him, some of them a few years older than himself, who were "locked in," and, because of their reputed ties to television work, were unable to get the kind of work which would allow them to break out of television and start moving upward. He was quite worried that he might turn into one of them.

> When I had been out here a year or so, I had done seven or eight television things—episodes, some work for a producer friend on a movie of the week, but I hadn't gotten a feature. I was crying the blues to my agent, you know, "I'll never get a feature, never." Let's face it, features are the big leagues around here, that's the step we all want to make. I was worried that maybe I was getting known as just another television composer, you know, people might start thinking: "He's working all the time at that place and that's *all* he can do." I was scared. A lot of producers see only television on your credits, no movies, and they'll think that you're *only television quality*—not feature quality.

He got a feature soon and moved into what he called "very exclusive television work"—pilots and movies of the week with considerable prestige. "I got the feature through a producer who knew my work. We had come up together at the studio. Then another feature came up at another place so I was really starting to move. After that it was easier to get features—once I had *done* them. Work leads to work."

Exclusive ties to television can limit a composer's talents as well as his career. Listen to this composer's reaction to some of his colleagues: "Now I know there are guys who do only television and no features. Their work, let me put it this way, is not that special. It has a kind of nice, meat-and-potatoes quality, but there's nothing that leads you to believe that they should be doing a feature, that they really have better stuff in them." The remark was made without malice, it was a straightforward assessment of talent. Composers generally retain considerable pride in keeping their music up to the level they've set for it. The man who coasts too long in television episodes and grows accustomed to the rather conventional dramatic scenes and musical solutions may retain the admiration of his clients long after he's lost the respect of other composers. Watching colleagues who continue to please their clients but not their colleagues, who become commercial "quacks," is a lesson to the young and talented composer. For colleagues to say, "I've heard it *before*, he did the same thing in his last show," is the most damning judgment they can deliver on one of their contemporaries' talent. This problem of circumscribed talent was discussed by a composer who admitted that he was accustomed to the comforts of television work early in his career, but then decided he had to do something for himself, something he really wanted to do—write for top quality films.

> When you're starting out you do what you can get. I had some modest success in this town and I'm now in a place where I can be selective.

I really don't want to work at [that studio] anymore. I could do a lot of television work there, but I decided to back off from that stuff. I did plenty of series there, some of their best stuff, and it got to the point where I was finding that unfortunately there's a stigma attached to some types of work, that is, if you show up and do every segment of a television show, you may be very big with *that show,* but that's it. You get nailed into that, that's what you *do,* you just write for a television show. This almost happened to me. You become a [name of the television series] *type.* I'd like to keep myself open for other jobs. You see, over time, if you don't do other work the typecasting starts to work against you, very definitely. Watcn out then. I know guys who have worked out nice arrangements with studios and they do all the work that comes along. [We talked about six composers at one major studio who are at the core of that company's television work. It was important to have a home base, he agreed: it was good to get known in that way, but only for so long.] After that, now they're doing a police-type show, a this-kind of show and that-kind of a show, but if they wanted to get into a film score, feature films, they would have trouble.

Important and consequential decisions result from occupancy of a niche at one level of the industry. Occupational expectations provide penalties for those who stay too long either buried in television or who remain year after year as active members of the "inner fraternity" at a particular studio. To acquire a reputation of this sort is to predetermine other possible locations and, as implied above, even compositional experiences in the business. Those who are left out of the charmed circle of film work are often explained away. In labeling others, there is usually contained the assumption that these other composers are peculiarly adapted to the particular jobs they have been doing up to that time. A composer learns that others think in this way. It is a corollary implication that others—particularly those who hire them—begin to think that those who remain in television too long are not quite fit for new projects to which they may aspire. Thus a major turning point can be the experience of getting trapped in a situation where one's options become closed off. Here is the view of a composer who was also concerned about the trap of typecasting.

The film business is a very exciting business when you start, and it lasts for five or six years of television. You get to do a lot of things, you learn a lot. But after a while you're looking at the same show every time: you did it before, you *saw* that story. It's frustrating because it's a very perishable item. The show's on one week and then it's gone. People in the business relate to you entirely in terms of what you've done. Some directors don't want people who work in television. I think some of them feel there's something about television scoring that's particular to television. The style, approach, way of handling the music is sort of background melodramatic filler. Although a lot of television scorers are very good composers—tops—their names are attached to a practice that for some producers and directors is tainted.

The experience of *being cast* as a certain type marks the end of the first period of a freelancer's career—that of struggling to get work and secure contacts—and the beginning of another, equally trying stage in which the perplexity of those early days gradually gives way to mild panic. Reviewing the first phase in the light of subsequent events, many respondents commented on how bizarre, and often inaccurate, the typecasting seemed. Few saw the danger at first in gaining recognition for a particular television or film project, or a string of television assignments, and they were pleased to establish a foothold at a television studio. At least, they reasoned, they were becoming known by a wider and wider circle of employers and establishing a reputation for professional work. But as they looked back, they saw other colleagues, some of them very talented, following a path which would get them recognition but would also taint and even trap them.

The Trap

A composer can get locked-in whenever he realizes that it would cost him more to change his current situation than it would to remain where he is.[2] While purposefully carving out a niche for himself in television, a freelancer often finds that he is digging deeper than he intended. Involvements are being deepened for him in other areas as well. He may find himself in the unenviable position of eliminating himself, as well as being eliminated, by typecasting and by not spreading his contacts into a widening orbit of employers. The processes of acquiring these involvements are partially unwitting and unintended, and they typically develop as unanticipated offshoots of his present line of work. Taken separately or together these additional involvements, these "side bets," constitute sufficient value for their loss to be a constraint on the composer. Doing more and more work, he gets used to the perquisites of the job; he adjusts to the ways of doing things, writes expected, even routinized scores for the television shows, develops rewarding friendships with colleagues, enjoys sponsoring others, and gains a measure of local eminence. His performance royalties continue to grow as he does increasing television work. A growing income from series, pilots, movies of the week, maybe a film or two, leads to financial investments, acquisition of real estate, leaping improvements in standards of living, expensive cars, expensive divorces, stiff alimony, and sizable responsibilities. Under these circumstances, trying to break into film scoring looks very risky, perhaps too risky. Reviewing this phase of their career, freelancers note the overlap of work and nonwork, for incidental side bets have been made in the private sphere as well. There bets look like bricks in a wall which could eventually grow to such a height the person could no longer climb over it.

For some it is only when a series falls through, when producers in television turn toward other composers, or when a competitor absorbs a share of potential jobs that they see the dangers. The following composer was one of the "inner fraternity" at a major television production headquarters. He was getting nervous about his involvements and responsibilities and the lack of work in feature films. After several years in television, he was still moving, but not quickly enough. He paid $18,000 in taxes one year, had been through a bitter divorce, and was still determined to "study" and enlarge his compositional talents, but he was squeezed by a complex of commitments: the financial loss connected with cutting back on television work in order to make himself available for films; the possible loss of contacts if he turned down television producers who were dependent on him; the dislocation of adjusting to new producers and new situations. Interviewed in 1973 he was delighted to be moving up into the center of work at the studio; in 1975 he was getting more and better projects while looking for a feature film which would help him "break out"; and by 1977 he was very restless and discontent about where he was and how slowly he was moving. He had just left his "home" studio in hopes of showing others in the business that he was available for a variety of jobs, that he wanted to redefine the shape of his current commitments. He expected to pick up a feature film assignment *soon*.

> I want to diversify now, so I don't become too subject to the rhythms of this marketplace, you know, so that I have more sources to go to, and don't get boxed in at [the studio], which I've found can be very destructive—both creatively and politically. The most important awareness I've come to within the last year was that I found myself thinking more about adding on to the garage and "This job is going to get me a new car," or "This job is going to pay for a trip back East," and the like. I stopped thinking about music the way I had thought about it initially, which is to get into your work and get back to the roots. I mean write music, for music's sake, not just to accomplish a five-minute chase or whatever. I'm really out of touch with that now, more and more. If this season is a light season for me, I want to get a project going where I can *write,* get myself back in touch with why I like to write music.

> After a few years, there's a trap in television. It's partly the time pressure, it's partly the enormous volume of work you have to learn to do, and it's partly your own way of thinking and how you handle your money situation, all of that. I've continued to do television and I must

admit, the grind is getting to me. What I'd really like to do is spend a
year soaking up electronics, soaking up rock, get into some new vocabulary, instead of writing this stuff from a voyeur point of view. You
always say, "I'll get to it sometime," but you never have a chance to
grow; there's no time. Once in a while when you're doing a feature,
sure, then you can spend a couple of weeks researching a certain style
of music, or a certain sound, or a certain idea.

He saw a greater opportunity to develop as a writer in feature films than
in weekly episodes of television. The economics of film work also seemed
to offer opportunity: "In features you're in a position where one feature may
pay $20,000, and then you've got enough money to pay the bills and subsist
for a season." He compared this with his present work. "At the rate of $2,000
or $2,500 a show—How many of those do you have to do to make that kind
of money?"

Looking for film work and trying to get out of television leaves this composer partly "in" and partly "out." He is cut loose from the many supports
and advantages of tightly-knit associations with other composers and a few
producers. The period of transition from relatively structured work at the one
studio to relatively unstructured and open freelancing on the market is painful
and the stakes are high. "I've got to get a film. I feel like it's time to get
on. It's not happening. And I don't want the train to pass me by and then
suddenly wake up and say, 'Why didn't I do *that?*'" He was going to meet
his agent after our interview and was contemplating severing that relationship.
He wanted someone else to represent him. "I can only improve in relation
to my goals." I asked whether he could not see himself doing another two
years of the same thing (knowing what his answer was going to be). "I don't
want to do it," he said with finality.

It is important to keep in mind that we are no longer looking at a freelancer
who comes to his work fresh and excited by the newness of it. This composer
came to many of his recent assignments flat and stale, worn down by the
routines and time pressures, and apprehensive about the disparity between
what he really wanted to do and what he was obliged to do in order to keep
going.

Each new season is a struggle. You want to move ahead, improve
yourself, and then you find yourself right in the same place you were
last year—the panic, the bills, the house, the limited time to write. If
you're lucky, you're right back where you started. If you're not, you're
broke . . . and you sell your house. I know some guys who have gone
under. All the contacts at the studios cut down, and there's no more
demand for their work. They either are out of touch musically with

what's going on or they're out of touch with producers, or their life style is out of touch with their earnings. It can be all that.

His talk of work, side bets, and money was shot through with examples of other composers who were living proof of being used, used up, and trapped. The freelance world is a public one. Everyone hears and evaluates his colleagues' work, and the world is small enough that close friends and even more distant associates can keep track of each other's progress or lack of it. Comparison is inevitable and as the composer watches others move past him on their way to better opportunities, he starts to feel like a failure, not an absolute loser, but a comparative loser. The difficulties of getting work become clearer, just when the need for competitive success becomes greatest.

The next composer was learning all of this. In three years he had moved from the fringe to a much more secure position in Universal television's "inner fraternity." He was aware of the Hollywood trap, the price to be paid when volume of television work increases, credits accumulate, reputation in television increases, and the money starts coming in, quickly. He joked about a friend, his sponsor at the studio, who had put in his four years, watched his money, and was very careful about the films he took. "His career has been spectacular," he said as we went down the other man's credits in film, "but it wasn't until last year that he decided to get a BMW. He's very stingy. I'm learning that you've got to be careful with your dough and not get locked in." He remembered the advice of one of his colleagues, an articulate and successful composer with over twenty film credits and a reputation for taking only high quality television work.

> He told me when I first got out here, "Don't get *stuck* in *television*. I've seen a lot of guys come out here and start living a certain life style, and to maintain that life style they've got to keep the ball rolling." When you have to keep the ball rolling you begin to lose control. You begin to get . . . you can turn into a hack, that's what it amounts to. You end up grinding out music like sausage. That's why he [his advisor] has limited his television work and whatever television he's done has been quality stuff, good stuff, first-rate.

> I'm a new guy in town, so to speak. It took me a while to see that there are television writers and there are *television writers*. There are composers and there are *composers*. For instance, F is ten times the writer that L is. [F was one of the top television writers at Universal and had six features to his credit. L had one low-budget feature and was doing a lot of series and episodic work, as he had been doing for the past six years.] You begin to see that a guy like F is doing all the quality films and a guy like L is doing all the schlep television. It gives you some

idea of the possibilities. When you start working on some series and that ball starts rolling you can get locked into *only* doing television, and what I'm saying is that even there the conditions are awful, you spend much of the season never seeing your family, days at the piano, heart attacks, and so on and so forth. You can get trapped by the lifestyle, for openers. You come out here and see things you've never seen in New York. You get used to a certain way of living while working, and then you're not growing in an artistic-craftsman sense even though your expenses and everything else are getting out of hand. You end up, you can end up, working for those expenses. You start taking many things you'd prefer not to take.

I next interviewed this composer's mentor and sponsor at Universal. He had graduated from television work two years earlier and was now picking his television assignments with care since his real interest was in films. By his own admission he was tight with money, fully aware of the dangers of letting things get out of control.

When you've done a lot of television and, say, you've got a lot of bills to pay you've got to take every show that comes your way and you learn about shortcuts and how to write a show in five days, or four days, or three. The quality of your work can go down. I know composers this has happened to, some guys have a wife or wives they are paying a lot of money to, the house in Beverly Hills, and then the Mercedes, and pretty soon they've *got* to do everything. I'm trying to avoid that, have been ever since I started to do more and more work. I live comfortably. I don't have lavish tastes. I tend to spend even below what I have. There's this kind of Jewish sensibility that this is all going to be taken away from me and I better be careful because bad days are going to come. You take it a year at a time.

He seemed to speak from the experience of long days of brooding upon his rise into a strong position in the business; he was seriously looking at what happens to successful others and their money. The danger of side bets, of digging in too deep and getting overcommitted to what he called "extra-curricular" or nonscoring features of work, had been slowly shaped and proved to him by others' fates and the traps they set for themselves. He had an image in mind from a television movie. Here's his version of what that show was and what it had to say about side bets.

There was this television show a couple of years ago, something to do with a $80,000-a-year trap. It was about a guy in advertising who's just been promoted to junior executive, and he's now making all this money a year and he figures, "Gee, I've got all this money." But yet in order to move into that echelon, to advance, you've got to entertain a lot, you've now got to wear the expensive suits, to let everyone know you're making it, and you go a little too far and suddenly making eighty grand a year has put you ten grand in debt—because in order to move ahead from the $80,000 you have to look like you're making $100,000, whereas when he was only making $50,000 a year he was *saving* some money. I'm sure it happens in a lot of businesses. You get ahead of yourself. It happens here and it can start affecting your work, how much you take and whether you move ahead.

This composer, like his colleagues, was well aware that the business was an uncertain one, and he had given a lot of thought to this. Outwardly he had lost none of his confidence or his characteristic fussiness about his work or stinginess about how he spent his money. But from the day on which the New York papers clobbered one of his film scores, something seemed to change in him. His face bore traces of the rising tension. He realized that a freelancer never finds a spot where he is "home free." Credits, contacts, typecasts, and commitments give only the first hints of what is to come as a freelancer moves into more work, with more filmmakers, with more labels (both positive and negative) attached to him, and with more choices about what to do with his cash. If the freelancer becomes aggressive, entrepreneurial, self-promoting, apprehensive, and at times paranoid, it is because these pressures can gnaw away at his self-esteem and talent the way radium infects the bone marrow of workers in clock factories.

Notes

1. For example, suppose that composer A is connected to producers B and C. Suppose further that filmmakers B and C themselves have ties with many film producers (D, E, F, G, etc.). Thus, composer A himself has only two connections, but he is tied with filmmakers who are themselves heavily tied into the freelance labor market. By contrast, consider freelancer X, a composer who works with producers Y and Z. Filmmakers Y and Z work only with X. The network of connections for freelancer X is sparse compared to the dense set of work ties linking A to B and C, and indirectly linking A to D, E, F, G. Thus, if we use the number of television or film credits to measure how well connected composer A or composer X are in Hollywood, we would find that A and X are equally connected in the market. This would not take into account the connections and networks of the employers with whom A and X work. Chapter 8, "Centrality in a Freelance Social Structure," considers the structure of tightly and sparsely knit networks and their consequences for career continuity and success.
2. On the social organization of commitment and personal change, see Howard S. Becker, "Personal Change in Adult Life." In Gregory P. Stone and Harvey A.

Farberman (eds.), *Social Psychology through Symbolic Interaction* (New York: Wiley, 1981); Robert R. Faulkner, ''Coming of Age in Organizations: A Comparative Study of Career Contingencies and Adult Socialization,'' ibid. A detailed and copiously illustrated sourcebook for students of television work and television credits is Alvin H. Marill, *Movies Made for Television: The Telefeature and the Miniseries, 1964–1979* (New Rochelle, N.Y.: Arlington House, 1980).

4.
NO MUSICAL REVOLUTIONS
Some Prompt Effects of
Commercial Conventions

Television is just not the place to stage a musical revolution.
— Thirty-two-year-old composer

Sure, I said once, "What's wrong with those dummies in Hollywood? Don't they know any better? Boy, that's really crappy music. They're not trying anymore." Now I know. Trying what? Trying to get out of this business? It's easy to stand outside and put it down before you know the conditions. A lot of it is just writing things that are expected, that have to be done on time, and that have to follow the format you're working in. It's just not the time to start fooling around.
— High-volume TV composer with two film credits

I would say that in episodic television, if you do something truly great probably no one's going to notice. If you do something not so great, they probably won't notice, either. The only thing you have to stay away from is doing something bad. So that gives you a great deal of latitude to try things.
— Barry DeVorzon, composer

The producers feel they must control the audience's interest every moment—that's why we get mediocrity. I'm not trying to be snide about it. We have a boatload of talent out here, and we're just allowing them to ape and mimic.
— Walter Scharf, composer

Hired hands—or artists? Are film composers subservient technicians skilled in working against time pressures and within worn commercial grooves, or independent creators able to balance the demands of commerce and creativity? Are they simple pawns in the television producer's master plan, or dedicated professionals who demonstrate their extraordinary range, stay away from "bad" work, and get the job done?

The commercial composer is all of these things. His career is shaped by the ways he handles these opposing tendencies. In the early going, he may find himself cast in the role of hired hand on someone else's project, or he may be asked to fashion a whole new musical approach to a television show. In either case he learns that to acquire experience as a professional he has to work with clients whose ideas about what they want differ markedly from his own, or those he thinks any composer would hold. He learns that to continue to work he must deal with filmmakers who are themselves hemmed-in by their own inexperience, ineptitude, or plain fear. The new composer gathers disconnected bits of information as he moves from one assignment to the next, and gradually he pieces together an image of his profession.

He quickly learns that what a film composer is, and when, depends on who he is working for, the conventions he is asked to work within, the dramatic materials he has to work with, and what he thinks he has to offer the project. His role contribution will vary enormously. Some filmmakers delegate large amounts of autonomy to him; others do not. Some projects are highly routinized; others are not. He may be able to work wonders at the spotting session with the producer and director and then minor miracles in the recording of the music a few weeks later, or he may be asked to do very conventional things by the producer and humiliated if he does not comply. He may be the hero of the project on the recording stage but the villain during the final dubbing session as filmmakers, sound personnel, and other interested parties start to realize that this is their last shot at making adjustments in "their" film, "their" series, and "their" own work. He may even find himself being blamed if the project dies a quick and horrible death at the box office or is unceremoniously axed by the network.

Out of such contradictions, the newcomer to the film business must form conclusions about the "normal" character of his work, and those conclusions will shape and define his entire career. He may conclude that there are no musical revolutions in television. He may give up certain points of view that were appropriate for earlier stages of his career but that now, under the pressures of day-to-day commercial work, are plainly inappropriate. He may find that to deal effectively and practically with the business he often has to satisfy his clients at the cost of denying himself satisfaction. And he often learns to live with these conclusions by distancing himself from his work. One young composer with three years' experience and a recent film credit, who had worked at Universal, notorious for being the greatest pressure cooker in Hollywood, said:

> The fact is that we're up against a terrifying medium. Universal's a great place to start, a great place to get experience. But the schedule is a killer. You have to learn how to work under pressure and not overwrite. There are things in episodic television that just do not demand more than a little flair for drama and a lot of speed in execution. Like other places in this town, they're not afraid to say, "Here's the show,

here's the timing sheet. If you don't like it, there's the gate.'' It's scary. [In many ways freelancers breaking in via television are indeed expendable pawns which is hardly flattering, but given the number of talented composers all trying for a shot.] You take what you can get and do your very best job. You learn that writing for television is a secondary kind of contribution. There's a reason for that—no one wants to take a chance, especially on *you*. So you are given assignments, as I was, by one of my friends. You are coached as to what to do. It's important not to lose sight of this fact, because, if you do, you can write yourself out of the business in a hurry. Sometimes you just have to cool it. *Usually* you have to *cool it,* as a matter of fact. I think we'd kill ourselves in writing complex music, if it would work, if it would be a contribution to the project. But on most things, like the weekly episodic stuff, complex music would be a big, big mistake. The producer and those above him want something more or less "expected." I'm doing a prime-time show right now where my friend's music for the pilot set the tone. Now that it's established, it's more or less standardized.

One of his colleagues with similar work experience used the same words, "expected"and "standardized," to describe the demands at this studio. "Television is a sort of a college," he said. "You learn a lot in a hurry, and you learn how to work under pressure, and you learn what you're supposed to deliver. You also see that in some cases it's just not that big of a deal anyway— it's on the air and then it's gone. You're under pressure to satisfy the requirements of the beast.'' This last phrase means turning out episode after episode, getting familiar with the working deadlines, and learning how to write with speed and accuracy to fill the turnover of products shown on the air.

Let's face it, if you start adding fugues and some intricate things, you'll most likely clutter up the soundtrack and get in the way of the dialogue— or at least you'll be doing something different from what they want you to do. Television is just not the place to stage a musical revolution. But occasionally you do something special, a good thing comes along— like last year I got the chance to do something fresh. But when you're just coming into the business you're an interchangeable part. Few guys make big splashes like Mancini did with *Peter Gunn* or Jerry Goldsmith did on a couple of his own shows at CBS, and anyway they put in their years in television before moving into better things, so why should I complain? I want to do more feature films, and who doesn't? In motion pictures you have more time and you get a different shot at the audience.

Writing music for a television series, particularly if one is added-on to the series is, as Lee Margulies of the *Los Angeles Times* once quipped, "sort of like building snowmen at the top of Mt. Everest": It may be art, but who is really going to notice? A few shows that caught on brought recognition and visibility to their composers—Henry Mancini's "Peter Gunn," Jerry Goldsmith's "Dr. Kildare" and "Police Story," Fred Steiner's "Perry Mason," Lalo Schifrin's "Mission: Impossible" and "Hawaii Five-O," Barry DeVorzon's "S.W.A.T.," Richard Markowitz's "Wild, Wild West," Mike Post and Pete Carpenter's "Rockford Files," Jack Eliot and Allyn Ferguson's "Charlie's Angels," and John Cacavas's "Kojak." But these are few and far between. And they typically involve the composer who comes up with the idea for the main title or the opening theme for the show. For the most part those composers breaking in through television are matched, either by colleagues or by filmmakers, to an already established series. They remain behind the scenes, consciously trying and being expected to write music that fits into the existing framework, music that does not call attention to itself. They may try to write music that will enhance what is being seen on the screen, but it must fit the style that has already been agreed upon by composer and television filmmaker. And the new composer must fit into this network of people who cooperate to produce that project.

The newcomer sees that the same people often cooperate repeatedly, even routinely, in producing and scoring similar series, specials, and television movies. He sees and hears just how things are done and learns the routines that make such cooperation possible. He then learns what it means to be a replacement: that those who sponsor him expect him to act strictly within these conventions so that the project moves ahead without time, money, and talent being wasted.

These conventions are essentially taken-for-granted agreements among all the parties involved in a Hollywood production.[1] To a great extent, they determine the music and the newcomer must learn how to use them. Thus there are a variety of conventional functions of music in film and the newcomer must learn each one. He should know how to write music which creates a specific mood for a specific character, music which evokes time periods, or the culture in which the action takes place, music which builds continuity from scene to scene or builds overall continuity, revealing the psychological makeup of character, by accenting, even mimicking, what is happening on the screen, or by underlining unspoken thoughts of characters or revealing the unseen implications of a situation. Composers must know how to use music to make a philosophical point, or set the audience up for a surprise, or even deceive the audience about what has actually happened. For instance, in an entirely conventional way, Williams's music in *Jaws* sets the audience up by creating the expectation that whenever the jagged, insistent rhythms occur the shark will appear. The sudden appearance of the shark without "musical warning," is doubly shocking.

Conventions also suggest the appropriate dimensions of a project, the size of the orchestra, the amount of time to be spent in recording the score, whether a given approach to the project can be adapted to the specifications of a three-inch television speaker, and what orchestration will achieve the desired effects. They also dicate the compositional materials to be used, whether the music will be twelve-tone, as in Leonard Rosenman's *Fantastic Voyage* and Lalo Schifrin's *Hellstrom Chronicle;* jazz-influenced, as in John Mandel's *I Want to Live* and Henry Mancini's *Peter Gunn;* rock and rhythm, as in Tom Scott's ''Baretta''; or lyrically romantic, as in Leonard Rosenman's ''Marcus Welby'' and Alexander Courage and Arthur Morton's ''Peyton Place.''

These conventions constitute a sort of code that facilitates work with the producer and director; it establishes agreement without having to go through the process of agreeing about which dramatic situations should be spotted, what materials should be used, and the form those materials should be arranged in and for how long. Decisions can be made quickly, leaving freelancers more time for their real work. Any television buff who listens to the music knows the predictability of the conventions. Here is one very businesslike freelancer explaining what happened on a popular series the year before.

> I decided that I didn't want any more of it. I was busy with a film and I tried to bring D (a young colleague) into the television show. You see, after we got the main title, the whole thing settles into doing the same thing over again and then doing it again. D understands this, he's very facile and has great range, but I didn't really have to spend any time with him. The show was fixed, almost locked in. The producers liked what I had worked out for the main character, sort of rock, hip, jazz oriented, and that was what we were going to go with. We had a small orchestra, the best performers in town. And the producer now doesn't want me to make any changes. If I did that it wouldn't make any sense. D took over and took it from there—it was his ball. It got him an in. He's now on his way.

The young colleague's view of all this was characteristic.

> I still had to write the music, but the thing was set. I know if I'm writing for this show—let's say it's some hard-nosed guy who goes around shouting at people, and maybe he has a little humanity here and there—I know what the producer wants to hear; the solution is pretty clear. I can't fool around, you know? I could write myself off this show, if I started to fool around. [He got up from the chair in his studio, went over to the piano and played a fast four-part atonal couple of bars.] No way [he shouted over the last bar], no way. The secret of writing for weekly television is knowing what *not* to write. You see, they don't expect you to write something to put in the vault that will be hauled

out in fifty years and played by a symphony. They want something that will work behind the scene. Due to the time limitations, you often have to write the first thing off the top of your head. And also, on something like what I'm doing now, what's being done is already set.

Work and experience. The newcomer develops ideas about the nature of the medium he is working in, but more important, he develops theories about how to make it work for himself, and conceptions of the people he has to deal with on a day-to-day basis if he is to get more and better assignments. He must also have a shrewd sense of politics. The following scenario was spelled out by a freelancer with almost five years invested in the business. He was just moving into his first feature, having lost a project to a competitor a few months earlier. During these years, he had seen several of his colleagues fall by the wayside. This had a profound effect on his own perception of himself as a freelancer and the choices confronting him.

"I've learned that you should know who the players are, who the figures on the big Monopoly board are out here." Politics, he maintained, was the difference between one very young and "hot" colleague-friend, who had recently won several Academy Award nominations, and another man trapped in television episodes. Describing the second composer, he said, "He is probably one of the most incredibly equipped composers ever to walk the face of the earth. Unbelievable. He can give you a Penderecki score overnight! He's a greater talent than any of the top guys in town." The incident had happened recently and was fresh to him and important. "He got an assignment to do an episode of a series, and he ended up writing a five-voice atonal fugue for it. It was great, fantastic, but *come on*. That's not being realistic at all. The show isn't like that." The result was that the score was thrown out, the producer threw a fit, and everyone got the message. The composer has not been invited back since.

These first experiences in a line of work provide a moral education in the politics of fear and conformity. The colleague with the amazing facility made a major, visible mistake at work. It was an error in judgment and an error of a particularly profound and social kind because he chose uncommercial trouble over commercial ease. Any producer is likely to resist something that starts to move out of the established groove, because he does not want to tamper with his sure thing. If the show is delivering its audience to the advertisers, if the people at the network are happy with the Nielsen ratings and the comparative share of viewers pulled in, and if the producer and director are pleased with the musical score *as is*, then anything new will be seen as deviant, even, indeed, an attack on the very nature of their success. A producer can feel betrayed when "his" composer startles him by suddenly composing music that is unexpected, different, and, what is worse, so different that he can actually *hear the difference*.

While the freelancer may share special knowledge, identity, and loyalty with his colleagues rather than filmmakers, he learns that his continued livelihood in the business depends on filmmakers. He picks up gossip about what has happened to those who insulted or surprised the producers. He learns to understand and deal with the pressures caused by filmmakers' own fears and needs to compromise. He must do what he can to increase his visibility, display a cooperative face, and hope they will call his agent. If he has the patience, desire, and stomach for slugging it out on these terms, the gift for locating what is technically and commercially required, and can deliver when called, the new arrival becomes a valuable commodity of the sort the industry breeds and is comfortable with. It is not a simple matter of ''selling out.'' Any person writing for film must understand his relation to the larger project.

> The film composer's obligation is to make what is on the screen come alive and to enhance it, not to clutter it up or to make it too diffuse [observed a veteran of six years in television with two film credits and years of commercial experience]. A lot of composers feel the screen is their showcase. It's not true. There are times to shine—on a main title or whatever—but if you're fighting sound effects or dialogue, then you've got to lay back. You have to know your tempos, how to get into and out of a scene, your timings, and you have to know how to write in between the holes, in between the dialogue. That way you won't get in the way. The hardest thing is to write as well as you can, every time, that's the hardest. A lot of it you can fake with orchestration. But the important thing is to write what you consider to be the right music for each situation. That comes from experience.

Part of the experience comes from exposure to and association with other composers. They are all great students of one another. They listen to one another's work and joke about stealing from each other.

> It's great being associated with the best, and I'm encouraged constantly to push just a little bit. You can look at a scene and say, ''Okay, this could be done this way and I've done it ten times like that before, so basically I can treat it that way again and it will work.'' Then you have to make that decision that may take you a little longer. Maybe I'll have to think a little bit more, do something different, and then I'll have to worry a few nights before I play this for the producer, and then maybe I've gone *too far*. If he likes it, I'm going to be happy with myself and my work, and I'm going to be propelled further.

The demand is to deliver—to write on time, on request, and on target. The bait is the chance to work—to move from scoring assignments that are often dull, repetitive, and highly predictable to those that are more interesting and challenging. The knack is to write in a musical and cinematic way that will be acceptable to the producer but will also give the composer pride in his work. This description of the film composer's entry to the profession shows the importance of compromise. It is all too easy to see such compromise as a lowering of the standards and values the composer begins with, but such a view is usually an inaccurate cliché. The compromise a film composer must achieve is not the result of a process of weakening but of strengthening his own craft—his talent and his ability to function in the Hollywood scene—to balance conflicting demands. A successful and productive freelancer must be responsible to both the fiscal and creative aspect of his job, and the job itself is one that requires a careful balance. Every composer wants to enhance the value of a film with his score, but he must do so within a relatively narrow range of dramatic and musical conventions. Both balances must be maintained; the composer must be responsible to but not enslaved by all the opposing tendencies inherent in his work.

There is no single, permanent resolution of the tensions in the work of a freelance film composer. His problems are genuine dilemmas, not merely characteristic of one special work situation, but intrinsic to commercial work. As a composer gets more work, he forms a conception of "normal" work out of the bits and pieces of experience he faces. Gradually he learns that the problems in his work world cannot be solved, only more or less successfully handled. His early socialization is one of learning to live within these dilemmas.[2] Since other freelancers are trying to learn to live with the same problems and trying out different ways of handling them too, they share problems and gather a common body of experience. In all important respects, they build a common culture through anecdotes and scenarios about their work and employers. "We all try to help one another, sure, we talk, we commiserate. We all know that at times you'll have a film and you see the chance to do something interesting but the producer will just be afraid of it. He'll ask you to do something more 'usual.'"

This composer was fresh from a successful string of work in television, successful at least in terms of volume and royalties. He was now eager for more film work and talked of "blasting" his way into that kind of work, which is a good indication of the degree to which he felt the need for a change in his career development. First, he did not want to get "buried" doing only television. Second, he felt that it was time to work on more "heavyweight" projects, more feature films of substance. And third, he was getting tired of the television projects he was associated with—"like recipes from a cookbook." One incident was used to illustrate the problem.

The producer will make the typical speech at the beginning of your work with him. He'll say, "This is something special and I want something fresh and original, none of that old stuff, no, no." But when it gets down to the short strokes he'll say, "Well, maybe we better not do that. Maybe we better play it safe." One television producer came up with a nice show a few years back. I had an idea for him. I described to him what I was going to do and he actually let me go ahead and do it. I did a score using some interesting combinations of instruments. It was a kind of hillbilly thing, a score I would have been really proud of. [I asked what had happened.] He threw it out, he couldn't handle it, *too different*. He made me add strings. You know the old saying, "When in trouble, add violins." That's the formula. I had to redo it. He paid for a huge orchestra and, yes, it was more or less the regular television movie music. That's a nasty problem. You deal with their taste; their taste may not agree with yours.

He continued by noting the technical demands that had to be met, that is, the professional and commercial requirements that had to be fulfilled. The discontinuity between what he saw as possible and what he was ordered to turn out showed him "just what I had to learn if I was going to survive. I almost found it *impossible* to write noodles behind some screen action. It was difficult. I almost struck out in my first few scores. It took all of my effort to write stuff that was sufficiently musically bland to go under dialogue. It got to the point where I felt I just couldn't write another dumb thing. I almost couldn't do it." I asked what his solution was. "Do it and forget about it. Do it and hope things will get better."

For many of the freelancers I talked with, whatever happens is worth it for what the future holds out; often it is worth it for the fun of working on a project, the excitement, the possible rewards. He hoped it would be that way for him. It seemed that he had made a lot of money but still had not made much progress toward doing what he really wanted to do. "There is a pain of not fulfilling the possibilities of what we might be able to do musically, yes, that's a dilemma." He paused. "Once you forget what you are being paid for you can get into trouble, immediate trouble. Reputations are made out here for being fast, efficient, for knowing what to *avoid*. Push music into the forefront and you won't get hired; it's that simple. It's a difficult lesson that has to be experienced, believe me."

At the most fundamental level this tension stems from the fact that film composers' work combines within itself what are probably the two major pulls of commercialism, tensions which seem to be radically and irreconcilably opposed. Hollywood demands both working according to conventions and working according to one's top expertise. These demands are fused, if not exactly into a convenient package, at least into a *way of seeing things*.

"In writing," said one composer, "you have an obligation to the film, to the man who hires you, and to your craft. Now you don't always write the right kind of music for a particular scene, that's impossible. And you don't function as an artist at all times, that's impossible. There are always fifteen different ways to do something, and you're not going to please everybody with what you write, but the important thing is to realize your obligation and then to please yourself with your music, have faith in your own writing ability, and hope that what you like is what the people you are working for will like." This young composer was describing his way of seeing things. A great part of the process of becoming a film composer is developing a conception of the industry and of one's role in it. All the interviews indicate that the successful composers develop a conception of the business that does not deny but does try to contain the conflicts inherent in it and develop a mode of working that somehow accommodates the tensions. Every composer will find his own accommodation, but all of them must be responsible to certain facts.

One of those facts constitutes a lesson the people I interviewed seemed to keep learning over and over again: artistic considerations are secondary to the demands of the marketplace, or more concretely, to those demands as they are defined and managed by people who own the film, hire the people to work on it, and try to get what they think they want from those they hire. This first fact is closely related to the second fact: freelancers have to serve filmmakers' needs largely in filmmakers' terms. Filmmakers are in control; they own the project being worked on. While the composer and filmmaker theoretically agree on the end product of their work—a good film score—their definitions of that may vary and, when that is the case, the filmmakers' terms will predominante. Composers cannot forget that once the score is completed, the filmmaker has the final say in how to use it. A producer or director can then do anything he wants with the music, because he does, after all, own it. He can turn it inside out, upside down, dub it louder or softer, spot cues in places not originally intended by the composer, or throw it out. The composer learns that over the long run the leverage is in the hands of the person who hires him.[3]

There are as many ways of accommodating these "facts" as there are composers. Take, for instance, the issue of conventions. A standardized demand for a standardized score may work to the advantages of both filmmaker and composer. It facilitates decreased cooperation, defines vision, and decreases mutual risk. The "formula" thereby insures, more or less, that the dilemmas of commercialism be kept within manageable bounds.

A neophyte to the commercial world quickly learns that the one element an ordinary producer on an ordinary project most wants to minimize in his work life is randomness. The producer calculates, plans, strives, "hypes," exactly in order to reduce the hazards of something unexpected or *too* unexpected. Reliance on musical conventions is a major part of the producer's effort to minimize randomness in the film project, but the composer's attitude is likely to be more complex. When the composer is starting his career and simply grateful for the opportunity to work, the producer's terms do not seem too restrictive. But as the freelancer meets other filmmakers and gains access to a greater variety of work credits, he starts to feel the difference between craft and art, between knowing what one has to do and what one wants to do, or could do. A choice becomes possible. One mode of working is plainly safe and the other full of risk and incipient danger—danger to status, reputation, and future connections and credits.

Not all composers I talked with are drawn to the risk side of the spectrum. They are the first to feel the compulsive attraction to routine, the comfort in doing what is expected, on time, and with craft. Their endless camouflage, good-humored resignation to most of their assignments, casual belittlement of colleagues, and matter-of-fact shrugs all suggest an acceptance of a limited range of performance demands. There is comfort and safety in being orchestrators of others' work and enjoying the cumulative effects of performance royalties. Such composers rarely chafe under the demands for a "formula" score for yet another add-on job; they are the routine seekers of the industry.

The ambitious neophyte sees these people all around him. In his own early television work he will see colleagues content to remain only in television whose work is written out of a desire to please the producer rather than stretch his own imagination. What for some is a simple sapping and leaching of the imagination and skill is for others a "home," a place of secure craft with limited horizons where the main challenge is to keep working. Faced with such models, the composer with some television experience and perhaps one feature film to his career line must begin to make some choices about personal preferences, and about where in this division of talent and labor his own special gifts will be most effective.

He starts to learn the real "script," and discards the illusion that his work will be autonomous and flawless. He may trim his conception of himself to a neater, more conventional, and perhaps smaller pattern, that accommodates the demands of others. If "television demands more technique than inspiration," as one put it, it also demands insight into when and where one is perfectly matched or, conversely, mismatched for a project. To be a professional, and display it, means to cultivate detachment, the ability to consider the views of powerful others and make an intelligent assessment of the exchange any project represents. "What can the employer offer me, what can I offer him?" The trimming of self-conceptions is not a question of "should" or "whether," but "when" and "how." The decisions a man makes as he adjusts to his early work experience are dependent on the kinds of projects he is getting, the degree of like-mindedness between himself and the filmmaker, and the reactions of others to his work. A composer shapes but is also shaped by his own career line and career choices.

Notes

1. Elizabeth Burns, *Theatricality: A Study of Convention in the Theatre and in Social Life* (New York: Harper Torchbooks, 1972); Howard S. Becker, "Art as Collective Action," *American Sociological Review* 39 (1974): 767–76; Barbara Rosenblum, "Style as Social Process," *American Sociological Review* 43 (1978): 422–38; Edward R. Kealy, "From Craft to Art: The Case of Sound Mixers and Popular Music," *Sociology of Work and Occupations* 6 (1979): 3–29; Eleanor Lyon, "Work and Play: Resource Constraints in a Small Theater," *Urban Life* 3 (1974): 71–97.
2. Erving Goffman has noted, in his discussion of moral careers: "It appears that conformity to the prescriptive aspects of role often occurs most thoroughly at the neophyte level, when the individual must prove his competence, sincerity, and awareness of his place." *Asylums* (New York: Doubleday Anchor, 1961), pp. 127–69.
3. As I will show throughout, transactions with filmmakers are a key to how the freelancer learns what the role requirements are, how to adapt to those requirements, and, with luck, how to eventually shape the demands toward his own interests. Important new interpersonal relationships must be learned throughout the development of a Hollywood career. Orville Brim laments the lack of detailed sociological studies of this process in occupational and adult socialization research. "Most of the descriptions of adult socialization in the family and in the community," he says, "deal with interpersonal situations and accommodations of one person to another. It is surprising, then, to find that for the occupational world there is no comparable body of information on the process of socialization which undoubtedly takes place between colleagues or between an employee and his boss." Orville G. Brim, Jr., "Adult Socialization." In *Socialization and Society*, ed. John Clausen (Boston: Little, Brown, 1969), p. 203.

5.

A SMALL ARMY
Career Mobility and Precariousness in the Middle Area

The middle area is really the toughest to crack. Breaking through into the big leagues becomes very difficult because you need credits and you need a film that will give you some exposure. By now, I'm known around town, but I'm not that much in demand, yet. I'm not a new face anymore, but I'm not being considered for the better films either. If you're lucky you establish some alliances with the people you work for and that keeps things going.
—Freelancer with four films between 1974 and 1977

I'm hoping that when they graduate to better films those guys [filmmakers] will take me along.
—Freelancer with three films between 1974 and 1977

Moving from the middle into the inner circles is no easier than breaking into the business originally. There is hardly any tougher task in this business than building a string of film credits and acquiring a set of alliances with filmmakers. Becoming known and getting access to more and better assignments is the industry's equivalent of jungle warfare. The key elements of success are talent, timing, persistence, ties with those who control the work, a capacity for dealing with different and often difficult people, a taste for risks, a thick hide, a chameleon-like ability to adapt to circumstances—and a lot of luck.

There is considerable inequality in the distributions of status, income, and power. Each step toward the center of Big Hollywood dramatically narrows the field. On the periphery there are 252 freelancers with only a single film credit. In the semiperiphery or middle area there are 150 freelancers with between two and six credits, but there are only around 40 highly productive figures at the center of work with seven to fifty films scored. The composer trying to crack one of the circles places his bets on many things. Tightly coupled alliances with film producers are key assets. But so are loosely coupled, one-shot ties across multiple filmmakers, because continuity of assignments rests in good part on multiple supports from wider networks of employers. By and large, the central figures in the inner circle have such a combination of ties. They are also known and proven quantities. They capture the market and score over 40 percent of the 1,355 feature films. The 150 standing just outside this inner circle competed for 35 percent (477) of the total number of movies scored over the twelve-year period.

The stakes vary. Producers with big-budget films are understandably reluctant to take a chance on someone they do not know, have not heard about, or think is inexperienced. With resources at his command and a lot of investment capital at stake, the filmmaker is under considerable pressure to hire those who have scored big-budget films in the past, and that means those with proven track records and a hefty string of credits. For other projects, a productive filmmaker may have a smaller budget, be unable to sign the freelancer he wants, and be encouraged to hire a new face in town. At the other end of this continuum we find producers with one or two credits themselves, a poverty-row picture to be scored, and an "el chintzo" budget for music and composer. As one of the busiest and most successful agents for composers put it, "If you're in that middle area, you don't stop and think if it's good or bad; you've got to do it because you need those credits. The credits at this point in a career can be good, bad, or indifferent, as long as you have them."

Mobility depends on recognition. Even if the recognition is based on inaccurate labeling, a lamentably common tendency of filmmakers, it is essential in order to broaden one's base and boost the probabilities for future ties. A broad base is particularly necessary for composers in this semiperipheral, midstream of the business since they work for producers with hugely diverse track records. Of the 477 features scored by those composers with two to six credits, 28 percent (134) were for the most productive filmmakers with five or more credits, 41 percent (197) for filmmakers with two to four films, and 30 percent (1946) for those who just made their first Hollywood feature film.

The colleague company is fast. Table 5.1 is instructive. There are 310 freelancers listed on 725 films scored from 1970–71 to 1975–76, for example, and 62 percent (192) have only one credit, 31 percent (96) have two to five credits, and 7 percent (22) are moving ahead with six or more feature films. Forty-four percent (52) are new to the film business in these years and have put together two to five credits very quickly. The allocation of jobs—with dominants and mainliners running far ahead of the marginals and contributors—combined with the aspirations and drives for upward mobility among all these composers, create the most unsettling of all Hollywood propositions: that many freelancers are called but few are chosen. Many freelancers get just enough work to keep their hopes high but not enough to satisfy their

TABLE 5.1
Who Gets Ahead? Career Productivity and Occupational Rank,
1964–69 and 1970–75

Composers' Productivity 1964–69 (630 films)	Composers' Productivity 1970–75 (725 feature films)						
	Dominants (11–24)[b]	Mainliners (6–10)	Contributors (2–5)	Marginals (1)	Not Scoring	N	%
Dominants (10–28)	36%	28%	36%	0	0	(14)	6%
Mainliners (5–9)	14%	15%	38%	14%	19%	(21)	9%
Contributors (2–4)	0	3%	24%	22%	51%	(67)	29%
Marginals (1)	1%	0	12%	13%	74%	(126)	56%
Not Scoring	1%	2%	24%	73%	---	(228 Composers --1964–60)	
N	(10)	(12)	(96)	(192)		(310 Composers --1970–75)[c]	
%	3%	4%	31%	62%			

[a] Rank is defined by a composer's share of the available market; a "Dominant" freelancer captures 1.5 percent of the available market during the six-year period; a "mainliner" .8 to 1.4 percent, a "contributor" .3 to .7 percent, and the "Marginal" freelancer .1 percent.

[b] This is the range of the volume of work.

[c] Total N = 442, 16 df, X^2 = 400, p = .001.

hunger for more and better film assignments. As newcomers move up from television and in from the outside, the displacement of those with a moderate line of work results in considerable anger and malaise, a work and career disenchantment that can range from moderate to devastating.

There are no guarantees. From the sixties to the seventies there is a pronounced shift upward in the middle area group as a whole, as indicated in Table 5.1. There is an increase of those with two to five films rising from 15 to 21 percent. Of the composers in the middle area, 51 percent (34) dropped out of sight. They failed to score any films from 1970–71 to 1975–76. Some dropped back into television and picked up former alliances with television producers and directors who had themselves failed to move into film work. There are no guarantees, and the bottom rung is precarious, but the middle rung in Hollywood is also dangerously slippery.

Let us turn now to work connections and the variety of ways they can influence a midstream contributor's career line. If every aspiring composer acquired work through advertising in *The Hollywood Reporter* or *Daily Variety,* or in an industrial "shape up" every morning before the gates of the major film studios, or through a flyer on the bulletin board at the local headquarters of The Association of Motion Picture and Television Producers, there would be little need to detail how these connecting threads between composers and employers are woven. I shall stay close to the original materials, particularly the interviews with contributors immediately below the top constellation of leading freelancers. Of particular interest are those who have made some fast steps in the late 1970s, since their views about what has happened to them are fresher, closer to the events that shaped them. A string of work and a series of encounters with employers allows the freelancer on the move to see clearly what has been happening to him all along. Trends, turning points, and position within the industry become apparent. A man with six films from 1972 to 1976 said:

> It's a funny business, and I didn't realize it at the time when I started out, but a couple of those early things really proved to be very significant for me, and also for some other people associated with the film. I did develop a good relation with the producer of one, he took a chance on me, and fortunately the film was a big success. There tends to be a snowball effect. People talk to people, producers talk to producers, you come to their attention. People notice you, your work. They notice you especially if the film is doing well. I mean, we're always subject to that. The first film I did with a big star in it was about three years ago. It became sort of a model for the things that followed. You hope that more things like that will come up and you'll be considered for the better projects.

Shared concerns are nicely brought to the surface in this statement. To make a real mark, the new arrival has to do something to engage the interest and investments of powerful filmmakers. The relationship between the midstream composer and his employers is essentially one of exchange, and unless producers see a composer as desirable, commercial, and marketable, he will not receive the projects that are absolutely necessary for extending his career line. His "worth" on the freelance market is proportional to his ability to command exchange value. Since few things succeed like a commercial hit in Hollywood, the object of career-work at this point, and all further points, is sufficient notice from trend-spotting filmmakers to get into a position of comparative advantage with the "better" producers in Hollywood, a position where one has some leverage and control over one's work. Such exchanges, commercial and otherwise, dominate the film business.

I will proceed by taking up the three problems that loom largest in free-lancers' discussion of their adjustments in midstream: (1) the problems of ties and alliances with single employers on various types of assignments; (2) the problems of visibility and confirmation for one's work; and (3) the problem of becoming chosen by circles of powerful and prestigious filmmakers.

Ties and Alliances

After studying at The Manhattan School of Music and in Paris with Nadia Boulanger, the following composer divided his time between commercial jobs and music in New York. He scored a project there for a young filmmaker friend, moved to Los Angeles in the early seventies, and broke into the business through television episodes, ghosting, and then an alliance with a producer on the rise. After a couple of package deals, he came to the attention of a top filmmaker; the man liked his television work and was secure enough in his musical judgment to give the composer a chance to score a $4-million schmaltzy romantic film calling for a full symphonic sound. The music was very effective and the film was a moderate success.

> That was a break. The man took a big chance and then gave me a lot of freedom to choose the orchestra; he gave plenty of positive input and didn't interfere. It is a slow process. A film works. Someone tells someone else about you. The big jump is into features. It's enormous and most guys never seem to make it from TV into films. There's a very mysterious set of frontiers and you need some vehicle that stands out. Everybody is trying to get across those frontiers, and the passport is knowing somebody who will trust you and *take a chance* on you. Filmmakers are usually reluctant to take chances; and they've got a lot at stake. When there's that much money involved, they are very cautious. Unfortunately, their decisions are usually not based on judgments

of your work. They are on what your work is associated with, the film, the project. They know you can do the job or you wouldn't be working at all, that's the first hurdle. What producers don't know is *how well* you can do the job, how good you are. The only way they can know that is if someone says, "I know this composer and he can do it, he'll be perfect." Producers need some *verification*. A director talks to a director, or a producer says, "I've worked with this guy and he's easy to work with; he's easy to communicate with, use him."

He looked over my list of composers that I had brought along to the interview. "Every guy on your list of composers is excellent."

"You assume craftsmanship, competence," I offered, "and then the matching gets made on the basis of what the composer has worked on and how visible he is."

You assume competence, you have to. The guys with tenacity, drive, whatever, are generally the ones who make out. If you want to be a film composer you have to keep doing it and keep doing it and know you're going to pay your dues, know you're going to be unappreciated for a long time. Then when it happens it's nice. And never think you've got it made, not in this town. Things change. You have to know what's going on, the styles, who's on the rise—there's a kind of Machiavellian intrigue that goes into getting a film. It is a market, and you're at the mercy of the people who control these projects.

He kept scoring, six projects in a few years. His batting average was pretty good, too: two were commercial hits, two were acceptable and paid back their cost with a couple of million, and two were disappointments. His batting average was over .300, and the top producers who took a chance on him were probably going to rehire him if a similar project came up. At present, he had proven himself with three projects between 1972 and 1976, was getting more and more television movies of the week, and was looking for a "good project" that would bring him visibility in the industry.

Getting a chance to play in the game itself can be difficult. The following composer had been in Hollywood for three years. Sponsored by one of the top composers when he first moved into work at Universal studios, he picked up the customary television episode work in the first year there, did a few pilots after that, and most recently had a well-received movie for television to his credit. He had worked closely with his colleague-sponsor since, was music supervisor on a recent film and, through that string of work, had come to the attention of several producers. One in particular liked his work and called him recently. The project was a low-budget horror film: "He's an 'el chintzo' producer; he's done a couple of features, all low-budget. So I go over and walk into his office and he says, 'This is a low-budget picture. This is a very low budget picture. This is a very, *very* low budget picture. Are you still interested?' 'Yes,' I said. So I sit down and it's the same old story; he wants to save every penny he can. He wants to put a *package* together. That's the way we get started; that's the way some guys get a shot at a feature.''

"Now the important thing about packaging," he instructed me, "is that the composer takes all the risks.'' He noted a horror film that had just been released. The composer had put together a total package for ten thousand dollars. That is very inexpensive by composers' standards. It is less than the man would get to compose the score alone, not counting rental of the studio, musicians, the copyist, and other costs. Two composers had been in consideration—that is, in competition—for the project. He continued, "The producer had liked my tapes and wanted to work out a deal. He kept calling and, after apologizing six times, would ask me if I could get a deal on a recording studio. I told him, 'Yes, I can get a third off at a place.' He then said, 'Do you know anybody who owns a recording studio where you could make a deal in exchange for another favor? Where you wouldn't have to pay *any* studio at all?' I said, 'No, I can't tell you that.' Well, the other composer obviously knew somebody who could, because he got the picture and I didn't. I heard later that he had scored it for ten thousand overall. Now the producer had mentioned something in the area of twenty-five, for everything, which is still considerably low, considering all the things we talked about—studio, musicians, copyist. And the picture has 45 to 50 minutes of music in it. That is a lot of music. I want to go see the movie just to see what he did. I think you have to be kind of desperate to do that, just to get a credit.''

For the man who got the job, it was his third film after a long hiatus. He had come up the ranks in television but broke out by doing a film with a major producer. The film was an Academy Award winner. In most cases this kind of work leads to something else, but for this composer it led to only two more projects before he was back trying to put together a package for a poverty-row producer. A year later, the freelancer who had been passed over got a chance. He was friends with a young director with whom he had come up the line in television. They both got their chance on a very low budget science-fiction film working with a young producer with two credits over the past three years. The music budget was $4,500 for everything—again, composing, arranging, copying, musicians, rental of the recording facilities, and so forth. Hungry enough now, the composer somehow brought if off. After the science-fiction film, the director was tapped by a filmmaker to do a medium-budget project, in the $2 to $4 million category, and he went to bat for his composer colleague. The composer got the job, was given a bigger music budget to work with, made some decent money on the film, and added another credit to his career string.

Certainly this is one way of getting started in films. But it is also full of risks. The composer can easily lose money on the deal. If the film comes to the composer late in the postproduction schedule, he may be under pressure to spot, make decisions about the music, write it, record it, and mix it with too little time to do any of these tasks. He may then have to hire someone to help him orchestrate the cues, and the cost of that comes out of his own pocket. The discretional control of the producer may also cost him money. The producer may reject the cues that are already recorded and refuse to pay for new ones. If the composer has not blocked-in his fee securely, expenses may skyrocket, and those expenses come out of the composer's already narrow profit margin or worse, out of his own bank account.

Though risky, package deals are nevertheless a way in which colleagues compete with one another for available films and for those all-important second, third, and fourth credits. On one recent low-budget production, I was told that a composer in search of his third credit had guaranteed the producer that the film scoring's total costs would not exceed $30,000. He had spotted the film, decided where it needed the music, knew what kind of orchestra he wanted, and made some careful estimates about expenses. Then, a few days later he found out that one of his colleagues, one in search of his second film, had gotten the job; his competitor promised to bring the film score in, complete, at $15,000. In a buyer's market competition can get even more intense; one composer (with only two credits) tells of being asked to spot a film and then meeting with the producers afterward to discuss possible hiring. He arrived at the studio screening room and much to his embarrassment met four other composers who had been also invited. They all expressed their chagrin at the open competition.

Resources and price have a great deal to do with the matching between the filmmaker seeking a composer and the composer seeking a project. The next composer started in the record business and had several commercial hits and a reputation as a fast, competent, and hip composer/arranger. The reputation brought him to the attention of producer T, a man who had made more than 300 films in 25 years and was one of the kings of the "B" film, particularly the topical, exploitation film. If a trend or fashion swept the country, he could have a film cast, shot, and in the theaters within months, even weeks. Up to the time he hired this composer, this producer had used a different composer on each of his films, freelancers hungry enough for credits to endure the filmmaker's shooting schedules and tight-fisted way with money. Like a couple of the other "kings" in high-volume, low-budget production, this producer rarely developed strong ties with industry composers. As the following scenario illustrates, it is often by dealing with employers faced with their own budget problems that a composer understands what business he is in, and what is possible and probable in his line of work. The composer had some experience with films because of the tie-in between major film studios and their record subsidiaries, but his freelance experience began with the filmmaker.

I started by doing a package job for him. I'm sure you've heard this from the other guys. Many of us start, have to start, there. One of my friends told me that to get into films seriously you start in the low-budget field and bid down low. When they told me how much money was involved I said, "You've got to be kidding. I make twice as much in records and I don't have to package anything." And my friend looked at me and said, "That's the way it is." Now you've got to remember at this point in my career I had been extremely successful. I had three number one, top one hundred records. I was more fortunate than some other composers trying to get into the film end of things. I was in a luxurious position of saying, "Take it and shove it," I mean, I wasn't after the money at that point. I was doing it because I wanted to get into the film industry.

But if you study the business long enough, you'll find that there is work that gets done because the price was right. I bid at the same price as the other guy I was running competition with, the other guy the producer was considering. As luck would have it, the music editor, whom I had worked with on some other projects, convinced him that I would be a better choice. So he gave it to me and we had a very, very stormy time. *Very.* But he loved the music. At that time I had my lawyer trying to get a contract signed, because you know the reputation of these guys—half the time you'll end up with little or no money. I had laid out all the money myself without a contract. His lawyer was stalling like crazy, and they wanted to sneak preview the picture on Hollywood Boulevard. So he wanted to open it, and I said to him that he better have his lawyer call my lawyer because we did not have a contract; we need signatures, rights, things like that—I need things on paper.

He said, "All right, have your lawyer call my lawyer." Have you met him? He's a caricature of what any producer would cast in the role of a movie producer. He keeps stalling. Eventually we go down to his lawyer's office to sign the contract. There were things in the contract that were just terrible, and my lawyer told me not to sign. We went until two o'clock in the afternoon with the producer and his lawyer; we haggled on and on. We finally signed, but I figured that this would be the last time I'd work for him. He was spitting, and fuming, and throwing things. So we went to preview that night, and he squeezed a smile out and I squeezed a smile out. He sent me my check and for some reason, I don't remember what, I ended up back in his office a few days later. I think one of the record companies had decided they wanted to put a sound track record out, off the film. So T had to call me to come in there and find out what he had to do. We met. He continued to fume. So I just said to him, "Wait a minute, T, all you guys do is steal money." I meant it, because these are the biggest thieves that ever lived.

I said, "I just figured out all my bills and paid everybody, and do you know how much I made on your movie? I made $45." That was clear profit in bucks. If you take the income tax on that and everything else in my bracket, I probably *lost* money. And he said that I was crazy. So I came back the next day with all my bills, all my vouchers, and I put them on his desk. "Here, you look at them, show them to your accountant," I said. He looked at them, and his accountant came in and he said, "You son of a bitch, you really made $45." And that was it: I did the next eight pictures he made. He never even thought of hiring another composer. Directors came in and worked with him and said they wanted so-and-so; he said "No." As far as he was concerned no one else was going to touch his music. He never asked to see a budget of mine again. All he wanted to know was how much it was going to cost, and, if it was reasonable, he said, "You've *got* it." The funniest thing about it was that I was the only man in his entire organization, all the way along the line, that he trusted. He never even showed up at the recording dates. He rarely came down to the spotting sessions. He never did a thing. All he knew was that the music was there, that it was going to be handled in a way he could trust, that it was done, that it was finished, and that it was right.

Their third film was a big commercial success in the genre—the motorcycle epic, the bikini, twist, rock 'n roll, juvenile delinquency genre. It cost around $300,000 to make, had a lot of music, some of it very effective, a large orchestra, and a sound-track album that followed the release. The film grossed nearly $2,500,000. After eight films for Mr. T, the freelancer had a reputation as someone perfectly comfortable with writing songs and scoring "contemporary themes," such as rock 'n roll and the like. He also had a reputation as a tough man to bargain with.

"We did a lot of very good low, low-budget films," he said with pride. "They all made money, a lot of them weren't as successful as the first one we did, but he *always* made his money on them." As for the pattern of association, "I continued to work for him, sure. We got along; when it came to music, as far as he was concerned, I was the gospel on it—especially after that initial confrontation when he just couldn't believe that someone had actually told him the truth. He was so used to people trying to make a fast buck and play games with him."

The producer died in the early 1970s and the composer's film work trailed off. He continued to work, however, doing six films between 1970 and 1973.

One was with a rising young producer, a former television actor turned filmmaker. The film they did together was a moderately low-budget exploitation film with a country rock type of score. The film made $10 million. The composer naturally hoped for a developing relationship on the basis of this success, but it did not happen because the filmmaker, now with a lot of money in his hands, decided to "hire up" and get a top-league "name" composer for his next film. Here is the war story scenario that combines all the elements of producers' choices and colleague competition for those choices.

> As loyal as [the first producer] was, that's how disloyal [the second producer] was. He's a very funny guy. He feels belittled and stepped-on by this business. After a success, he felt that he was just going to get back at a lot of people. So the second picture he did following the hit we had, he showed to me. It was horrible. He showed it to me, and then told me he had other composers in mind. I said, "What is it, a contest? What do you want me to do?" He said, "No, no, I just want to tell you that I'm thinking of a few others, and I'd like your opinion of them." I said, "You've got to be kidding." I told him if he hired some of the top guys in town, "then good luck to you, you've hired three very good people. If you hire anybody else, forget it. I'm better than they are. What more can I tell you?"

The producer ended up hiring one of the top thirteen composers, a man with several nominations and one Academy Award, whose métier was the lyrical score. The film was a middle-level budget film, again, in the motorcycle, young-love genre. The composer poked at his lunch, and for the first time in the interview became visibly angry. "He was about as right for that film," he said of the colleague who was tapped for the film, "as the waiter over there." He was quick to qualify his remark. "I mean, he's a lovely man, he composes nice music, but this just wasn't his kind of picture. It wasn't his style of movie, it wasn't his *bag*." The film opened to bad reviews in Los Angeles and New York and then disappeared from sight. The failure offered little satisfaction to the composer who was passed over:

> It was a lousy deal he pulled on the last thing. You see, I did him a real favor on that first thing. I mean, I did not charge him anything close to what I should have on the picture. You know the story, the producer pleaded poverty—it was his first picture, the whole deal. He had all these records he wanted to use. No one advised him as to what these records would cost to use in his film. Nobody told him that you have to get permission of the record company and the artists—if they're still alive—and all of those things. So I felt sorry for him and, being a nice guy, I did it dirt cheap for him. This is a kind of business where you make your bets. I figured, okay, *next time* he'll maybe have some

money. As it turned out the picture made him some money, a lot of it. So he owed me one, I figured. What happens? Next time out he decides to hire a guy with a big name. So sometimes your bets pay off, and sometimes they don't.

This time they had not. He felt that he had given too much of himself to someone else's property and someone else's success. Perhaps he had done too much too soon in the business, seen too much of how some high-rolling producers operate, worked with a man who gave him a lot of autonomy and succeeded too easily in those first projects and, then, maybe he figured he could purchase the loyalty of his next employer in much the same way.

Alliances, associations, loyalties, ties are the cause of enormous concern in the middle ranks. Most freelancers hesitate to say so, but if pressed will admit that the prime ingredient in their intense personal scramble for credits and ties to employers is fear. Peering into an uncertain future is a prime Hollywood hobby. A fear of sliding backward into episodic television is one fear; the inability to get more work and, hence, move forward into a film career is another. Composers know they are highly dependent on the opinion and choices of employers for practically everything they do or hope to do in this business.

The wary and often depressed outlook of contributors in midstream is pushed to the edge of paranoia as the composer comes to understand rudiments of hiring decisions as well as the limits of loyalty under these circumstances. Everyone knows the gravitational pull is toward the inner circles; producers have a pronounced tendency to hire "up," once they get enough money and resources to afford the more expensive and more experienced freelancers. The filmmaker's treatment of the previous composer is a good example of the limits of loyalty in the face of that tendency. Sometimes it is simply a matter of power; few producers and film directors on the move are strong or independent enough to demand that their early colleagues be employed on their new film projects. There is cause for depression and paranoia but the only basis for action is hope. A freelancer must continue to place his bets, betting that a certain film with a particular producer will pay off in the future, hoping that as the producer moves into bigger and better assignments he will take him along.

It is not an easy position to sustain. A future grinding out pot-boiler features and low-budget packages can look bleak. Also, a person can start to feel locked-in by the routinization and specificity of his tasks. In much the same way as a television composer fears getting typecast, a man working on rock and roll epics fears getting known as "just a motorcycle, beach-blanket bingo" kind of composer. But then there is the excitement, although rare, of working on a challenging film with, perhaps, a filmmaker and director who really know and understand music. One such experience is enough to keep a dedicated composer going for a long while.

The middle position raises both aspirations and fears. Sizable jumps in self-confidence as he acquires more work, growing hunger to escape from schlock jobs, and increasing resentment of rivals who get the better projects all put an edge on the composer's desire. He knows what better assignments are like, and now he is sure he is ready for them.

Visible Effects

"I'm ready, and I'm also mad as hell and I'm not going to take it anymore," joked a 36-year-old freelancer on the lookout for that all important breakthrough project. He had come up from Universal's television core group, had done five films in four years, and had several, strong ties to producers and a growing reputation as a lyrical composer that was scaring some of his colleagues in the inner circles. He was ready, and he also knew some major producers, but had not yet been tied to a commercial success that would attract the attention he needed.

His first film was done with a filmmaker who had also started at Universal. It was a moderate success, nothing special. His second film was for a megalomaniacal producer, full of superhype, vague directions for what he wanted and illusions about the importance of the project. The film was overpromoted and did only mediocre business. The music, however, was singled out in several Hollywood trade reviews as rising above the disaster that surrounded it—supplying a degree of excitement and tension not always evident in the film itself, to paraphrase one reviewer.

The third project was an inexpensive package deal that a producer with four previous credits put together. The man had very definite ideas about the kind of music he wanted, going to the extreme of carrying an armload of records into one of their meetings where they talked about the cues and the approach to the film. To the extent that their aesthetics diverged, they experienced difficulties. It was a stormy relationship, one of those occasions for controlled conflict or antagonistic cooperation. Somehow they managed to arrive at mutual solutions, and the recording took place in two three-hour sessions with a small orchestra at one of the lesser-known and worse-equipped studios in Hollywood. "The guy was scuffling," the composer recounted, "and I sort of liked him, once I learned to deal with him and his ideas." They had not worked together since.

The next film, number four in the string, was with a major filmmaker, a man the composer could really collaborate with, a producer knowledgeable about musicians and music. "I had worked for a record producer out here in Los Angeles, and he just happened to know [this producer] who was looking for a composer for his film at the time. Apparently they had someone else to do the score and they had run into problems. So I had ten days to do the scoring. The budget was $12,000 and it was around forty to forty-five minutes of music. So I said, 'Well, the best way to handle it is not to think about it, just do it.' It called for a classical type of composition which I'm comfortable with." To the extent that their aesthetics converged, the composer and producer experienced a good working relationship. The film opened to good reviews, recouped its costs, and, it was rumored, the composer was in line for this man's next project.

Number five was a big one. There were several freelancers in competition for the job. He had the inside track, however, because he had worked with some of the key people associated with the project. Songs were to be written by a major recording star, and at one point it looked like the singer was going to be trying his hand at *scoring* the film. "He didn't have the background as a composer of orchestral music," the composer said, "so the job pretty well fell on my shoulders to develop an orchestral score, and the film called for a considerable amount of music, all of it in a symphonic style, which, of course, I was very much at home with." That became obvious to everyone who saw the film, for the score began to attract more attention than the project in which it was embodied. "The film was not a great success," he said a year later, "but the album was a great success, and that gave me an enormous leverage into the business. A lot of people became aware of my work and my contribution to that score, so I started getting some calls." In retrospect, that project seemed to be the beginning of the freelancer's success.

I tracked down one of the freelancers who had been passed over for that film, a freelancer in his late thirties with seven credits from 1969 to 1976 who occupies an interesting social position in composer circles, significantly superior to those with two or three credits, because of his hits in television, but not within range of men in the inner circles, because of his relatively low volume of films. He was still hungry for a breakthrough project. He had plenty of experience in dealing with producers, understood the rules of the game, and was cosmopolitan, eclectic, somewhat detached, even distant, toward his career, but willing to share his concerns. In the spring of 1978 he was signed to do a major production for one of the top filmmakers in town.

"If that film takes off . . . *if* . . ." he said, nodding his head, "then who knows? There are no guarantees in this business. I'd certainly like to have something like that. I would like to be in a position to get my share of good pictures, good films—to me that's the toughest plateau. It might work out and it might not." Much will depend on other producers' reactions to his work, and those are difficult to predict and harder to influence. There are difficulties in establishing a reputation for one's talent and a presence in the commercial marketplace. "Many producers have a very narrow view of music.

Most deal strictly on a kind of monolithic view of it. 'If you've done X, Y, and Z pictures, then you're automatically qualified to do my picture.' That's all. It's on the basis of what you've done lately and what people *think* about what you've done. That's *the* judgment factor with your work—you're continually subject to that.''

Because a man's work is always tied to or encapsulated in the shell of the project, freelancers can become at times desperate for quality film projects. "I'm not in any position to be choosy," he continued. "I'm not that well known in those networks. And like everyone else you want to get something you can do something with, a film with a better chance of taking off. You at least want to get into an industry situation where you're being considered for projects with major directors, major stars, a budget, a major producer, and high production values all the way down the line," he concluded with the deliberate emphasis and faint amusement of someone who has learned a foreign language. New language. New interests. In this mid-career area, the major outlines of the freelance picture—a collage rather than a picture—are clear: the film project is the means to influence opinion which in turn influences the future availability of resources; the visibility of a commercial project is a crucial factor affecting the status a composer enjoys in employer networks and so the rate at which his career develops.

"You've got to keep the career moving," said one of the top agents for film and television composers as we talked about several of his clients in the middle area one afternoon. He emphasized that getting more work, getting access to better films, securing some leverage in the business by virtue of visible success, and being considered by the top circle of Hollywood producers were all mutually reinforcing concerns. He illustrated his point by describing one particular composer who had come up the line at Universal with a reputation as one of the most respected young writers in television. His film credits were not extensive, and he lacked what this agent took to be the most important ingredient, "a breakthrough film," an association with a commercial and critical success that would launch this composer in "the top leagues," that is, the inner circles.

"Sometimes ability is not enough. It's fate, luck, or personality. There are a million factors that go into who gets trapped and who breaks out," he said referring to breaking out of television and into the center of film work. "About a year ago we sat down and we had a meeting, no holds barred. Now, obviously, he is not unhappy generally. He is only unhappy in one area, and that was not the financial area, because he was doing all these television shows, all the good stuff, pilots and all that stuff, but, as you know, there comes a *time*." Sponsored by the head of the music department at the studio, this freelancer had done over fourteen films for television and many pilots and television series from 1968 to 1972. From 1972 to 1976 he had done only three feature films, though he had scored over ten movies for television and accumulated a very sizable string of television episodes on which he wrote the main titles and themes. It was *time* to move into the bigger leagues.

"They were all *good* projects," he said in his characteristically optimistic tone, "but none of them really took off—and that is the measure of success for a composer's life." He paused. His voice changed. "You've got to have a film that takes off." He continued with the scenario: "Up to that point in his career, the features he had done, well, they looked good on paper but unfortunately nothing happened to them." They were good on paper because two films had been scored for two very young and very hot producer/directors. "You see, it's not necessarily the music he writes," he cautioned. "The ability is there, but the *picture it's attached to*. So we decided to make a really tremendous attempt at getting him that *first* really breakthrough picture. As it happened, a few months ago I got a call from a friend of mine, a big producer, who had previously used another client of mine but now wanted somebody new and fresh. Very rarely does that happen, as you know. Most of the time producers and directors have preconceived ideas, generally, within a certain group of people, about who they want, the top league, whatever. In this case he was wide open."

The agent talked about his past work with this one top producer: "I've worked with him for many years and we're friends and he asked me what could I do. I said, 'If I were producing this film, I would use [the composer].' He said, 'Doesn't he do a lot of television?' So I told him not to worry, that this could be the film for him, you know, 'He's looking to do that film, to get *away* from all that.' And I gave him the whole thing about [the composer] personally, his talent, the type of man he is and so forth. The producer said, 'Send him over.'"

The producer hired the composer, and they were working on the film at the time I talked to the agent. "It's a major film," the agent noted, looking both pleased and hopeful: pleased that the composer was finally attached to a film that looked like a winner, pleased that he had broken through the producer's preconceptions about whom to hire, and hopeful that the project would expand his client's reputation, breaking down the early typecasting that tends to get transmitted from one producer to the next.

The film's budget was over $5 million, and the project had a major star and several very capable supporting actors and actresses. It was the producer/director's first release in years, and many were waiting to see what he was going to do. The filmmaker, I heard, was pleased with the composer's score and their work relationship was open, honest, and professional. "I know he'll do a sensational job on the score." With some justifiable pride at having arranged such a fortunate match, he added, "It's the right time and it's the right vehicle."

He was right. After five or six, maybe seven, years of trying to crack into the inner circles it was time. An unexpected opportunity like this can shave years of struggle off a career, if the film is successful. It was not. Though the composer put in a lot of time and energy on the score, the film was a flop. It was supposed to be a big, exciting adventure but ended up looking like a crass rip-off of some other films in the same genre, lumbering along with a few impressive special effects but with little energy in the script and little skill in the directing. A commercial failure, and the composer was quiet for two more years. So was the producer/director.

Thus, when film people talk about their work, they talk about specific projects, specific employers, and prompt effects. They consider whether a job moved a career along or slowed it down. Composers are not unique in focusing on individual events and individual employers: the whole spectrum of hiring in Hollywood is geared to the individual, and every project is a separate piece of business—people maneuver in swift currents as they move from project to project. At first, much of what happens appears to be a one-shot proposition. Then with more work and experience, participants see that single projects can lead to lines of work, and, more important, that the line itself is merely an instrument to reach another, deeper objective.

Fast Company

"The whole object is to get into a position where they want you," summed up one freelance composer whose career had taken a sharp rise during the late 1970s. The real targets of a career line are networks of work relationships: the "social circles" of ties among employers that result in snowball effects or a credentialing again and again as a sought-after composer. It is the changing of those alignments among producers that is sought. "If you're going to make that leap into, let's call it the big time, then you have to be in the running for the best films that become available. Obviously if you're being considered by the top people in this industry you're in a much different place than if you're doing the kinds of things we all have to do in order to get something going. I mean if I know François Truffaut is considering me for his next film or Ingmar Bergman is considering me for his next film then I can see where I am." He added Robert Wise, Walter Mirisch, Blake Edwards, Robert Daley, Robert Chartoff and Irwin Winkler, Ray Stark, Alan Pakula, Martin Scorsese, John Badham, and others to his list.

When better work comes it can create a snowball effect and this composer speculated on why that happens. "You see, the fact of your being busy creates more work for you because then producers don't have to make decisions; any one of them doesn't have to stick his neck out. So they can say, 'Look, he's done this and this, he's worked for this producer and that producer, he's coming off a big hit, let's use him,' instead of wondering whether you're ready or not. If a composer is working, if he's busy, then the producer has the confirmation of other producers who have hired him. That makes these decisions about what composer to use much, much easier.''

As producers' decisions are made more easily and quickly, the freelancer's career develops at an accelerating rate. What before were mutually reinforcing concerns are now mutually reinforcing effects, and all at once it seems the composer develops accounts with top filmmakers and moves out of the small army toward the inner circles of sought-after colleagues. He simultaneously gets away from mediocre work assignments by moving ahead of his rivals; and he increases his income and his work satisfaction.

> Obviously, if you're being hired by someone who has done *Jaws, Star Wars,* or something very different, like *Turning Point,* you're in a different league, I would think, than if you're working on these lesser kinds of film productions. This is not to say I would automatically turn down a project, a little, wonderful film with a producer who is just trying to get started. I don't operate like that. There are many, many films that you would work on for almost nothing, just to have the chance to be of the film. But in the business a lot of people pay a lot of attention to what you're doing and who you are working for, absolutely.

His own outward circumstances were changing. He was making more money now than he had ever made in his life. After seven years he had a growing reputation and position as a dominant and active composer. Under the surface there was the anxiety of slipping back into those dark moods of inertia and self-doubt that can plague freelancers, heavily dependent as they are on employers for continuity of work. There was a fear of isolation, of being hopelessly adrift while he waited (without the faintest idea of when or from where it was coming) for another series of assignments that would keep his work improving, and keep the snowball effect going. "It's not easy," he continued. "For every good film done these days you have the Class A guys trying to get it. And if you're a top producer you're trying to hire the three guys who happen to be really hot at the moment. The rest of us then fight over the crumbs."

The result is that most composers must struggle constantly for those jobs that will hopefully bring critical recognition and all-important commercial visibility. A look at *Variety*'s "Big Rental Films of 1977" suggested to this composer the odds he was running against. Only a few of the one hundred or so features released each year return impressive grosses to their producers and, by implication, recognition to almost everyone who works on them. The first twenty features returned around $597 million in distributor rentals from the U.S. and Canadian markets during that year. The 118 movies that ranked next returned $408 million in rentals. Thus, out of the top 138 feature films, 14 percent (20) accounted for almost 60 percent of the business. Put another way, twenty producers made big-money films during this period. Of course, fewer than twenty film composers scored those films because those in demand get first shot at the big-budget projects and always do more than one film a year.

6.
SYMBOLIC INTERACTION

Here is a copy of the score which I tried to make bright, dissonant, elegant, entertaining, full, rich and sonorous, historic, spooky, hollow, informational, intellectual, light-hearted, lush, lyric, mocking, mysterious, powerful, questioning, romantic, unorthodox, unsettling, and occasionally upbeat. A tall order, but on listening to it quietly at home, I think I may have succeeded in part. I hope you agree.

Your ersatz Oriental Mahler.

There is a story in film composing circles that a filmmaker once said to David Raksin, "Write me another Laura," *to which Raksin unhesitatingly replied, "First, make one."*

Hollywood filmmaking is full of tall orders, as these stories suggest in their own ways. The "ersatz Oriental Mahler" is a key informant and close friend. He is blessed with a keen eye for the ironies of commercial careers and the fact that only a small proportion of the output of the film industry achieves box-office, hit status. He also knows that few composers achieve big successes and that most of the work in films is carried out by freelancers and filmmakers who work together once and never work together again. He has been in the business for over thirty years. His best years were some time back when he averaged $80,000 a year doing several television shows, documentaries, and features. He had at that time strong ties to a handful of film producers and directors. We saw each other every summer and it was during a recent visit (in his spacious study in Hollywood) that he showed me the "Oriental Mahler" letter.

"Tall orders," I noted. He shrugged. It was a gesture that I had become familiar with. Indifference, resignation, contempt, call it what you will, what it boiled down to was that demands such as these are normal troubles and taken for granted in the business. The more work a freelancer does, the more familiar he becomes with a variety of producers and directors, their projects, their knowledge of film scoring, their appreciation of music, and their specific demands.

Working in commercial worlds presents extraordinary potential for conflict with producers and directors. There are no statistics here, no percentages to show how many freelancers square off against which producers. Nor is that the point. The point is that certain composers have problems with certain filmmakers when they have worked together, and everyone in the business knows it. The question is whether those mismatches and conflicts are grounded in particular personalities or are inherent in the nature of freelance social organization. Are the "buried grievances" so many composers feel for their employers rooted in the typically nonrecurrent, short-lived contractual nature of this market? Why are producers so nervous when it comes time to "cast" or hire a particular subset of freelancers for their film projects, so stupid in the spotting sessions when they have to talk to and make demands of their composers, so high-handed in the postproduction of their films, and so concerned with the visible results of others' decisions? Why do composers often act like resentful professionals, like physicians who have been told how to perform particularly difficult operations by their "lay" patient as client?[1]

These conflicts are not remote mysteries involving a free-floating occupational culture, cut off from the tangible social organization of the freelance market. These conflicts and uncertainties are locked into a short-term contracting arrangement which places the filmmaker in a position of dependence on outsiders—freelance specialists—with the attendant risk of having to trust the professional judgments and craft instincts of these employees.[2]

Music and musicians are the last artistic elements to be added to the film as it moves through the production process. The composer is shown a rough cut, as I noted in chapter 1. In his specific work with the filmmaker, a freelancer's job is to talk about the film, its dramatic value, what he as a music writer might do, can do, and probably will do. Without a score to discuss, their mutual task is inevitably unspecific; it draws heavily on intuition and chance and is subject to revision at a later date—when the composer has completed the score. Seeing the film and talking through the perspective on the film, composers must interpret client wishes and try to understand their changing and often bizarre requests. Finding common terms to describe the film may be a problem.[3] If they have never worked together before they may even find it difficult to abstract out of the film the same kinds of concrete features.

The classic story—and "war story" among freelancers—involves David O. Selznick and composer Dimitri Tiomkin while working on *Duel in the Sun*. For a scene involving some off-camera sex, Selznick called for some "screwing music." Tiomkin's cue at this point had a windy, rasping sound. In spotting it, both had agreed on what the scene was and what it needed as background music. "Dimitri," Selznick announced, "the music doesn't have enough shtup. It doesn't sound like the way I make love." Tiomkin answered for himself: "You love your way and I'll love mine. To me that's lovemaking music."

On *The Reivers* (1969) composer Lalo Schifrin and producer Mark Rydell thought they saw eye to eye and were defining the picture and its score in the same way. Schifrin wrote what one of his colleagues admiringly called "a brilliant, neurotic subtext score," to underline the neurotic features of the William Faulkner characters. Rydell, however, wanted something else, but obviously did not work with his composer hard enough—or did not really tell him—and was expecting a pleasant, Aaron Copland-like approach to the music. Schifrin's score was thrown out and John Williams hired to write another.

On *Torn Curtain* (1966) composer Bernard Herrmann and producer Alfred Hitchcock thought they were in agreement about the music, but upon hearing the main title during the recording session, Hitchcock got up and left saying that his long-time collaborator had missed the point of the film. John Addison replaced Herrmann.

"Film, whether for features or TV, is a business of personalities," commented one composer with six credits in the last five years. "Film composers are not stamping out cars on an assembly line. Each project is different— different people, different values, different story—and each calls for a different musical approach. All this is the sum of personalities working, and working under pressure. You're there to help and you've got to pick their brains sometimes to find out what they have in mind."

It is a business that requires elaborate modes of cooperation among specialized and variously talented personnel. Composers want to view it as a craft in order to reduce equivocality and restrict the range of feasible approaches. The initial definitions of the film the composer makes and his sense of who the filmmaker is and what he "sees" are all-important. These definitions and interpretations do not necessarily determine all the events that follow in film scoring, but the early readings of project and producer do play a fundamental role in the work process, for they provide the framework within which the composer begins to develop the concept of his score. When asked specifically what they look for in the filmmakers they work with, it becomes clear that filmmakers' words and actions are closely scrutinized for their practical content. Often, producers and directors do not know how to get the effects they want, yet they insist on telling the composers how effects will be achieved. Other times they cannot express what they want, and the result is a series of "tall orders" strung together, one after the other, as in my opening example.

In any event, communications and directives which are incomprehensible, shallow, and contradictory are of little use to a composer. Collaboration is difficult. Composers have ideas of the possibilities in any film, and beyond that, an idea of the filmmaker and the film as a means of developing their own work. In "talking through" a film, "picking the brain" of the filmmaker, shared meanings are built up. "Many of us have a lot of experience," the composer with six credits continued. "You ask them what they see, what kind of music they relate to, and you're either dealing with someone who understands and knows something about music or you're not." His colleagues all agree that they may read a film differently than its maker does. They also agree that those statements and expressive signs which fail to communicate concrete ideas have little, if any, authority. An example from the "ersatz Oriental Mahler": "It's rather difficult to be asked by a director to write music that is like Spanish tile roof—a *Spanish tile roof*? What would he like me to write for the celli?" He shrugged, again.

His tone speaks for itself. Without help from the filmmaker, the composer is thrown back on intuition, chance, and guesswork. As I will reiterate throughout, much occupational behavior is situational in character—freelance composers constantly face the possibility of "troubles" in "tall orders" and the nature of a client's demands strongly affects their work satisfaction. In the course of one production season, a composer on the move can work on two to three feature films, one or two to a dozen movies for television, a couple of television pilots, and other projects. This will bring him into working relations with as many as eight to ten filmmakers. Some are knowledgeable about music. Many are not. Some can discuss what they want. Many cannot. Some make very specific and detailed demands for the score they want. Some give the composer leeway, room to make an innovation or two, a chance to nudge his vision onscreen and on the sound track. But innovation is risky, since there are enough gambles in the business of film without handing over the dice to composers—support personnel who are, producers reason, only one part of the final project.

Calling it a "collaborative medium" does not exactly fit the ups and downs a composer experiences in his itinerant travels from employer to employer, project to project, film score to film score. Sometimes it is; sometimes not. From the retrospect of a happy ending it seems that well-meaning filmmakers and "flexible" freelancers can come to some mutually beneficial definitions of the film (and its possible music), can work out some agreements in a language they both understand. But the more work he does, the more likely he is to run into tall orders and hustler-producers who have a gift for making the deal but little talent for discussing the film's music. Composers become highly skeptical of employers who indulge in "hype," "talking the talk," and overselling themselves and their project. In filmmaking fast talking, self-aggrandizement, and deal making have long been elevated to the level of a creed, a style, an industrial ethos—so composers must accept it up to a point. They still have to face the problem of concretely defining the film on which they will work. When the talk or expressions about the project are vapid and empty, when talk between parties leads nowhere, and when discussions fail to provide any information and focus, the composer foresees trouble. Composers dread the employer whose knowledge about music is nil and whose demands lack specificity, details, and even taste. The composer sees him as an occupational idiot, a prima donna who communicates through a thick cloak of flamboyance and exaggerated hype.[4]

If this "symbolic jerk" is troublesome because of ignorance and vague directives, the next type of producer—the "Plus-Music Boy"—is downright dangerous. The trouble he makes for the freelancer is in his explicit demands. If a problem with Hollywood is that "everybody knows his own job, plus the music," as Alfred Newman used to say, then this is the filmmaker who thinks he's in command of both the managerial and artists' side of freelancing.

If power is what allows people to modify the conduct of others in the manner they desire, while preventing their own conduct from being modified in ways they do not desire, then the plus-music people have power. They have clout and they use it. Anecdotes and stories of musical ignorance coupled with insistent demands for rock and roll sounds, country and western flavor, and "crossover," are legion. These determined filmmakers may overlook the fact that a way of seeing is also a way of not seeing; that limiting one's purview of musical alternatives to A and B—which happen to be "hot" and in fashion at the moment—also means ignoring alternatives C and D.

To be sure, there are times when freelancers try to get such demands turned around. There are times when they try to force concessions from producers. But there are hidden costs to squaring off against a plus-music boy whose competence is problematic, at best. Next time, when employment time rolls around—when the deal is put together—a producer will turn again to those he has dealt with. Any composer with a bad work experience, and maybe too much integrity, can find himself saddled with a reputation for being slow, arty-farty, too much of a perfectionist, obstinate, and worst of all, costly.

These kinds of filmmakers seem to have popped up over the past twenty years in the industry. Their appearance was quickened by the decline of the studios and the disappearance from the production chain of the music director. Nowadays freelancers work directly with producers and/or directors and enjoy no buffer or intermediary. Men like Ray Heindorf at Warner Brothers, Alfred Newman at Twentieth Century-Fox, Stanley Wilson at Universal, John Green at MGM, Morris Stoloff at Columbia, and others, acted as both bridge and buffer between filmmakers and composers. Now producers and directors go directly to the source—the composer—and they bring their unadulterated problems with them.

Comparing the hyped up prima donnas and the demanding plus-music types is not difficult. The prima donnas would say, "I don't know that much about music, but I know what I like. Make this larger than life, this is an important film. Go write it, then I'll tell you if I like it." The latter, because of his or her presumed expertise, might come up with the following line: "I want a score just like *Star Wars*"; or "My son's been playing Emerson, Lake and Palmer, that's what I want"; or "Give me Copland, you know, that Marlboro stuff." From the viewpoint of the composer, the prima donnas are vague to the point of meaninglessness. A sickening feeling sets in; yes, his music does have to be "lyric, mocking, historic, lush, unorthodox, and occasionally upbeat." With the second set of "instructions" the composer suffers from too much specificity rather than not enough; he is given little elbow room to work. It is almost as if the filmmaker said, "Here's what I want, here are the cue sheets, here are the timings. If you don't like it, there's the door." When it comes all the way down to this—what one respondent called "the short strokes"—the freelancer feels like a hired hand, cut off from the very skills he thought he had to offer, and forced to make estimates about his own survival with this kind of an employer. But personal preferences for film work are secondary to the much more pressing problem of attracting a clientele and getting on with the business of building a string of credits. There are, after all, hundreds of hungry competitors eager to take the job, often at a cheaper price, and the client-employer can always turn to someone else if the composer becomes hesitant or unwilling to deal with him.

The primacy of position over work preferences does not always result in opposition between the parties. Some filmmakers are highly knowledgeable about music and may even provide the composer with autonomy in their work relations and plenty of room to even experiment. Some are even informed about the dramatic value of music, can talk intelligently about instrumentation and orchestration, and want to be continuously involved in decisions about scoring the music. Demands, and therefore highly specific scoring alternatives, now come to rest in the mutual work of composer and filmmaker.

By combining the dimensions of client knowledgeability and demands in the work situation, we can construct the following ideal-typical set of categories. These help discriminate different kinds of filmmakers as well as the context of the negotiations which give rise to either unity or opposition.

Working Situation and Demands	Filmmaker's Knowledge of Music	
	Perceived as Knowledgeable	Not Perceived as Knowledgeable
Extensive demands; low ambiguity; clear definitions; fixed choices.	*Collaborators*	*Plus-Music Boys*
Truncated demands; equivocation; vague definitions; shifting choices.	*Partners*	*Prima Donnas*

These categories are, of course, on a continuum. Obviously, it is in the composer's interest to try to move the plus-music and prima donna types over to the other side of the ledger, and such efforts at training clients do take place with variable success. Retrospective constructions of what happened are often vague, full of reevaluations of filmmaker-composer cooperation in the light of subsequent events (whether the film was a success or not), and always subject to composers pushing *their* claims in accounting for what "really" occurred. Nevertheless, at one point on the spectrum we find collaboration in which the filmmaker is knowledgeable about film scoring, where the authority of a composer's expertise is likely to be recognized and paid attention to, where there are extensive and thorough demands placed on the music writer by the filmmaker as to the specific music desires, when choices for alternatives are narrowed and fixed accordingly, and where negotiations between the two are highly developed and informed. Filmmaker understanding of music and scoring can ease collaboration. Not all producers and directors are very specific in their instructions, and working partnerships arise where the informed filmmaker makes very few detailed suggestions, remains circumspect and occasionally vague about what he wants, and, as we saw in the last chapter, gives the composer plenty of support to arrive at his own solutions to the music.

At the other point on the continuum of clients' knowledge and their demands upon projects we find relationships where the filmmaker cannot fully, if at all, participate in the professional's culture, where his grasp of film scoring is weak, yet where he continues to give very detailed and thorough instructions about what he wants. Under these conditions "client training" is difficult. Generally, the plus-music boys with a clearly understandable project in a well-defined genre with a finite budget, and with a credit for work, are preferable in the freelancer's view to the more evasive and undependable prima donnas.

Collaborators and Partners

Here's one of the top five men in film scoring. He has nearly thirty films to his credit over the past ten years, moving quickly through television work at one of the studios under the sponsorship of a powerful colleague and with the help of the head of music. Confident, relaxed, and cooperative, he is a respected figure in the music world of Los Angeles. He likes to talk about working with specific filmmakers; one in particular was on my own mind since I had just seen one of his films and was knocked out by the twelve-tone jazz score of this composer. I asked him, as I asked everyone, about the ideal relation between a composer and a filmmaker.

It would be ideal if you had a kind of relationship with a producer where you could run the picture with him, discuss the film, and then you do your job. Then you record it, and maybe even surprise him— in a pleasant way, of course. But you learn from experience that you can't do that. You can't surprise a producer, he doesn't want to be surprised. Someone once explained to me that the film is out of a producer's hands while you're working on it and you may be ruining it for all he knows. A former studio head, a great man, once explained to me, "You have to *take partners*." He meant that you have to let the guy know how you're tackling his film, and how you're approaching it, and what you're doing. Tell them what you're doing. The best relationship with a producer is one where you can communicate with him. Some of us do it better than others, to be sure. I would like to go in, talk about the film and then go away and get lost, go away somewhere and do my job—writing. But you should collaborate and there should be no surprises on the recording stage.

He then talked about a director he had worked with on two films.

He's very articulate and we understand each other. He's probably one of the few directors who really understands music. What I did mostly was talk about character themes with him, it wasn't necessary to get that precise where I say, "Yes, that's *his* theme." There's a problem in that picture we worked through. The picture is not what they intended it to be about. They wanted it to be about this guy, and it turns out to be a lot more, there's a lot more activity than that. In fact, he isn't on the screen all that much. The theme turned out playing on the guy selling the guns. We were playing the yellow car he drove. Every time you see the yellow car—music. The main title ended up being con- structed the way it was because it was trying to tell the story of this holdup, to use that footage to set up the bank robbery, while the titles are going. We figured you might as well have that information in front. It takes a long time, I started off very soft. Then we had the holdup theme—while the guys look at the bank—then we hit a new key when the Brinks truck comes into view, right *there*, a different feel, and we continue the theme over that and we end on the director's title. It seemed to work, we liked it. And I wish I could always say that, "Yes, this and this and this and we'll definitely do that." I wish I had that kind of vision, but I really don't and probably never will. You work with the people, talk about it, and hopefully the solution is reached. It's such an indefinite sound with this picture, it was a very indefinite kind of a thing for me working on the film. I believe there are eight ways to do it, to do any film. There are many concepts which will work, some maybe even better, and it's a matter of talking through it, a matter of choosing the one you think is right. I spent a lot of time thinking about it. It was nice to work with someone who also understands. I'm a procrastinator, a great one, and I did that score four days before we had to record it.

Similar sentiments and experiences were encountered by a younger colleague with three credits. He had just broken out of one of the major studios' episodic work and had several television movies to his credit line. He and his producer friend rose up the ranks in television together, they had formed a working relationship early at the studio, they were both on the move. Three years after this interview they did a film together that was one of the top money earners of that year.

"I've had the good fortune to work with him," he said of this producer friend. "He knows and loves music, and it's a great help *to me* working with him. I can play him the theme, we talk it over, like today just as you arrived we were finishing some work for this movie of the week. We've done a few things together and I played him the theme a couple of days ago and he didn't like it and he had *reasons why* he didn't like it. And I saw what he was trying to do and I agreed with him."

"He could talk to you and tell you why?" I continued.

"Right. I played him the theme today and he said, 'That's it.' He helped me find the right tone, where with most of the producers or directors I've run into you could just play them one thing or another and they would say, 'Sure, sure, great.'"

"That could lead to troubles later?"

"Sometimes, yes. The guy then comes back and says that's not what he had in mind or it's not right for this scene or that scene. This guy's an exception. We went to school together and he's a personal friend and he cares about the music and likes to come and hear themes."

There are other forms of successful collaboration.

This year I've been fortunate to do some films with one producer who goes a little crazy. We'll argue and fight about the music and he'll ask me why music should be *there*, then he'll say he wants this or that. He'll either hate or love what I've done and this is increasingly gratifying because it's the meeting of minds and we'll decide together what is right for the film. One project I played for him what I thought might work, but it didn't feel right. Then little by little we settled on what was right.

This collaboration is what I enjoy, where a director tells you that the music is wrong for what's up on the screen and then I can argue that the screen is not working for my score, you know, that it might be better another way. This give and take about what I can add in terms of coloration, style, emotional impact is all-important for the betterment of the film. I believe in this. In one case recently this director reshot an opening scene to accompany the music I wrote. This is rare, as you know, but it means the music meant enough to him so that they redid the beginning and I thought the total effect was that much improved. He was that kind of a filmmaker.

The composer is called upon to do an indefinite task to the extent that the approach to a film score cannot be fully programmed or anticipated *before* it is written and recorded. The meaning of a film and the possible score is not there for the taking. It must be talked through, defined, argued out. Every composer I talked with noted that a test of the congruence between talk and realization is crucial. This test takes place after the spotting session and after some work has been done by the composer. It functions as a further check, a means of giving the producer and director a fuller sense of the direction the composer is taking. The freelancer, like others who deal in a marketplace, not only must keep on top of matters but must also convince his client that he is on top of things. Part of his job is to calm the filmmakers' anxieties, and he often spends a lot of time doing this. Because anxieties are high at this postproduction stage, and because the film is out of the filmmaker's direct control while the composer is working, the latter must assure the producer and director that their confidence has been well placed. He cannot entirely explain the process of writing music to them, but he can tell them what he is thinking about. He can tell them what reels and scenes he is working on, and they can glean from him some sense that puts some of their apprehensions to rest, for the time being. The composer may play some cues for them or run through selected and important cues. The main idea is to get the filmmaker interested and committed to the freelancer's *concrete* treatment, thus avoiding interference, meddling, and producer unhappiness at later stages.

"You find that some guys are very musically knowledgeable," said one of the younger freelancers with a string of work in episodic television and two film credits. "I just worked with a producer on this project; he's not the honcho but he's the second guy in line, and I was amazed. He was talking about Stockhausen and Boulez and what not. And he knew music like the back of his hand. He said before spotting, in conference, 'I'd like something like the slow movement of the Bruckner Eighth, something like that.'"

"And there's another guy at the studio. He not only knows all the repertoire pieces, he also knows film scores. He could hear a film score, four or five bars of it, and tell you exactly who it is, whether the guy got an Oscar for it or whatever. This guy was over the other day and we had a Brandenburg on and he said, 'Hey, that's the Brandenburg Three.' I said to him, 'You are already at the top of my list. Any film producer that hears about twenty seconds of Bach's Brandenburg Three and knows that it's the third and not the second or fifth, is at the top of my list.'''

There were problems with a too-well informed producer. "This can make him a little bit difficult to deal with," the young composer said carefully. "But he's very opinionated about what he wants. And sometimes he will back you into a place where you'd rather not be. On the other hand, I'd rather have that every single time than someone who doesn't really know what he's talking about. This is something that everyone has to deal with and some composers deal with it better than others."

Whether they can "talk" about music itself seems to be an index to the producer or director's ability to see a composer's point of view. Honesty, tact, and experience in dealing with composers are important parts of the work relationship. Whether they understand what music is and what a composer does is the most crucial question. The point of the composer's and producer's mutual labor is to get a film score that will advance the dramatic action and contribute to the movie, so the composer judges the extent of the filmmaker's professional experience and estimates the degree to which that experience can advance their mutual labor.

The next composer is moderately busy in television; he has a dozen film credits and has been active in television recently. He is very close to five or six film producers who try to get him on their films when they can. He acquired a reputation as something of a perfectionist, as someone who had trouble letting go of a cue sheet, and as a composer who could cause trouble by not finishing all the cues by the time a recording date rolled around. He told me this in a matter-of-fact way, as if he were now on top of these problems. He was happy to be back working with one producer/writer, a friend with whom he had done many television shows and a couple of films.

We had just come out of a morning dubbing session and were on our way to the commissary. The morning's events had been instructive about the tempo of work and temperament of both filmmakers and composers. The two had known each other for years, but still, the two fought, often openly, in dubbing. The producer was faster at the quip, the muted demand for moving the session forward; he was obviously the man in charge. He was respected by the mixers, sound editor, and his friend, the composer. But sometimes they battled for two minutes, way too long, over a thirty-second music cue. Nuances were critically important; the balance between sound effects, dialogue, and music had to be just right. At one point, the composer wanted to hear one cue better—it was not cutting through the jet airliner and was not blended suitably with the dialogue. Encounters in dubbing are tense, sometimes brittle, but rarely loud or passionate. They are more like diplomatic negotiations couched in polite language whose inflections carry an enormous amount of weight. The search for the perfect blend of music, effects, and dialogue ended with the producer saying, "Alright, it's fine, for Chrissake, it's not a bass solo." The freelancer nodded agreement and went on to the next reel. "As you can see," the composer said as we walked into an empty cafeteria, "we get along pretty well, it's open, no bullshit. He's got a tendency to want wall-to-wall music, too much scoring, not too much subtlety." We started the interview.

> The producer will hire you for the film and you'll see the film together. Then you embark on discussions about where the music is going to go, and each composer will have a different approch to the same problem. It's nice to be working with this person because we see eye-to-eye most of the time—at least we can talk about it if we're going in two different directions. I think it's important to have a relationship to a producer so that this can happen. It doesn't happen *that* often—unfortunately. You know, they say they love some types of music, modern music, and you'll be playing something like that over cocktails and they'll start to complain about it. It's never ending.

> You have to read the filmmaker. It's *his* film. Your job is to help. Now I know that a lot of the talk with them is really superfluous because you can't deal in specifics or I should say that in most cases you can't. You try to convince them about your approach. You want them to feel confident about what you're planning on doing. You try to get through in dramatic terms. You've got to be talking about the same general topic, in the same general area, and if you have questions or if you start leaning one way, try to tell him about it. Otherwise, you'll think you're in agreement. Sometimes you bury your doubts because you're anxious to go to work, and you like the film and see some things that can really work out. If you have misgivings you better get it cleared up early. Get his reactions; maybe one word, an idea will all of a sudden put things in place.

The freelancers experience this in conferences time and again: two intelligent people, two skilled craftsmen, each with a different angle on the film. They talk and talk and are apparently at cross-purposes, until, if they are lucky, one phrase clarifies their views. One might say, "Oh. Well, now I see what you're getting at. Why didn't you tell me that before? I know what to do with that idea." Now there's the meeting of minds mentioned earlier by another freelancer. No matter how intelligent the two are, the discussions are a kind of groping for common ground and a fix on the film and its individual cues. They have to be patient with one another because when the composer says "jazz," it may mean something entirely different to the filmmaker. Becoming a professional is becoming educated in this use of words, this hit-and-miss, try-again, inductive method of moving from a film's specific reels to the general approach for the score. This makes "taking partners" crucial. For it is in the hit and miss, the give and take, that their mutual work becomes interesting.

The problems of talking through a conception, getting the cooperation of the filmmaker, and seeing eye to eye were stressed over and over by these composers. During the interviewing sessions in the early seventies a premier composer had a score thrown out by a filmmaker. The responses of several composers to this event were similar. The following excerpt from a long interview is representative of these reactions. I asked this freelancer if, after working with a filmmaker on several projects, you find out how to "read" him and what he wants.

> Yes. But it's a vague art, you can't say, "Okay, here's the score I'm going to do for you," and that's it. You have to start somewhere and you get to it by degrees, but you still have room for misunderstanding. I can think of one composer who is a close friend of a major producer-director. This guy did the producer's first film I think, and just recently did a score for his latest picture. The producer threw the score out last week. He brought in someone else to do it. That can happen between good friends. Not only is the composer this guy's favorite writer, but he is also a close friend. Apparently they just hadn't discussed it enough.

I asked, "They didn't communicate and when they got to the dubbing there were surprises?"

"I suppose the producer said to himself, 'He'll know what to do, he'll know what I want.' And the composer figured, 'Well, this is obviously what he wants because in his last film I did this neurotic score and it worked.' They probably thought they both agreed."

Like most of his colleagues, the next composer ends up for the most part in antagonistically cooperative or cooperatively antagonistic relationships with just about every producer or director he works with. He has worked with one director on five of his films—all of them treating themes of respect, retribution, masculine control, and violence. The two have a great deal of admiration for one another. Each is outspoken, often very difficult to deal with; each has a definite point of view.

"I have to *fight* for what I want with all of them," he said. "And I don't mean to presume that working for him is a bed of roses. It isn't. In order to keep the best things in his pictures I've got to throw chairs at him and fight and scream, you know, all *that scene*," he said, noting the utility of fighting fire with fire. "His judgment is not better than anyone else's, it's just that I have more respect for him. I'll take more from him and he'll take more from me. I have no fear of him. We call each other the most horrible names you can imagine and a lot of hitting goes on. But that's all in the course of the thing, and we understand that.''

He paused. ''It isn't that easy anywhere else. But I'll do his stuff and keep doing it because he cares and it's worth all the fighting.''

This composer was always ''in trouble,'' as he put it. Outspoken, honest, unwilling to put up with the clamor of socializing in Hollywood, he was blunt about his likes and dislikes. He was, at times, in need of some diplomacy: ''I'm still a little too frank for some people's comfort. That makes me not too lovable in certain circles. I cannot stand bullshit and just won't. That's it. So my scope is limited to a few guys, with whom I've developed a kind of rapport. And they also care.

''Care,'' he emphasized, naming three producers ''whose pictures are not really all that good, but who are *willing* to spend a lot of money for what they consider to be very high-class, quality stuff.'' He then named one of his recent films. ''A dreadful picture but the best score I've ever written.'' He then ticked off some titles of films that contributed heavily to his recent volume of credits. ''They're all good, very good scores. I'd hold them up anywhere in the world.''

''What about the caring?'' I asked.

''Well, you ask for fifty-five musicians and he says, 'Why not start with seventy-five?' The time is never compressed, you never feel the rush. With some producers you are a *specialist,* you are something special.'' He reflected on this recent experience with satisfaction. ''They don't treat you like a schoolboy, a hired hand, and they figure, whatever they pay you, you know what you're doing and they're going to let you do it. They would never overrule you.'' All of which points to the eternal goal of film composers: to find a filmmaker they can work with sympathetically on a project with whom they feel, as several put it, ''at home.''

This next freelancer worked for one actor/producer who demanded a rock score, and then proceeded to make life difficult for him. ''I would never work for him again, never, under any condition. On the other hand, the project I did with [a top Hollywood screenwriter], I did for no money at all—nothing. I worked half a year. And I'll go back and do everything else he wants, I'll break my ass for him because I believe in his projects.'' Another film he did in the past year won several prizes. He also did that work for virtually no money. ''That's just the kind of man I want to work with, that's just the kind of project I want to do. The guy knows what he's doing, *he knows,*'' he said slowly and with respect. ''He's probably the most knowledgeable director I have worked with in the business—one of them, at least.''

There are others whom film composers talk about. Franklin Schaffner (*Patton, Planet of the Apes*) is knowledgeable, easy to communicate with, and respects the important role music plays in his films. Robert Wise (*The*

Sound of Music, Sand Pebbles, West Side Story, Hindenberg, Star Trek: The Motion Picture) is a former music editor with a keen appreciation of film scoring. George Roy Hill (*Butch Cassidy and the Sundance Kid, Slapshot*) is also mentioned; he was a music major at Yale. Steven Spielberg, Francis Ford Coppola, Alan Pakula are acknowledged collaborators and good partners with useful insights and sure instincts about film scoring.

Here is the composer who did the score for one of these sought-after producers. He is in his mid-forties, came up through the ranks of television, starting out as a performer in the studio orchestras. An alliance with one producer he worked with in television carried over into feature films; one of their films was a gigantic success which launched the composer's career. Fresh from another success with a young filmmaker, he compared his recent work to his partnership with the older veteran. The composer was concerned about getting to work on a score for a big blockbuster. "Not all the films you work on in a career are like that," he reflected, noting that he had worked on many unsuccessful films up to that point—unsuccessful in terms of commercial standards and the integration of his own craft with the demands of the film and filmmaker.

> By being at home I mean being stylistically comfortable. You feel that the picture is good; you feel that the director is going to understand, appreciate, and *use* the music. You feel that the picture has a good chance at the box office, that it's a healthy work situation, that you're not flapping your wings and working hard for something that's going to sink before it gets out of the harbor—which is a feeling you can have with a lot of projects. This feeling of "at home" is a feeling that you've got a chance *to write* and *do things*. The film is going to have a chance at some success. That's a good feeling.
>
> Most of the music that I've done for films doesn't represent my own private tastes. I think I'm always looking for films that I can write a little bit more—a little more idiosyncratic. I'm thinking in terms of the style of the music. I think that you have to be a kind of musical chameleon to be successful in this business. You have to be able to have a good sense of what will work in the film or who you are working with, and not simply what you'd *personally* like to write, but what can survive. And you want to do something with those people where you can contribute something to their film. And it may be in a language that has nothing to do with your own personal handwriting or thumbprint or whatever—that's what I mean by idiosyncratic.

He had a way, then and throughout his career, of molding the commercial and aesthetic demands of film work to his needs rather than the other way around. With more credits, access to better projects, recurrent work with more intelligent and talented producers and directors as their work became more commercially successful, he was increasingly able to resist projects which required too much of a compromise on his part. He had learned very early that some compromise was necessary, that the freelancer had to be a "kind of musical chameleon," and that some of his colleagues had difficulty molding themselves to this role.

> Some composers make the mistake of trying to *impose* their own personal style on situations where it can't possibly work. [He continued on the composer's obligation and the importance of working with collaborators and good partners.] One needs to have a very keen sense of what the *noise* of the picture ought to be: the way it should sound, what kind of noise it should make. Obviously, there is always more than one way to approach a film. You have to try to hope to find one that will work and is good. But I think that's the difference—that's the area where the film composer often has the most agony. He's often writing in an idiom that is not his pet thing. But if you're lucky, you're working with people you respect and again, back to Benny [Bernard Herrmann], one can always say, "No." No one's forcing us to work.

These remarks have implications often overlooked by new composers in Hollywood. One can always say no, but that, of course, implies that one has been asked. We'll explore this later for those who make the big jump into the subset of the 40 freelancers doing the majority of feature films. The 150 who have moved out of the first film into a line of two to six career "points" develop a heightened awareness of the problems composers have in common. More work tends to generate an appreciation of the difference in films and the variety of styles of filmmakers. The hazard at this stage of a career is that in meeting the expectation that he collaborate and contribute, the composer on the move can come to present himself as an expert to clients. He might try to appear infallible once he has committed himself on some point, some approach, some "noise" for the film. He strains to develop and deliver this conception. But he frequently becomes impatient for applause, knowing the difficulties of extending his string of work into four, five, six, and seven credits. If so he tries to force acceptance of his ideas and his approach—maybe even pushing the stylistic features he is most comfortable with. He might then give anxious and suspicious filmmakers the impression that he is boxing them in, that he is trying to get them committed to a style that might not be right for their film. Of course, filmmakers resent the implication that after many years of struggle for their own credentials they now need the guidance of a relatively inexperienced and somewhat rigid newcomer. When this sore spot is touched, collaboration cools. Composers thwarted for these reasons see their own failures, and inabilities to play musical chameleon, as a result of the "ignorance" and "rigidity" of their clients. Thus freelancers can create their own problems and shift the blame quickly to their employers.

All the freelancers I talked to noted the importance of "staying in shape," expanding one's skills, and keeping fresh and sharp. This is not just a matter of professional pride or personal idiosyncracy. It is an external demand made by the setting in which they work. In order to handle any film they not only have to be willing to collaborate but also prepared to select from a wide menu of skills. As a central figure with fifteen credits in the 1970s put it, "A good composer is open to the dramatic values of the film, knows where his own strengths lie, and can make his musical contributions because of those strengths." He went on to note the pernicious effects of typecasting but also the fact that some composers feel comfortable in one or two idioms and can feel out of place when faced with a dramatic film "calling for something else, an approach that may not be the composer's métier."

To get trapped as "just another jazz guy," or a "twelve-tone freak," or "a composer who can write a big, lush, orchestral score" is dangerous because the filmmaker quite rightly fears personal and stylistic narrowness in a composer. In this respect collaboration is the ability to mold one's self to the aesthetic and dramatic demands of the project, the willingness to get along— and at times go along—with the producer and director, and the professional facility to see their film on its own merits.

The image of collaboration as one big, happy accommodation, in which film composers simply sell out and "go commercial," is misleading. The misapprehension exists largely because commercialism is being looked at from the outside. Looked at from the standpoint of the subordinates—the sellers of talent in the market—collaboration and power seem more like related structures. The extreme displays of power, or the "last resorts" of filmmakers—throwing out a score and hiring someone else—serve as reminders that the filmmaker is in final control. He is continuously present in the work lives of all. Composers' attitudes toward clients are continually influenced by their awareness that filmmakers can give or withhold very valuable resources—market validation, prestige, and future projects.

Listen to one freelancer who is on his way to developing a good working relationship with a top film producer-director. The composer has sixteen film credits over the past twelve years, six recurrent ties to this one filmmaker, the six giving him career continuity. Five of their films have made over $4 million; the producer-director keeps his budgets down, is loyal to those who are on projects, and is known for his fast and efficient work which makes money for his investors and himself. The language of business is always in the foreground with this composer. Early in the interview he noted that some of his colleagues failed to realize what he called "the requirements" of the business as well as the absolute importance of technical flexibility. His entrepreneurial zeal is engaging. The tone is open, honest, and direct:

I think you have to understand who you are working with and you have to try as best you can to figure out what a producer is trying to achieve. It's your job to help; that's foremost. If you're going to have a career and get anything going for yourself in this business you have to help them—the people who hire you. Some of my colleagues, who shall remain nameless, feel that they are compromising their integrity at times. But that's because they don't recognize the situation. They don't realize fully what they are brought into work for. There's no use swatting a fly with a sledge hammer. Look at this realistically. How many great films are being done? If someone asks me to write a score, and maybe they have a sort of Guy Lombardo arrangement in mind, I'm not going to try to bring *all* my experience to bear, I'm not going to work out a complicated six-part invention. That's silly. You know it and I know it. They want a Guy Lombardo arrangement.

He made the comparison with other filmmakers who were not so detailed and specific in their demands.

Most of the time they don't even know what they want, but that's just another problem for us. I don't *have to do* what they want, but I accept the job for what it is and I use my experience to give them an arrangement, a score, that's going to sound like maybe what they think they want with the film. Sometimes it's inconvenient, sometimes they're incomprehensible, but you try to figure out what they're saying in the film, talk, and then deliver. If a composer accepts a job and takes the assignment, then at that point if he feels that he's compromising his integrity or whatever, he did it long before. He did it when he took the money to do the work. That's when he compromised. So your job is to come up with what is demanded; that's where the business integrity is very important.

Sometimes it is easier to resist these pressures than others.

I know that you've got to work and that's important. A lot of it is not the greatest—we all know that. But let's not get confused about what we're hired for when we're hired. If you want to go outside the business and write in some idiom, that's fine too. Don't confuse your frustrations about that with the fact that you're hired to do something as is and you have to be ready to do that. Maybe some composers are more artistic than I am. I don't know. I would say that with some exceptions I've enjoyed almost every picture I've done. I've watched the budgets, I've tried not to cost the producer too much with a huge music budget, and with a couple of producers and directors I'm able to get along and do what the film calls for.

"Well, what about work dissatisfaction?" I asked, growing a little impatient with the discussion of business and comfortable adaptations. He stopped, glared at me, and then asked me how well I knew any producers in the film business. Not waiting for me to answer he then said he would tell me about what he and his colleagues were up against, project after project.

> We're up against guys who'll tell you, "Something's wrong with the, er, strings, or uh, the piano, the melody, something like that." Really it can get ridiculous. Then you have a guy like the one I'm going to be working with starting next week. On our last film, last year, well, he would challenge me and ask me to explain every note I was going to write. He wanted to hear my ideas, see what I had in mind. He was very open to this. He would be one of the finest to work for—demanding, but you enjoyed the work. So that's very satisfying and the first one I mentioned is very unsatisfying, *really unsatisfying*. With the other producer, you see, once *he was satisfied* with my explanation, he let me go ahead and do it, he got out of my way, and that made me satisfied. He was a very knowledgeable guy, so that's very satisfying. In fact that's rare.

A strong producer can be an important positive force in movie making and film scoring by, first of all, bringing the right people together, and then, once they decide on an approach for the film, seeing that they follow the concept through. Good filmmakers contribute in the definitions of the possible approach. They reduce the composer's own uncertainty by bringing an engaging or interesting filmmaking intelligence to bear upon the subject. Composers recognize that attempts to analyze even in retrospect what makes a film work or not work are very difficult; and they know that the responsibility for the total effect is clouded not only by who has the final cut, but by the compromises and accidents of production. What is in the end important to the freelancer, because it is the hinge upon which his work and career depend, is the relation with the filmmaker. There are strong producers who are knowledgeable about film scoring and who try to be too helpful, but they are, by freelancers' accounts, rare. The most common complaint and source of work dissatisfaction is an unproductive kind of strength and power based on lack of knowledge, driven by fear, and nourished by the uncertainties of whether or not the music will contribute to the success of a project. Let us turn to these situations.

Projects and Problems

With more work and credits comes more experience. With more experience comes a finer-grained knowledge of commercial requirements and those who can operate within them. Composers profit from these relationships in many ways, not all of them related to film scoring. Some producers are very shrewd businessmen and judges of talent. Talking to them and watching them deal with composers can be very enlightening. Some, almost by nature it seems, combine business acumen and creativity as though they were *intended* to be mixed. Others exacerbate the potential conflict. Obviously, to have a score scrapped by a filmmaker who has only a rudimentary grasp of the nature of dramatic underscoring is embarrassing and irritating; to have a knowledgeable collaborator or partner throw out one's work is deeply humiliating.

Here is a composer who in the late 1970s broke out of television into features. His first couple of films were low-budget features scored for two producers who had worked with him earlier when they were all doing television episodes and movies for television. The third and fourth films were bigger productions, bigger budgets, and with actresses and actors who were nominally known to the public. The filmmaker on the last project was not always easy to do business with, because he was unpredictable and mercurial. He could be helpful, polite, and cooperative—or indecisive, suspicious, and impatient about film scoring. It was a difficult assignment, "an education," as the freelancer put it. The producer on the third film was sometimes blunt— even imperious—in his dealings. Nonetheless he was always professional, honest, and to the point. The composer liked him and thought he would work with him again given their mutual openness and directness. The producer's latest film was in the motorcycle, bikini, chain-saw massacre genre and, quite surprisingly, was doing fairly well in the drive-ins. The freelancer's score for this film was even singled out in some reviews. He was now admitting to restlessness. He did not want to get typecast as a motorcycle rock-cum-jazz-cum-jagged strings type of composer.

> Many times, I've found, you're dealing with people who don't have any idea about what they're looking for, and they're ill-educated about music, really. You're also coming from two different sides of the thing. He has his ideas and you have yours based on what's up on the screen. You can be saying one thing but he's hearing another. In one way or another you're always facing a problem of communication, they have their area of expertise and I have mine. It's the exception where you find a producer, or even a director, who really knows music. You have to almost drag it out of these guys at times. You see the film and tell him what you see, but the man either understands music or he doesn't. If he hasn't got it, then you just can't predict what's going on, or what's going to go on. He may think that the big bands were the greatest thing going, or that Glenn Miller is it; well, at least you have some reference there. You can get up against some directors who will open up with something like, 'Give me something real, real modern!' And you're trying then to figure out what they mean and it turns out the guy thinks Tchaikovsky is modern, as the old story goes. You know, the producer

who says, 'I must have something new, something fresh, different, it's got to be different, like Bela Barstock [sic].' It's your job to understand the film and what the guy's trying to do up there, and then you've got to read the guy and figure out what he's talking about when he talks about music.

"On that film," he said, referring to the fourth project, "it wasn't easy. Things kept changing. He wanted this, then that, then I could do whatever we had talked about. Very difficult. I don't think he really knew what he wanted and like I was told by some of my friends, other composers, these guys [filmmakers] will learn a couple of phrases and start using them, and you're trying to see if they *really* understand what this means or what that means." He mentioned the way filmmakers indicate intentions by using *types*, such as "Give me a *Wild Bunch* type score."

To the composer most of his clients seem musically ill-educated, although to varying degrees. Filmmakers may acquire some musical knowledge and appreciation of what the composer can and cannot accomplish. For most, however, the music is just one more part of the film. The viewpoints of producer/director and composer can never be wholly the same. As our composers recognized, filmmakers have their own problems, presuppositions, and assumptions. Sometimes filmmakers think they are helping but are not. Here is a classic story from a recording session.

You are in the recording studio, and the singers are singing and the band is playing and the producer stops everything and says, "Could I have it a little higher please?" So the composer is transposing like mad up a half step, right? But the guy says, "No, no, hey, you don't understand—higher, I want it *higher*." Okay, they take it up another half step. The musicians play it and the guy says, "No, no, I need it higher." So up they go another step and everyone's transposing like crazy and trying to read the music and the producer is shaking his head again, "No, *higher, higher*." The composer says, "Well, geez, if you go much higher the singers won't be able to sing it." The producer says, "Just try it a little higher, okay? That's what I want." They take it up another half step, now they're up a minor third. And the guy finally stops and says, "No." The engineer, sitting in the booth, says, "Wait a second, play again." And the engineer just turns up the volume. "That's it, higher, higher," screams the producer. "You got it!"

That kind of semantic problem happens all the time. From spotting on into dubbing it can occur. [He had run into the problem very recently while doing a television commercial. The producers had told him that the music should be] "contemporary, with a moderately classic approach." What does *that* mean? You don't know what they're talking about. So I try to pin them down. "What do you mean by that?" I ask

them if they want this, or this, or that. Somebody asked me a few years
ago to do a Baja marimba band sound. I said, "Okay," but I wanted
to know what specific Baja marimba band, "cause guys go home and
listen to records and they come in and say for a commercial, "Can you
do a sound like Neil Sedaka?" You have to know *what they're talking
about*. And if you're writing episodic television you're not listening to
Neil Sedaka. That's another thing that sets you apart, you're not really
tuned in to what's the latest hit at the moment whereas in commercials
you've got to be constantly on top of it. When they do a commercial
they're listening to something that's usually two months behind what's
right on the top forty that moment. Six weeks. So they start asking for
something and you know it was a big hit six weeks ago. You get all
kinds of semantic problems with the producers. You have to know how
to deal with them, and I usually just try to pick their brain by asking
them what they like.

Anecdotes about directors' attempts to "talk music" are a rich part of occupational lore. The following two examples illustrate the downright silly
side of filmwork—as composers are often required to see it.

   Bernard Herrmann (composer of the music for *Citizen Kane, Psycho, Obsession*) refused *The Exorcist* not only because he hated the film but also
because director William Friedkin's idea of collaboration and role allocation
was to hum and whistle the effects he wanted. Presumably, Herrmann would
then go to work with these directives as a guide. To make matters worse,
Mr. Friedkin also wanted credit as cocomposer and music director and a share
in the music royalties. Hugo Friedhofer (*The Young Lions, The Best Years
of Our Lives, One-Eyed Jacks,* and many other scores) tells of a music
conference where the producer announced to him, "Now, since this story is
set in France, we should hear lots of French horns."

   As we shall see in chapter 8, producers select freelancers for reasons that
have little to do with the film itself. Composers constantly complain that
filmmakers are unduly attentive to what is fashionable and making money at
the moment. To be sure, their job is to make money. But in hiring freelancers
filmmakers appear to suffer from what has been aptly identified as trained
incapacity—their skills function as inadequacies. Concern with sales potential
of sound track albums leads producers to hire many pop songwriters, whose
only proven ability is that they can write a hit record. But writing a hit album
or song and composing a film score are two very different things, a difference
many producers are unaware of. From watching and imitating other producers'
hiring preferences, inexperienced filmmakers draw fallacious conclusions about
a composer's skills and talents. Thus, composers are urged to write hit songs
for their scores while pop musicians are pressed into service to compose film
cues. One composer with ten credits between the late 1960s and 1980 was

very candid about the plus-music boys: "Everyone is an expert in the area of music. That's something we commiserate about. I just finished a film with a man who's an old line writer-producer. He knows absolutely nothing about music, and he keeps saying it—which is refreshing. We need more of this, this honesty. When a producer stops being a producer and starts acting like an *artist,* you're in trouble."

Task uncertainty is thus complicated by another contingency: some film-makers try to "sell" the composer on themselves and on the artistic importance of their motion picture and television production. The zeal and emotionalism with which this is done is annoying, not so much because of overevaluation of the film, but because delusions of "artistic" importance undermine the composer's ability to define the work situation clearly and comply successfully with the demands. As one composer expressed it: "It's difficult to deal with a person who is all worked up about his project . . . it can be rewarding if the person cares and listens to you and you can discuss the thing. It can be agony, also. He won't make himself clear, nothing you do will be *enough,* things can keep changing and you then have the score thrown out. You accept this as part of the job." The following are descriptions of the problem by a freelancer with over twenty film credits from 1968 to 1980. He summed up his perspective on communication and the conditions under which it becomes nearly impossible to plan a score.

> Unless you're a musician, it's very hard to talk to another musician. The picture was a two-hour movie of the week, a rush job where three days before I was going to score it—I had already written most of the music—I had a meeting with the director, who had been out of town and had just come back, the producer, and the head of the music department who had hired me. We had lunch. And the director said, "First of all, what I really want in this picture is a very thin, eclectic, very sparse kind of music with a lot of . . . uh . . . how can I put it?" In other words I had three people who I had to answer to and three opinions. I said, "I don't believe this!" Anyway, I told them that they hired me because I was the expert on music and that I would write what I thought was right. As it turned out, they loved it. But the director, who is a very talented man, is basically a music *hater.* There are people like that. They don't want much music in their pictures. They consider it an intrusion. I underplayed what I did to the point where he liked it.

> That was very lucky, and unique. Quite often you'll do something and the guy will say, "That's not what I had in mind—at *all.*" That hasn't happened to me. It happens. I'm sure it will happen to me. Then, I'm very fast at repairing things on the stage. I can make a lot of changes. You run into trouble because the guy thinks it's the greatest film ever made. It is not, but he thinks it is. This makes your job tough because

you don't see the same thing up there . . . also . . . the producer has been working on this film for, let's say, a year—or years—and has lost all objectivity. Then you're called upon to provide the "magic." You know, it's something about a teenage . . . ah . . . cowboy . . . who has astigmatism.

An angry veteran had this to say about his work satisfaction:

You go into an interview like I did today and as the thing progresses with the director or producer, you know you either want to do it or you don't want any part of it. If I don't want it, we blow out of the water right there. I say to myself, "This is impossible, we'll get eaten alive on the project." I mean there's no point in kidding ourselves. We're not turning out great art here. The film in most cases has nothing to do with it. I mean I don't mind working on a crappy film so long as everybody *says it's crap*. What I don't like is the pretension, the pretension that up there on that screen there is something great happening— when it isn't. Now when you can't be honest about the guy then you're in trouble. How you relate to the producer has a lot to do with the whole thing. Now when a producer says, "It's kind of a dumb film, but we had this budget, this problem," and so forth—that's perfect. I don't mind working on a crappy film, that's all right. But please don't tell me it's great, it's art. Let's understand each other clearly.

The overevaluation that producers do is more than attention-gathering theatricality in the service of the "big pitch" for the "big project." From the composer's point of view, it is a major barrier to open and explicit communication between himself and employers. Still, the accent on show business euphemism is viewed as a normal feature of film work. It is a necessary evil when working directly with people who face the conflict between the business and creative side of filmmaking. Freelancers note that the excessive use of metaphor, gloss, and euphemism has no simple, invariant relation to lying or deception. It is occasionally used to mask motives and conceal the merits of a film whose quality is questionable. Communication with clients is often through a specialized shared language. Composers become skilled at assessing the authenticity of the producer. Consequently, the nonrecurrent relationship between composer and "client" is a precarious admixture of mistrust, dependence, sycophancy, and impression management. One composer talked about several recent encounters with some major producers of a top television series.

The whole music conference was taken up with a big discussion about the project and how important it was, and what the music's role would be. And after a while in this business you learn to read these signals pretty clearly. . . . Let's say it's a schlock show, but it pays good, *fine with me,* let's get down to business—*how much* and *when do you want it?* Let's be honest about it. Don't tell me a *long story.* None of this something larger than life or "I need a score that has never been done before." Say it, but get serious. If the producer has a pretty good idea about what he's doing and doesn't get into all the clichés, then it's okay. Or he gives you the line but you know he wants an uncomplicated score and he wants it on time. Sure, I'll talk the talk, but then we get down to the small strokes and stop the show biz. Fine, the project's important; *fine,* you'll have all this freedom. Now that we've *said* it, what about terms? And what about the emphasis? I got to get a reading from him so I have an idea.

"Talking the talk" and "PR" (public relations) suggest that communication across occupational lines is characterized by intentionally or unintentionally transmitted false information. Euphemism is a valuable facilitating device and its presence reveals the uncertain nature of the film product (and its controller). Unless the reader appreciates that "talking the talk" and dramatic emphasis are quite a normal part of the loosely structured pattern of commercial film work, he/she will misunderstand freelancers' attitudes toward the turbulent features of their work situations and the recurrent problems of coming to terms with filmmakers on one-shot projects.

Producer/director talk may contain not only a dominant or overt definition but also counterthemes. These counterthemes qualify the expressed definitions of the project offered by the filmmaker. In some cases, they run in opposition to the stated definition and these contradictory definitions must be accommodated by composers. Knowing euphemisms are used and knowing how to use them in turn gives the composer some help in negotiation under conditions of uncertainty.

Composers interpret euphemisms or show business talk as follows: (1) if a filmmaker asks you to give him something "new," he really wants you to be imitative and follow the "now" style for the genre worked on; (2) when asked to "let yourself go," you are being told to repeat yourself; (3) when a producer says that he is not concerned about money, you know that the film has to turn a profit; (4) a directive to "do something creative," means "not *too* creative," or (5) when asked to "do as you please," you are being told to act as you must, after all this is what you are being paid for. To disregard these assumptions can represent the failure to "read" intentions and discover the line that gives direction and meaning to each new filmmaker's behavior. Moreover, euphemistic niceties such as these are read as indicators of prospective trouble with a filmmaker. Learning how to see and parry manipulative misinformation is an important part of career socialization.

Composers are not immune to the politics of persuasion. They too dramatize their own expertise, exaggerate or stretch the truth a bit, and "talk the talk" to quickly increase the filmmaker's confidence in them. Given that in the majority of work transactions, filmmaker and freelancer are trying to work together for the first time, "hype" is a Hollywood medium of exchange—a common language. Freelancers try to be cautious and refrain from reaching overly facile conclusions in this atmosphere of exaggeration. All this makes knowing whom they are working with important.

The "management" of cooperation with plus-music boys and prima donnas is a precarious enterprise. Often the efficacy of a composer's work can be discovered only retrospectively. Since the producer or director is in a position to reject the music for a variety of reasons—ranging from "too conventional" to "not conventional enough"—a composer cannot fully predict the consequences of doing things differently. It is easy to see how a profusion of up-front ambiguities in these nonrecurrent transactions creates an ad hoc affair in which participants make do, improvise as they go along, and then make sense out of what they have been doing after some of the details are finally in.

This chapter has focused on freelancers' ongoing experiences with different types of employers. A professional knows that the struggle for control of the work relationship is finally the *definition* of the relationship. Jockeying for advantage goes on in every type of expert-employer work relationship. Freelancers learn that this is a fact of life, that there are many times when they can come right out and frankly fight for control, that filmmakers are not all of a piece, and that losing a few battles, even having a score thrown out, is typical, normal trouble for composers. One can hardly improve on the perspective of a composer with six credits from 1971 to 1975. "I've learned," he said, "you have to be objective about your work, know who you're working with and know what you can contribute to the relationship. After that, there's only so much I can do. I'm just there to write the music. I may never work with the producer again. I think that's one of the emotional hurdles you have to move over if you're going to function effectively—or at all—in this kind of collaborative medium." He added, smiling, "I've learned to be more detached about all of this, occasionally at some cost to my ego." The next chapter details some of the sources of this new-found objectivity and detachment.

Notes

1. Client work, as E. C. Hughes has made clearest, furnishes the possibility of conflict between specialized experts and those they serve. Students of antagonistic cooperation have paid close attention to how people define each other, construct the subjective meanings attached to their work, and engage in concerted action. The

literature is extensive. O. D. Bigus, "The Milkman and His Customer: A Cultivated Relationship," *Urban Life and Culture* 1 (1972): 131–65; J. Bensman, *Dollars and Sense* (New York: Macmillan, 1967); J. Browne, *The Used Car Game* (Lexington, Mass.: D. C. Heath, 1973); J. E. Carlin, *Lawyers on Their Own* (New Brunswick, N.J.: Rutgers University Press, 1962); F. Davis, "The Cabdriver and His Fare: Facets of a Fleeting Relationship," *American Journal of Sociology* 65 (1959): 158–65; R. Fox, *Experiment Perilous: Physicians and Patients Facing the Unknown* (New York: Free Press, 1959); L. J. Henderson, "Physician and Patients as a Social System," *New England Journal of Medicine* 212 (1935): 819–23; B. Barber (ed.), *L. J. Henderson on the Social System* (Chicago: University of Chicago Press, 1970); E. Friedson, *Profession of Medicine* (New York: Dodd, Mead, 1970); "Dilemmas in the Doctor-Patient Relationship," in A. M. Rose (ed.), *Human Behavior and Social Processes: An Interactionist Approach* (Boston: Houghton Mifflin, 1962); R. L. Gold, "In the Basement: The Apartment Building Janitor," in P. L. Berger (ed.), *The Human Shape of Work: Studies in the Sociology of Occupations* (New York: Macmillan, 1964); S. J. Miller, "The Social Base of Sales Behavior," *Social Problems* 12 (1964): 15–24; S. Y. Fagerhaugh and A. Strauss, *Politics of Pain Management: Staff-Patient Interaction* (Menlo Park, Calif.: Addison-Wesley, 1977); A. Strauss et al., *Psychiatric Ideologies and Institutions* (New York: Free Press, 1964); W. F. Whyte, *Human Relations in the Restaurant Industry* (New York: McGraw Hill, 1948); B. Glaser, *The Patsy and the Subcontractor* (Mill Valley, Calif.: The Sociology Press, 1972).

2. Professional workers often find that many of their clients make demands on them that are (1) inconsistent and conflicting, and (2) strikingly incongruous with workers' claims to expertise. Such difficult or troublesome clients threaten professional autonomy and control over work tasks. See H. Becker, "The Professional Dance Musician and His Audience," *American Journal of Sociology* 57 (1951); 136–44; id., "The Teacher in the Authority System of the Public School," *Journal of Educational Sociology* 27 (1953): 128–41, reprinted in *Sociological Work: Method and Substance* (Chicago: Aldine, 1970); M. Griff, "The Commercial Artist: A Study in Changing and Consistent Identities," in M. Stein et al. (eds.), *Identity and Anxiety* (New York: Free Press, 1960); L. A. Mennerick, "Client Typologies: A Method of Coping with Conflict in the Service Worker-Client Relationship," *Sociology of Work and Occupations* 4 (1974): 396–411; H. O'Gorman, *Lawyers and Matrimonial Cases* (New York: Free Press, 1963); H. L. Ross, *Settled Out of Court: The Social Processes of Insurance Claims Adjustment* (Chicago: Aldine, 1970); C. R. Sanders, "Psyching Out the Crowd: Folk Performers and Their Audiences," *Urban Life and Culture* 3 (1974): 264–82; D. H. Zimmerman, "Tasks and Troubles: The Practical Bases of Work Activities in a Public Assistance Organization," in D. A. Hansen (ed.), *Explorations in Sociology and Counselling* (Boston: Houghton Mifflin, 1969); J. A. Roth, "Some Contingencies of the Moral Evaluation and Control of Clientele: The Case of the Hospital Emergency Services," *American Journal of Sociology* 77 (1972): 839–56; F. Baker and R. Firestone, *Movie People: At Work in the Business of Film* (New York: Lancer, 1973); C. Higham and J. Greenberg, *The Celluloid Muse: Hollywood Directors Speak* (Chicago: Regnery, 1969); R. Corliss, *Talking Pictures: Screenwriters in the American Cinema* (New York: Penguin, 1974); Ralph Rosenblum and Robert Karen, *When the Shooting Stops . . . the Cutting Begins* (New York: Penguin, 1980).

3. The idea of communication under conditions of bounded rationality refers to human behavior that is "*intendedly* rational, but only limitedly so," as H. A. Simon has

said. See his *Administrative Behavior* (New York: Macmillan, 1961), p. xxiv. Participants to a transaction sometimes lack the ability to communicate successfully about the nature of the materials before them and the nature of the transaction itself through the use of words or symbols that are contractually meaningful. The requisite language may not exist or the individuals concerned may not have access to it; moreover, the individuals concerned may be organizationally limited in their ability to acquire the language, expectations, and definitions of their collaborators. Discussions of bounded rationality can be found in: R. M. Cyert and J. G. March, *A Behavioral Theory of the Firm* (Englewood Cliffs, N.J.: Prentice-Hall, 1963); H. A. Simon, "Theories of Bounded Rationality," in C. McGuire and R. Radner (eds.), *Decision and Organization* (Amsterdam: North-Holland Publishing Co., 1972); J. G. March and J. P. Olsen, *Ambiguity and Choice in Organizations* (Bergen: Universitetsforlaget, 1976); A. V. Cicourel, *The Social Organization of Juvenile Justice* (New York: Wiley, 1968); K. E. Weick, *The Social Psychology of Organizing* (Reading, Mass.: Addison-Wesley, 1969).

4. As long as either uncertainty or complexity is present, the bounded rationality problem arises and in Hollywood the solution is often to introduce "hype" and exaggeration *as if* this language of dramatic accentuation carried large amounts of meaning with relatively few symbols. Despite their best efforts, then, parties may find that language fails them and resort to other means of communication. For moderately complex problems, such as talking about music, the number of alternative paths is very large; in talking with filmmakers neither the alternative paths nor a rule for generating them are easily available; and a final problem is one of estimating consequences, for the consequences of alternative ways of scoring a film's cues are difficult, if not impossible, to estimate from the composer's point of view. Approximation replaces exactness in his decision making as he does not fully know what he is going to do until he does it; he does not know what the filmmaker will make of what he has done; and neither composer nor filmmaker can predict the music's contribution to the film's success in the popular culture market for neither knows if the film will "make it" or not.

7.
DUAL INTERESTS
Opposing Tendencies and the Positive Aspects of Conflict

It's important to keep working and stay in shape, to keep fresh, and be open to the values of the film. But I don't ever think it's wise to agonize unduly over what you've done. A project is just a project. You do your best and after that you have to forget it. It may be recut and reedited. Your music will end up in places you didn't write it for, and you just can't let it bother you.
                                    —Composer with over twenty film credits

The more you work, the more you learn how to handle the different sides of this business. . . . If you get too close, you can lose your objectivity, what they call your third eye: the ability to stand back and see the total project and your own job in an objective way.
                                    —Composer with six film credits between 1970 and 1977

The effects of continuity in the freelance labor market are direct and nontrivial. With an absence of employment difficulties a freelancer retains dual interests in individuation and integration into networks of filmmakers. A composer wishes to have both work connections and independence. He wants to gain experience and credentials as well as freedom from undesirable work relationships and the stereotypes or labels that credentials often confer. He quickly learns that he is simultaneously tightly linked and loosely linked to the business of film. He finds that filmmakers and freelancers come together, as much by accident as by design, do the best they can together, then go their separate ways and often never work together again. Nonrecurrent or one-shot ties with producers are a normal feature of freelancing as a loosely coupled hiring system. But recurrent and stable alliances can develop between freelancers and filmmakers as partners. If he is lucky, the freelance composer develops a combination of both strong ties (recurrent alliances) and weak ties (nonrecurrent connections) across multiple film producers. Given the dual tendencies of commercial work, it follows that diversification of accounts provides conditions under which a freelancer can match his dual interests in individuation and integration to a changing market situation.

With the absence of employment difficulties a freelancer encounters more choice points. He takes additional responsibility for integrating more of himself into the organization of connections and film projects. He learns that he is asked to write music that is different, but not *too different*. He is also pressed toward doing too much, but at the same time must remain selective about his film assignments. He has to work to stay in shape and stay fresh, but too much work can result in going stale. There are pressures to become recognized and visible, but not *too visible*. That is, he knows that in order to "make it" he must be conspicuous to filmmakers—he has to attract their attention, but the attention and publicity he draws may entrap him. With increasing strength in the market, he takes steps to ensure that his competitive position is preserved. By the choices he makes, in response to freelancing's dual tendencies, he actively shapes the looseness of the hiring arrangements themselves. He enacts the work ties which become strands in the network of Big Hollywood.

By the stance he takes toward his specific job assignments, he also enacts the conditions under which dual interests can be realized. Not only does a freelancer wish to have individuation and centrality in freelance networks, he also wishes to have flexibility and stability in writing the score for a film. Given these dual interests, he learns to be a chameleon, as several composers put it. He quickly learns to adjust to the film projects he chooses, projects requiring different levels of musical skill and taste, different degrees of cooperation and antagonism with his employers, different acts which influence his definition of freelance behavior. This chapter will describe how the successful composer's perceived control over work and the self facilitate such chameleon-like adaptation as detached concern.[1] I will look at the dubbing session as the nexus of many of the pressures I have described. Finally, I will turn to the talking freelance blues because in such talk a work culture is enacted or built up.

Acquiring a "Third Eye"

Composers with a line of work experiences instantly learn that their music is only one part of a larger endeavor, that it often gets the lowest priority in the dubbing session, and that all of this is part of the way things are usually done in Hollywood. After some experience and exposure, a freelancer concludes that justice does not have much to do with film scoring, that producers and directors often react more to the total project and its commercial fate than to the composer's specific efforts, and that maybe this is the way things should rightly be. They become more objective about their work, themselves, and what happens to their music after they score and record it. They learn not to take personally a lot of what happens to them though they can hardly not take it seriously.

No freelancer is without stories about adjustment problems in this difficult and delicate area of film work. Some problem areas—such as the felt discrepancy between some imaginary, ideal state of affairs and the practical circumstances in which they see themselves—are old. Some are a hangover from their early television episode days when they were scuffling and trying to break in. Some—such as their complaints about different producers—are continuous. And some—such as access to quality work that allows a closer tie between aesthetic and commercial opposites—are newer and more urgent.

Here is a freelancer going through all this. His career is on the rise and his past feelings toward work were good objects for reflection. They allowed him to review just how far he had come in this business. When it was all new, he said, it was difficult for him to handle. Some problems were self-induced. Others were the result of demands made on him by various employers. And still others were the result of his ideals of who he should be and how he should work on expensive projects.

"Has your relationship to your work changed, or your feeling about yourself and work changed since that time?"

> It went from dealing with the business very poorly to dealing with it very well. You know what I mean? I went from not dealing with it very maturely, I think, to having much more control over it and myself [noting the difference between the work and his reaction or response to it]. It's something I'm sure everyone else has told you. It's unspeakably frightening about committing yourself to a project where you know there's been a lot of money involved, many thousands of dollars spent, and now it's put in *your hands*—a piece of the film budget has been invested in *you* and you've got two weeks to be brilliant, and there's a time, money, talent conflict that hits you like a bomb and the second you're signed the clock starts ticking. Many logistics have to be worked out, let alone the music, the style, the musicians who are going to play it, where you are going to record it, and all of a sudden your life isn't simple anymore, you know? I used to deal with that very poorly, I used to totally fall apart.

"Under the pressure of those things?" I asked. "All of them mixed together?"

> You're right, they're often in conflict. Usually there's not enough money to do what you *want* to do, and that's frequently the case when you're starting, and there's not enough time to do what you want to do, and

you can't always get the people you want to get on the [recording] date, and that's not even to mention the problems of *writing the music for the film*. You know, a lot of guys panic under that. You just fall apart and then pull yourself together and try to cope with it. Or, I think most guys, as a result of that, write up to the last minute. They're always writing the night before and sitting up. I used to do that kind of stuff and then I read an interview with a top composer somewhere who said he doesn't do that. He finishes his stuff two days before so he can relax. I was thinking how mature, how enviable.

"You mean what great work habits he must have?"

"Yes. I'm always hearing about these other guys and their work habits," he said, talking about three or four of the busiest and most successful composers. He jokingly talked about the ideal schedule. "These guys get up at six in the morning and run two miles and then write music for two hours and then have the rest of the day to swim and socialize. Anyway, at first, it seems like everybody's work habits were admirable and mine were totally screwy."

"What helped you the most in this transition?" The answer was simple:

A growing sense of confidence from having coped with so many disgusting and lovely people at different times [he included filmmakers, musicians, contractors, and production personnel]. You know I can kind of deal with the people better now. I mean, I've worked with some monsters in my time and some really lovely producers and you know you kind of learn that this is going to be a monstrous situation and how to cope with that, and then, this is going to be a lovely situation and how to cope with that. You learn about the money involved, how much they will spend for the score, the amount of music that has to be written in a given period of time for a given amount of players.

Freelancers on the move claim that, looked at as a whole, their reaction to these difficulties is not as intense as it probably would have been when they were working on their first series of projects, that their experiences with filmmakers, budgets, time pressures, and the quality of projects have curbed their tendency to react emotionally: "You know, you're much more interested if you're working on a project that you feel you can contribute and be part of something of quality. You find that's pretty hard. I mean there are not *that many* quality movies made over a year's time. So with a lot of the films you get, don't make more of it than the job requires. Why knock yourself out on a score that may or may not be heard all the way through or where you're dealing with difficulties?" The difficulties were, again, limited budgets, low production values, and troubles with the employer.

Whether their aim is to integrate the aesthetic and commercial sides of the situation or simply to acquire more credits in a career line, the composer learns how to accept, even manipulate, client expectations, how to keep his long-range career interests in mind, and occasionally put a great deal of distance between himself and his work simply in order to keep busy, to keep his skills in shape, and, as the next quotation suggests, to do the work in the first place. "You can lose your perspective," he said. He went through his major film credits and at the conclusion of the list he summed up some "lessons" he learned.

"I feel very lucky to be working in the business at all. I'll always have that feeling because every day you look around and somebody has either a coronary or an ulcer or something," he said. Not only did they take too much work, but they got too wrapped up in their own problems. "So I'm trying to cool it," he continued. "About three or four years ago I decided that I wasn't going to work myself into that state of madness. I was going to back off from that frantic thing. It's all right if you can take everything you get if you're busy—take it and *not worry about it*. That's fine."

High volume and increasing levels of worry were dangerous. He had been through it and had arrived at some conclusions about himself. "They are not exactly great pieces of work. I think that helps to get through it. It is that vague kind of contempt. To be able to sit down—because you're putting yourself on paper, and you're going on the block by virtue of writing the music. You're making a statement and that's your main title up there, you're responsible for it—and write, just write."

Insecurity and a sense of inadequacy frequently come after spotting the film and before the actual writing begins. "Now there's a thing that happens to me," he said cautiously. "I'm not all that secure. I feel I know what I know, but I dodn't know if that's all I *should* know. So I have to get that basic thing going that says, 'Well, let's face it, *it's just a movie*; that's what we're talking about, a movie'—in order to be able to write."

"Nothing's good enough," I said.

"Nothing. So you sit down and write it. Bang. And that attitude has helped me. That's not the perfect answer. The perfect answer would be for me to have all kinds of self confidence and great work habits and say, 'Of course this is what you really want to do—now write.' But a dose of contempt has helped me. And I find as the years go by I have a better attitude towards the vernacular 'they' or 'them,' you know, 'I'm fighting them' or 'they're going to get me,' and so on. This kind of thinking about the producer or whoever it is. . . . I have much less of that now, so it's a better attitude personally for me."

It is easy to assume that a composer should always be deeply attached to his work, that at least ideally the image of self and of work should be closely linked. This is a limited and uncritical view of the world of work; it obscures important differences in the psychological tie between a composer and his projects.

First, when the freelancer does move on to more work and new associates he is not likely to be told explicitly how to handle himself, nor will the facts of his new location in the division of labor determine his stance toward that work without some consideration. Ordinarily he will be given only a few hints about how involved he can be toward his own effort. If he follows the stories about tall orders and plus-music boys he is sure to be misled. If he simply assumes that all work should be self-fulfilling he will be sure to be disappointed. For the composer, socialization and learning what the business is all about is not primarily a matter of mastering details but of learning what his own strengths are and being able to manage any project and any producer he is likely to be matched with. One way of managing, as suggested above, is to put some space between one's self and one's work. Just as producers and directors who get all worked up about a mediocre project are treated with disdain, so too a composer runs real risks if he forgets that some projects are simply pieces of "work." We have a source of *distancing*: a tactfully limited involvement in the task, a concern for modulating one's skills with the demands of others, and a flexible sense of the level of effort required on any one project.[2]

Second, in the matter of task distance, the filmmakers themselves will often cooperate by acting in a professional and respectful fashion, letting the composer know that they understand what their mutual labors are all about, and even helping the freelancer not to make more of his job than the project requires. It is the unsophisticated that draw rigid lines between "them" and "us"—as the previous professional described in his own moral education.

Third, the freelancer's ego may get in the way of his grasp of the film itself; he may be so concerned about showing off that he misses the point of the film and, probably more likely, the ideas the filmmakers are trying to tell him. He may also be committed to and comfortable with one or two musical styles and idioms. This can limit the range of aesthetic responses to a film, rigidify positions in negotiation with film producers, and encourage oversimplified ideas about commercial work generally.

More generally, a professional freelancer is a person who can function successfully in *any kind* of situation because both his skill and sense of himself have grown since he entered the business. What Hollywood promotes and produces is a relatively small number of composers who get beyond scoring the one film, who cash in their first set of chips, and keep on trying to play the same game with the same style and personally comfortable idiom. For a few, as long as film producers keep coming back for the same commodity, they have nothing to worry about. But freelancing is volatile. Films and filmmakers change. A composer has to change also in order to extend his string of credits and his connections to employers. A pro can do many things. The flash-in-the-pan composer is one locked into a limiting tie between himself and his work. He is unable to balance the need for stability with the need for flexibility. The pro can alter himself and his relationship to his craft, adopt new roles, and work to exploit talent few guessed he had. He is always surprising others; at times he even surprises himself. Flexibility of craft and outlook, openness and adaptability to changing ties and typecastings, and circumspection in the face of turbulence are unmistakable attributes of detached concern as career survival.

These compositional skills and talents are not acquired easily nor uniformly. Some of the most productive composers I talked with admit they found dealing with the film business difficult. They were, they said, rather sensitive, even touchy, about anything in their work environment that interfered with what they wanted to do, which was to write the best music they could. But with more work and more experiences with filmmakers, they find that some assignments are restrictive and obdurate. The tasks and immediate constraints of the fifth, sixth, seventh, and eighth credits were difficult for the next top composer. He is at the top of most filmmakers' lists. One of the top ten in Hollywood, in terms of continuity and visibility. Changes in work habits are important, he noted, as is modification of aspirations for success. The constant pressures to produce help an ambitious composer become more detached from the responses of others toward his work.

He was, he said, getting more objective about his work. He thought a film composer in Hollywood ought to be able to see his efforts from the perspective of the carpenter Faulkner once described who had built a henhouse. "You have nothing to say after you've done your part on the film, so there's no need to hold on to it; after all, it's not in your hands anymore." He then voiced an opinion that I had heard before from composers involved in record production. "Look," he said, trying to set the frame around the details. "It's not your album, the film is the *producer's thing*—not yours. You are there to help. You do the very best you can, try to feel at home with it, but there's no need to agonize unduly about it. I mean, after a certain point your job ends."

"I had to realize," he continued. "I could only make the effort; I wasn't responsible for the *ultimate results*. There were a lot of things that I *wanted to do*, there were a lot of things I would *have liked to do*, but I really didn't have the final say-so in it and that's the way it *is*. If you want the final say-so go into production yourself, don't be a composer. Also I stopped thinking of myself as the center of all the other possibilities revolving around me. I started to see after more work that somebody else is going to be responsible for picking a composer for the film. Many of the choices are out of your hands."

A freelancer can hardly consider himself the center of things when all the way down the line he has to deal with the choices, uncertainties, decisions, and resources of other people. Ultimate control is never theirs. The spotting session is a study in antagonistic cooperation; the dubbing session is a study in controlled conflict. Detached concern is most necessary for the composer's dual interests at both points, but especially in the latter stage. Up to this point in the production process, it was all talk, all concept, and negotiated terms about something that did not exist. Now, on the recording stage and in the mixing or dubbing of music onto the film's sound track they could talk about concrete things, such as "louder," "softer," "more strings," "less brass," "too slow," "higher," and all the other words that can pinpoint something. At this point in the work process it is vain and presumptuous to claim absolute autonomy for one's work and how it is treated in the final film product, especially when the score's individual cues are clearly visible and audible to everyone who is working on the dubbing. On the other hand, the freelancer does not lightly hand over the treatment of his own work efforts to others, a practice which would be inconsistent with the ethos of craftsmanship and his personal involvement with his composition. In light of such considerations detached concern is a necessity and anything else is the betrayal of professionalism.

> The point where everything gets intensified is in the dubbing session— adding music, sound effects, dialogue, and putting all of that *together*. Sound effects. That's where you run into trouble because dialogue is more or less there, you know it, it's in your timing cues. You've got to stay out of the way. You know what to expect there, but you *never know* what's going to happen with effects, or what kind of a heavy hand the mixer is going to have that day. I mean he can wipe out all of your music if he decides to go heavy with effects, or you don't know what the perspective of the director is going to be that day, or the sound supervisor. I welcome a second perspective, sure. The director's got to call the shots, really, it's his picture, it's not my album. Some directors and producers are totally logical about that kind of thing. With the producer-director I'm working with now, there was a truck in one scene, it had to be there, and we'd get the music out of the way of it and try not to fight it. It would be horrendous if you tried to cram too much on the sound track at that point. You see it from his point of view, and in this case he's absolutely right.

Another colleague who had just moved from the core at Universal television into feature films hastened to add that dubbing is a good place for freelancers to learn how to see the project from the viewpoint of the other people involved, and consistently how to put some emotional distance between himself and what happens to his score during these mixing sessions. He was a composer who let it be known how he felt about getting along with others.

"Look," he announced toward the end of the interview one afternoon in an office at Universal, "you're not there to fight 'em, you know? Dubbing is a place where you can learn a lot. You can see how good your timing sense is and how successful you were with the score and that sort of thing. As far as influencing the game in the dubbing stage, it's a place where you can get destroyed if you are really worried about your *art* at that point." It was clear by the way he pronounced the word *art* that he had no affection for composers who refused to see the situation for what it was. The mood was sardonic. There was no need to brood over these circumstances, to continually think about what one could have written, what could be more highlighted on the sound track, or imagine what would happen after the dubbing session and the film was released. Spotting sessions were difficult many times, he noted; composing the music was usually a lot of fun, but after that he placed a partition between his work and what others did with it at the next stage.

"If you were worried about preserving everything that you wrote and tried to sustain it over the next stage, you would have your legs cut off," he finished. "There are times," he qualified, "when you'll have a scene that you've discussed with the producer you're working for, where you shoot for something, where maybe there's no dialogue and you're trying to make something out of a scene where you might get involved in that way. Those things happen and they are very pleasant experiences where you put the music *up* on the sound track and let it do its job."

He then returned to his first stance. "But again," he said more disinterestedly, "they have paid a lot of money for the script and the story and the actors and the recording and the reshooting of scenes because someone mumbled, and then *you* come along with a bunch of music and they *are not* going to take a chance that every word the writer wrote isn't going to be heard. They will not sacrifice any of *that* for your music."

"In a sense," I added, "You can see their point of view."

"You *better*. Look, there's no conspiracy going on here," he said having in mind some of his colleagues who might have difficulty in cutting loose from their work. "It's a pragmatic point of view on their part," he noted about filmmakers. "The priority on the sound track is dialogue, sound effects, and then the music. The last two are competing with one another. The first is almost always given top concern."

Growing connections with filmmakers deepen a freelancer's appreciation of weak and strong ties; numerous spotting sessions and discussions with filmmakers increase a composer's ability to deal with knowledgeable and unknowledgeable employers. Dubbing sessions bring home another important lesson to the music writer: he's part of a larger project. He's surrounded by numerous craftsmen and powerful employers when he walks into the dubbing studio a few days after having recorded his own music. He'll see three or four sound mixers, the producer, a music editor, a sound supervisor, the projectionists, and a few hangers-on and maybe a gofer. The session is costly. It is important to keep everything running smoothly. Sometimes his first reaction is rooted in the illusion that anyone trying to mess with his music must have a personal motive. He may even think that sometimes the creative tension between himself and his employers boils down to simply tension. But gradually he learns that there is nothing personal about it. Sometimes he wins, sometimes he loses; he has to know when to make a request, how to make it, how to talk to the mixers, and when to stay out of the way. It is a sobering experience, one that directly confronts the newcomer with the limits to his own autonomy. He also learns that it is important to take the point of view of others. In so doing, the composer begins to change, to lose some of his awkwardness. He becomes more professional, leaner and tougher. A thick hide begins to grow in order to maintain relative equanimity in these commercial situations.

Composers' detached concern, arising as it does out of the context of work, changes as that context changes. Spotting, scoring, recording, and then dubbing, all call for different attitudes and create different problems. In the first instance, each composer will face his employers on his own, alone. In the second, he will be all by himself writing the music. Then he will join with his performing colleagues on the recording stage and perform the music he has written. The scoring is essentially a process of arriving at a music solution to a dramatic problem, then executing that solution. The recording session is the concrete realization of that solution. It is realized in the company of musical colleagues. After that task is accomplished, the composer goes into the dubbing session where he faces different problems with different company. His fellows will either already have reached decisions about how to treat the music, dialogue, and sound effects and thus treat the freelancer as just one among many with interests to be handled, or they may have little sympathy for his professional interests. Either attitude makes the session more difficult. Alternatively, the composer may find himself in good hands, a fraternal crew that knows its stuff and tries to be flexible, compliant, and objective. Fighting with producers, sound mixers, sound editors, etc., seems most agreeable to those who are either strangers to the politics of dubbing sessions, newcomers who are inflexible in their demands, and, more generally, any composer who is overattached to his single contribution to a collective endeavor.

Failure to understand one's limited role in the making of a film is often wishful and narcissistic. Detached concern must be related to practical occupational interests as I have shown here. It must finally rest on the realization that in any kind of collective and purposeful work, overinvolvement can be inefficient, often uncontrollable, and downright obstructive to the attainment of the freelancer's own interests. It is true that a composer's basic commitment to private and individual expression is tested in the commercially dominated ambience. It is also true that some feel their creativity is placed in a collective straitjacket, which turns their art and work into something secondary, bland, insidiously impersonal, and dramatically insipid. But the necessary adjustment can be achieved with a modicum of disenchantment and anger. Composers have all the experiences they need to build a personally useful stance toward their work. First, a composer has limited powers to compel compliance after the dubbing session is over. Second, he has no control over the merchandizing, distribution, and exhibition of the film. Third, he has no control over the sound system in movie houses in which his score will be played. If the production calls for twin-channel, stereo-optic soundtracks processed by Dolby, that is all to the good, but more likely his score will be run through an ordinary and outdated mono-optic system with deteriorating speaker systems in the movie house. He knows, for instance, that "95 percent of the industry sound standards today were set in 1935," or so said Fred Hayes, chief sound engineer and vice-president of Todd-AO. Fourth, the working conditions in sound recording and dubbing studios are awful. One is encouraged to make do and keep one's mouth shut. The freelancer trims his expectations. He says to hell with it and makes some highly agreeable music, occasionally even terrific music in spite of the troubles. The message is quite plain: overattachment and unrestricted grasping for responsibility to one's film score during dubbing and beyond may be nice, and even eccentric, but it gets you nowhere. The perfectionist, the man incapable of cutting loose and never looking back, creates many difficulties for himself. He may also find that employers and television studios find other, more flexible freelancers much easier (and less expensive) to deal with.

The apparent, outward detachment of freelancers probably disguises a great deal of discontent coming from dampened aspirations for their score, demoralization about the sometimes marginal quality of the complete soundtrack, muted resignation about what the whole soundtrack will sound like in theaters with antiquated equipment, and their own private knowledge about what is theoretically possible versus what is probable in commercial work.

After a music writer has been in the film business long enough to acquire continuity and connections to different filmmakers, he becomes cynical and skeptical about all the hype and sluggishness in Hollywood. With a number of credits behind him he begins to anticipate more and better work, but those anticipations quickly outrun any concrete means available for their realization. Just as confidence in one's craft and competence is being tested, long-run career interests become uncertain and increasingly difficult to predict. Just when a freelancer is learning how to function in his work, he is denied those

desired opportunities that would make his career really happen. As his resources increase, he finds himself in direct competition with composers in
the inner circles. The gaps between short-run successes in work and long-run
successes in project career have potent effects.

First, they render him vulnerable to the anxiety of future exclusion by
producers and studios as better projects go to the more visible and tightly
connected composers in the "top leagues" just ahead of him. Before he was
only trying to get work. Now, with movement in his credits and visibility,
he wants to "break through" into the exclusive networks of those in demand
for the best projects in Hollywood.

Second, delay increases the competitive threat from colleague competitors
in the swim of things—at his own level—and also by those now on the move
from the periphery toward him—freelancers quickly coming up, like he did,
from the industry's Sprinkler Drain(s) or coming in laterally to film assignments. The issue *now* is to get ahead of the hundreds he is surrounded by.

Third, all these anxieties forcefully bring home the instantly learned fact
that most potential employers do not always pay that much attention to him
and his unique musical accomplishments, but rather, are driven to their deal
making on the basis of how "hot" a so-called creative person is at the moment,
the commercial success of his latest project, and whether they can get him
at a price they can afford. By every yardstick of film-producing deals, composers in midstream can be had for modest fees and by film producers with
modest track records. The two sides of the market are matched. From the
freelancer's viewpoint, at this level big money matters considerably less than
the chance to be associated with a quality project which would give maximum
exposure to his talents and, with luck, provide him with some longevity in
the market.

It is hard to find the right distance from such a situation. Composers can
make the error of becoming too involved, too attached, and too enthusiastic
about their work and the corresponding project. They can also become too
distant, perhaps too businesslike, and too remote from what they are doing.
The knack is to join these opposing tendencies. Considering the shifting
currents of commercial work to do otherwise is either emotionally foolish or
cognitively immature. Thus the exigencies of the market breed freelancers
who have dual interests and are detached but concerned about their work.
They are realistic but idealistic about their long-run prospects in a mercurial
business, and close but remote to a chameleon-like professional persona they
project outward into an uncertain market.

War Stories: Talking, Conflict, and Shared Culture

Like members of other occupations who work directly with clients, freelancers share stories and images of the "ideal" client. They actively use this

image and fiction to shape their conceptions of how their work ought to be done, how much leeway they should be allowed, and why all of this should be so.

The more a man works, however, the more he comes to see just how greatly filmmakers vary in their work styles, candor, communicativeness, demands, and knowledge of scoring for films. Only a small part of the freelancer's total work assignments will even remotely approximate the ideal conceptions of who the filmmaker is and how he should treat the freelancer. Composers tend to type clients by their distance from this ideal. These scenarios about successful matching and disastrous mismatching go back at least as far as the days of D. W. Griffith and become part of the lore of this industry.

There is always some mixture of reality and distortion in these war stories. At some point in his career, a freelancer must cope with tyrannical, corrupting, uncaring, and exploitive people and situations. It is hard to sort out such experiences, and a freelancer frequently vacillates between extremes of blaming others (for suppressing or ignoring his talents, for telling him what to do, for threatening him with no future work if he does not "go along") and blaming himself (for feeling inept, lacking control over his own circumstances, and being unable to seize the initiative and do something to improve his lot). When these external demands and internal conflicts are at their height, it is difficult to get a perspective on what one is doing and how to do it better.

Paradoxically, this mixture of reality and distortion is matched with a mixture of good and bad filmmakers as shown earlier. The larger the freelancer's share of the market, the more people he works with, the better his judgments about producers and directors will be, for he is able to compare them with one another. A composer with over twenty-five credits from 1971 to 1981 talked about some filmmakers and the way in which they taught him something very important about the relation between himself and his work.

> I could sense that there were certain producers whom I worked for, whom I admired for what they had going. I think a lot of what I admired was the way they were as people. There was a way of acting. Nobody is running over them, nobody is pushing them around, but on the other hand they're not really pushing anybody else around either. They had found a middle line where they're out front with you, they're as honest as one can be under the circumstances. They express what they want. They express their opinions in a way that recognizes you as a professional. There's an openness about it. Now when I was around someone like that I admired it. I admired those qualities in that person. And I saw them under stress, you always have to add *that extra ingredient* of stress in this business. It's one thing in a nice clinical environment to say these things, but it's another when you're in a very stressful environment. It's an uptight business, you know?

I admired them and I thought to myself, "Gee, I'd really like to be able to handle myself that way." I respect it and I admire it. And it's not an easy thing to do, and not all the people you work with do it, by any means. I learned as I went along. After a couple of years, one thing I learned is that the lines between, say, self-assertion and arrogance, flexibility and being obsequious are thin. They're in flux and they're difficult. But the people, some people I'm around in this business, have managed to put it together. You learn from them that there are ways to handle difficult situations. There are ways to do it. And sometimes they are the easiest ways to get a handle on it and you have to try your own style. What works for one composer may not work for another. But the fact that a producer, a composer, whatever, operates effectively, with respect, with humor, and a high level of professional ability, I respect that. You know it when you're around it. You can sense it. You know that some people have some conclusions about the way they are going to handle *their thing*.

He paused, listed several of his collaborators and partners he enjoyed working with and from whom he had learned a great deal, then said, "This doesn't come in the beginning. In the beginning you're too busy trying to show off. You're too busy trying to get somebody to just notice you and not get your name wrong. And you go through all those kinds of rejections. But you don't work in a vacuum here. There are a lot of individual styles, you find all the human factors involved in this profession as a profession."

People who work in this "profession" love to tell stories. Most of the stories, as we have seen, have to do with themselves and their work experiences. A career as a line or succession of work assignments is an adventure, and a key part of becoming a full-fledged member of "the industry" is getting assignments and being able to exchange stories with colleagues. In a kind of show and tell, the filmmaker as benefactor, even mentor and guide, is one subject from which stories are made; another kind of material is about the bête noire scenario. This latter version of filmmakers and films operates on a number of levels and has its roots in the persistent dilemmas of commercialism.

The first and foremost function of tales of troubles with film producers and directors is to reveal expertise or, more fundamentally, to reveal what a film composer *does* and who a film composer *is*. This may seem very straightforward—film composers write film music—but the discussion has shown that not all film producers and directors can or want to see things that clearly. Questions of whether composers are artists or employees, even hired hands, get tangled. Tensions between routine and innovation are never resolved. Composers are anxious to advance their claims about themselves—And what better way to show how talented they are than by revealing how they are misunderstood, mistreated, and mismatched with their employers? Stories about working with prima donnas and plus-music boys allow the freelancer to define foreground (himself and his "profession") and background (the "bad guys") more clearly. In these stories, a self-image is advanced, carefully fashioned to lay claim to expertise, and advanced against something clarified by opposition.

With the backdrops firmly in place, stories about "successful" work situations and employers as benefactors can be moved into the forefront. The informed employer is something of an anomaly, but for that very reason stories about him further define the distinctions between useful collaboration and destructive meddling. As one of the busy freelancers put it, not without considerably irony, "I'm suggesting that producers who understand are almost nonexistent. I could tell you stories that would curl your hair."

He proved his point with war stories about three plus-music boys and one prima donna, but concluded with the following long tale about the informed client: "I did a score ten years ago for a producer. At my first interview we looked at the picture and he asked me what kind of music and I said, 'Somewhere between Richard Strauss and Schoenberg.' He said, 'Terrific.' Now first I could say that to the guy and have him understand what I meant— that's already a major step, a *big step*, believe me. We checked notes and I did the score; the protagonist was the devil incarnate and I based this theme on a tritone. A tritone in the Catholic Church in the twelfth and thirteenth centuries was called the devil in music—*diabolus in musica*." He got up from his desk, went to the piano, and played some bars.

> We got to the first day of the recording session and the producer walked in while we were recording the main theme and he heard the theme and ran over to me and grabbed my hand and said, "That's marvelous, the devil in music—*diabolus in musica*." I stared at him . . . I just stared at him. And to this day I have *never* run into anybody in the business like that. I have never run into anybody who had the vaguest idea what I was doing. That's the one guy I've met in ten years who brought enough knowledge to my idea to say, "I really understand what you did, that's marvelous." It's never happened since. I can give you the opposite, I can give you the opposite by the numbers.

Third, stories such as *diabolus in musica* are often the groundwork for a moral lesson. A succession of tales about producers hiring song writers who could not score dramatic films, nasty shifts in fortune among those who were once at the top of the business, effects of typecasting, are frequently pointed out as some hard-earned wisdom. Thus, the bête noire serves to display heroism, occupational adulthood, maturity, and sophistication. After one tale of trouble on a recent project, a veteran slowly summed up with the following opinion: "As far as being a 'media composer,' I say don't come to this town unless you're prepared to sacrifice yourself to it, because I think that most of us who jump into this business sacrifice ourselves enormously, and not just this business but I suppose anything today that you believe in and want to do something in and operate at a reasonable level and have a reasonable amount of integrity about yourself and sleep pretty well at night. You really are in for a struggle if you come to this industry. It's a life struggle out here."

Fourth, stories indicate the relative importance of things. Freelancers agree that they are in a struggle, and the struggle is for more and better work. Most feature films are not great artistic achievements. Many projects are cinematic turkeys—routine films worthy only of routine treatment. To spend any more than routine time with them is unnecessarily boring and demeaning. Stories abound about the mistake of investing too much effort and energy in this kind of work. As one freelancer said about some recent encounters with prima donnas: "The guy is showing you something like 'The Devil and Miss Deep Throat' with a little karate thrown in and then he's asking you to write something 'important, very important.' "

There are many responses to the chronic indifference or ignorance of the filmmaker. Some composers react with the ironic understatement of the ersatz Oriental Mahler; others indulge in caustic derision. Still others rely on witty depictions of malapropisms and Hollywood's own show business euphemisms which try, usually unsuccessfully, to bridge the opposing tendencies of art and business. Tales of the bête noire, as well as the benefactor or collaborator, are entertaining. Many composers develop a wit in order to cut back their anger at how they are treated and what is asked of them. Such wit is another protection against the bitterness and disappointment they feel.

Producers and directors know what the game is about—control over work. "Collaboration's fine, sure. But I have a double standard about this: while I think it applies to me that I should be left alone, I don't think it necessarily applies to those who work for me," said a candid Bob Rafelson, whose credits include *Five Easy Pieces, The King of Marvin Gardens,* and *Stay Hungry*.

All freelancers with enough experience and perspective on the business of film work understand this double standard. Freelancing forces a person to learn—socially—how to survive in a complex environment of dual interests. Every picture is a separate business, and composers learn how to handle different personalities, how to see the demands placed on them, and figure out how to respond to these requests. At times, the personality of the client is complex, demands are equivocal, and the project sets up associations that a composer is not comfortable with. At other times, producer and composer talk the same language, the demands are unambiguous, and the composer knows and likes what he is writing for the film. He also sees what the completed project looks like. But work is rarely this clear-cut. Dual tendencies

have been mentioned insistently (e.g., preserving versus breaking with received conventions; overt antagonism versus cooperation; dissolving the work
tie versus retaining the tie), and the point has been made repeatedly that film
composers have to deal with opposed tendencies throughout their careers. To
emphasize the possible cooperation between composer and filmmaker may
be misleading, because the materials suggest that work with an informed
filmmaker allows each to express dependence and independence, *both* cooperation and antagonism. The composer, for example, is able to shift back
and forth, within the work exchange, between his own interests and those of
his client, between his own juggling of business and artistic requirements and
those of the filmmaker. The more the project and work relationship allow a
freelancer to express both independence and dependence, both antagonism
and cooperation, the greater his involvement in the project. The implications
of this principle are interesting. As opportunities for shifting back and forth
decline, as the occasions for cooperative antagonism fade, and as the distinction between writing for one's self and writing for the employer is blurred,
there is less satisfaction with the task and the relationship. A project in which
film composer and filmmaker easily cooperate should be less satisfying than
a project in which they alternate between fighting and seeing eye to eye,
between proposing a line of action (an approach to the music for a scene),
meeting resistance, having to ''convince'' the producer or director about its
merits, and generally being able to argue in an intelligent and mature way
with the client.

Greater involvement in work and greater work satisfaction happen when
composers are forced to compete and cooperate with their clients. A supreme
achievement would be to transform a plus-music boy into a collaborator; it
happens every once in a while. Transforming a prima donna into a partner
is a noble ambition, but one almost never achieved. The inability of freelancers
(again, *some* of them) to tolerate and handle personalities and demands that
run counter to their career interests and musical preferences may well be the
most important cause of trouble in their work with their clients. The basic
raw materials are just plain difficult to talk about—film scoring is a vague
art indeed. And the state of the employer, nervous about his film and apprehensive about losing control of it, compounds the difficulty. The unwillingness
to deal with opposed tendencies often produces egoism, nonadaptation, isolation from the dramatic values of the film, and negative stereotypes on both
sides.

As in all lines of work, the easy way out is to suppress one or the other
side of dual tendencies or interests (business versus art; routines versus innovation; equivocal versus unequivocal demands; recurrent versus nonrecurrent ties; altruistic versus selfish motives). But in commercial work, both
sides of these pairings are necessary for survival and must be actively ac-

commodated. Facile duplicity with the plus-music types can destroy a composer's self-respect as well as some of his obvious compositional strengths if he reaches the (false) conclusion that this *is* what Hollywood is all about. On the other hand, extensive collaboration with a filmmaker can wipe out the creative tensions that first attracted them to one another as work partners. A work relation between employer and composer that permits informed expression of strong, and often polarized, opinions about a "musical solution" is healthy because it avoids easy compromise and the appearance of mutual agreement. Such apparent agreement is frequently dangerous because it obscures the genuine tensions underneath, which if properly acknowledged, are the source of much excellence in film work.

As in other lines of client work, the composer's ideal solution is to transform the employer into something of an "insider," at least someone who understands and appreciates the exigencies of writing music for films. Jerry Goldsmith said, "Film scoring courses are given to the wrong people—they should be given to directors and producers, not composers."[3]

Different kinds of matching with employers and different kinds of dual tendencies have a lot to do with a shared outlook or culture among Hollywood's film composers. By "culture" I mean the shared understandings generated in the company of fellow colleagues. It is an ethos, a stance they develop together in their experiences and act on in defining the industry and their networks of employers. Appreciating and sharing war stories, scenarios, and legends help freelancers make sense out of what they know about the organization of work in Hollywood. These stories contain scenarios which help participants remember what filmmakers and composers experienced in the past. They facilitate filling in the gaps in their knowledge with educated guesses, and help predict what will occur in the future. Stories reassure the freelancer on the move that his image of himself as a freelance composer is shared by others. War stories and scenarios serve as a means for regulating members of the occupation. They point to exemplary conduct of some, the abhorrent behavior of others. They direct newcomers and central figures alike to an occupational script in which they can articulate and reconcile conflicting interests or opposing tendencies.

It is when a freelancer becomes integrated into the colleague group and its discourse—when a he becomes someone with something to show and tell, a script to offer, as it were—that we speak of cultural integration into the industry. The scripts and scenarios contain lessons and define a stance toward commercial work; listening to and telling such stories a composer sees that for better or for worse, he is stuck with his clients and their choices. He has to learn how to handle this and his own emotion-laden involvement in his career. Just how involved or wrapped up he gets in a particular line of activity varies from filmmaker to filmmaker, but the range of response is delineated by the lore and the composer who listens to it attentively sees a script and blueprint for realizing his dual interests of individuation and integration. The script says, in effect, to be neither too distant nor too emotionally invested in the projects, especially in these unpredictable market outcomes. Also, by telling stories, laying out proscriptions for conduct, and depicting stories of success and failure in the industry, premises for practical action are developed. Through actively choosing which stories to tell and by shaping work experiences into stories, a composer defines his general interests in relation to ongoing work. His personal knowledge of employers and projects, far from being merely a desultory array of anecdotes and jokes, functions as a powerful scheme of interpretation. Every composer with a string of credits and concrete transactions with employers starts to acquire a good ethnographic grasp of the business. That is, by shaping practical experience into scenarios and scripts to tell colleagues about, a freelancer develops sharply defined typifications without sacrificing interest in and respect for individual variation. Every employer and project is always viewed as a particular instance of a class—neither merely unique nor merely a type.

The freelancer moving into the inner circles takes on assignments in hopes of enhancing his reputation and increasing his career's resources. He also works to keep his name socially alive in client and colleague circles. The work and business transactions are primary; but the composer also needs new material for detailed, witty, and above all fresh, factual, and believable stories about current spotting, recording, and dubbing sessions along with his recent dealings with partners, collaborators, and the dreaded bête noire. In this way opposition with filmmakers provides a source of refined unity among Hollywood's freelancers. Sharing anxieties, trading horror scenarios, discussing recent mismatches, talking freelance blues—all enrich the stock of knowledge among the craft and artistic specialties in Hollywood. The coexistence of opposed tendencies—art and commerce, personal autonomy and social integration, public persona and private self—generates positive-negatives, that is, tensions which result in mutual problem solving and culture building by freelancers together. War stories are a potent means for creating normative, instrumental, and affective commitment among the industry's labor force.

Notes

1. A phrase first used by Renée C. Fox to show that the process of becoming a professional, particularly a physician, involved a distinctive blend of closeness and remoteness to the object of work. My use here derives from Fox's, but my analysis of distance between self and work, between cognitive expertise and emotional neutrality, is slightly different. See her *Experiment Perilous* (Glencoe, Ill.: Free

Press, 1959). Concepts such as "detached concern" and "antagonistic cooperation" draw attention to forms of association in commercial work. Donald Levine
writes that "the concept of dualism" is a key principle "underlying Simmel's
social thought." Levine explicates Georg Simmel's dualism as "the assumption . . . that the subsistence of any aspect of human life depends on the coexistence
of diametrically opposed elements." Chapter 8 additionally suggests that the particular patterning of an individual's freelance connections defines his points of
reference and (at least partially) determines his social identity in this work world.
See Donald N. Levine, "The Structure of Simmel's Social Thought," in *Essays
on Sociology, Philosophy, and Aesthetics by Georg Simmel et al.*, ed. Kurt H.
Wolff (New York: Harper & Row, 1955).
2. This idea of distantiation should not be confused with "self-distantiation" or the
sequences of concerted action which result in a person becoming estranged from
himself.
3. Quoted in Thomas Backer and Eddy Lawrence Manson's "In the Key of Feeling,"
Human Behavior (1978):63–67.

8.
CENTRALITY IN A FREELANCE SOCIAL STRUCTURE
Career Performances and Professional Networks

Direct observation does reveal to us that . . . human beings are connected by a complex network of actually existing relations. I use the term "social structure" to denote this network of actually existing relations.
— A. R. Radcliffe-Brown, *On Social Structure*

When sociologists speak of social structure or social systems, the metaphor implies . . . that the collective action involved occurs "regularly" or "often" (the quantifier [sic] being implicit, is non-specific) and, further, that the people involved act together to produce a large variety of events. But we should recognize generally, as the empirical materials require us to do in the study of the arts, that whether a mode of collective action is recurrent or routine enough to warrant such description must be decided by investigation, not by definition. Some forms of collective action recur often, others occasionally, some very seldom. Similarly, people who participate in the network that produces one event or kind of event may not act together in art works producing other events.
— Howard S. Becker, *Art as Collective Action*

Who is in the *center*? Which particular producers, composers, and projects gather in this productive and visible market? What are the processes associated with market continuity, transactions, and career success? To this point I have confined the discussion of social organization and career to the distribution of credits and the perspectives freelancers have of the reality of their work lines. I also looked at what they do in their work projects in addition to what they feel they must do to accumulate connections, information, and industry accolades. I suggested that new entrants into the organization of Hollywood are impeded by the lack of expertise, by the difficulty of upsetting established ties between composers and producers, and by the absence among potential contenders of a known performance record—a "track record." This situation accurately reflects the circumstances and career problems of approximately 75 percent of the composers who have ever scored a feature film in this industry. The Hollywood work community, like most work communities, is dominated by an elite. It manifests severe inequalities in the control over resources; and few careers exceed toehold proportions in Hollywood.

Those making a successful climb are few. They are very productive, visible, and often conspicuous in terms of their connections and rewards. The social organization of the highly visible and productive few brings into highest relief the loosely structured networks that are the distinctive feature of freelance work. As major contributors to the film industry, the ambitions, attitudes, and career interests of the central figures are as much dependent on their work connections with film producers as they are on the successes of their projects in the external product market, in the mass market in which films are cultural commodities. Hollywood's executives, money backers, producers, and directors—and others—watch the financial and critical reception of projects, and connect the personnel with the success or failure of films. The filmmakers read box-office grosses and film rental information first. They read these as carefully as Roman soothsayers read entrails.

Since the composer, not the particular film score, is the principal force in this social market or publicity system, the independent merit of a film writer's music recedes into the background. Since the basis of industry visibility and being in fashion rests heavily on what others make of a busy composer's line of films, the freelancer becomes vulnerable to the consequence of this judgment and labeling process. Since the film score is embedded in the marketplace project, it is the project which is typically brought directly into judgment and evaluation. Filmmakers look at a freelancer's past successes and failures. They pay attention to what other filmmakers say about the person and his/her work. They see whether the freelancer has been nominated for Academy Awards. They go see the freelancer's films—a long list of considerations come into play. In making their selections, they refer to the conventions of hiring and typecasting to make their decisions simpler and less costly. Their alternatives and final choices are a form of social control.[1] They choose their work associates on the basis of their resources and preferences. And often more important, they choose with whom *not* to associate. The presence of work ties produces networks of careers for both producers and freelancers. The absence of work ties produces "empty spaces" in the social structure. The absence of action provides a background against which clusters of networks clearly appear.

In being selected and agreeing to work on film projects, film producers and freelance composers develop reciprocal relationships; two sides of the market are joined. The composers are linked to the film industry through two principal social bonds: to industry culture and conventions by the labeling and typecasting process, and to Hollywood filmmakers through existing work transactions. Composers in turn help make a network of the film business by linking through themselves the producers linked to them. Each film composer is a member of the unique network of each film producer to whom he is tied. His membership in these networks connects a number of different social circles. A diversity and breadth of ties facilitates indirect access to an even greater number of producers, film projects, and commercial rewards. Continuity and centrality in networks are not always recognized as status qualifications in Hollywood's film business, but in the long run they are, and with extraordinary regularity.

When market transactions between employers and employees involve recurrent demand for the services of a few, the organization of rewards becomes concentrated in the top tier. These freelance artists and specialists then have more opportunities for controlling exchanges with their employers or clients. Centrality is directly associated with a freelancer's perceived scarcity as a resource by these filmmakers. The networks that result in centrality find their basic precondition in scarcity. The fewer the film scorers in relation to the number of producers that must hire them for their films, the greater accumulation of resources. The greater the perceived scarcity of a composer's expertise and visibility, and the more inelastic the demand for those talents, the greater the freelancer's ability to cash in on a favorable climate of opinion. The end result is a synergy: connections and credits build the demand which builds the continuity which in turn builds reputation and centrality.

There is an upward spiral that narrows the field with every turn. The spiral of involvement is composed of three features: (1) the freelance system of short-term performance contracts for sets of work activities; (2) a climate of opinion for transmitting information about producers' and composers' performance capacities, and for certifying competence; and (3) a means for maximizing benefit to cost ratios in the hiring of particular composers by film producers.[2]

Big Hollywood—the matching of top-level projects to the central circle of name composers, and the matching of visible and productive freelancers to expensive projects and their powerful producers—narrows the range of collective action so that participation is permanently restricted to a chosen few. The people who form the networks may change from decade to decade, but the centralizing social structure itself persists.

Only the Best Will Do: A Resource-Alternative Theory

The top of the Hollywood list is dominated by people who are in fashion and have proven their worth on film project after film project. Fashion was once described as a taste shared by a large number of people during a short period of time. In the film business, any commodity perceived to be both perishable and universally desired becomes highly valued, and often over-valued, in the networks of Hollywood. Wage differentials exist among composers because a few do something that others cannot do.

An important determinant of aggregate demand for the fashionable and "hot" is their cost against overall budget expenditures. Put simply, the larger the amount of capital advanced on a film production, and the larger the budget, the lower the relative costs of highly valued—and priced—freelance composers. Producers are sensitive to the value of the labor power—as variable capital—applied to their film projects. A freelancer is an important, but by no means overpowering piece of the action. The price of big-league composers is hard to estimate, but it is pegged anywhere between $25,000 and $50,000 for composing and conducting. On a major film, the overall music budget also includes the costs of orchestration, studio recording time, freelance musicians, copying costs, and editing the final product. Depending on the minutes of music required in the film, the size of the orchestra, and the amount of studio time, expenses for music run into thousands of dollars. They still comprise a relatively small proportion of overall production expenses.

Exact dollar amounts are very hard to come by when the top producers and freelancers start talking about money in Hollywood. Some rough estimates may prove useful however; the following proportions seem to hold true across all kinds of film productions. *Meteor*—the Sandy Howard and Samuel Arkoff, and Sir Run Run Shaw production—cost $17 million, and required a $10-million line of credit from the Bank of America to finance its completion. Another science-fiction extravaganza with expensive special effects and lots of music was Steven Spielberg's *Close Encounters of the Third Kind*, costing $19 million. *Star Trek: The Motion Picture*, produced by Robert Wise, cost around $20 million. It is possible that Laurence Rosenthal's fee for composing and conducting the score for *Meteor*, along with the combined costs for orchestration, studio recording, musicians, and so forth, totaled around $60,000. It is possible that John Williams, and the costs of music production, totaled around $70,000 for the score to *Close Encounters*. And finally, it is possible that Jerry Goldsmith's work for Robert Wise cost somewhere in the neighborhood of $80,000. For each of these three, expensive productions, the total music budget, including the composer's fee, is less than half of 1 percent: .003, .004, .004, respectively. These figures may be underestimating expenditures for the production of film music. Still we can *double* each budget for music and composer and rarely climb into one percent of the overall budget category. Thus, big-league producers can get the central composers at a relativeley low per-unit cost.

We saw this principle working before in the low-budget film projects: here a filmmaker may have only a million dollars to spend and is not particularly sanguine about a music package—composer, score, orchestration, studio, musicians, and editing—that exceeds $20,000, or around 2 *percent of his total expenditures*.

This principle determines the hiring process. Al Bart offers a continuity of perspective across the industry's film productions. He heads Bart Associates, an agency which serves composers and lyricists, representing such top freelancers as Fred Karlin, Walter Scharf, David Shire, Henry Mancini, Elmer Bernstein, and Bill Conti. He said that film scoring is being taken more seriously by producers, but that not all filmmakers *can afford* the services of top composers.[3] Much of the matching of filmscorer to film project (and its controller) concerns the total music budget against the film's budget.

"Assuming we're discussing a medium-budget film which has a fairly decent allowance for the music," Bart said, "I might ask for $25,000 for my client to compose and conduct. The producer might respond that $25,000 is his whole music budget which includes studio time, the cost of musicians, copying, orchestration, tape, everything. Well, he might like to have Elmer Bernstein, or Henry Mancini, but there's not enough in his music budget to afford them."[4]

The relationship between resources and alternatives of Hollywood's filmmakers is hard to pin down; nonetheless, it is clearly present and I suspect that it is getting stronger all the time. In broad strokes, the greater the level of capital resources at the command of a filmmaker, the larger the entrepreneurial risk; the larger the risk, the less freedom of choice.

"Producers are investing the money, and I don't think they feel very courageous about being daring and experimental. I don't blame them. They want to be safe," explained Verna Fields, a former film editor and now production executive at MCA-Universal. "They know that *Jaws* made money, so *Jaws II* is sure to make it. And if *Jaws* can do it, *King Kong* can do it. They want a best-seller book, something proven. I can't blame them for being nervous about trying anything new."[5]

Box-office receipts act as market signals directing filmmakers toward film ideas and industry personnel, helping filmmakers isolate the ingredients that created the commercial success in the first place.[6] Reliance on market outcomes and film rentals is an attempt to decrease the uncertainty of filmmakers, and their perceived need for the best-seller and the best-selling specialists and craftspeople is a way to reduce the overall risks incurred while putting together a production. Reluctant to hire people with the liability of newness, filmmakers are driven into making choices among the successful and visible few. A consistent flow of ties begins to shape a network of cooperative action. Producers and freelancers circle around one another, with the filmmakers hoping to reduce the risks of their investments by anticipating the combination needed for the "hit" film. These filmmakers rank freelancers and other specialists according to their perceived performance capacities, indexed by their association with successful films, by their current reputations among their own colleagues, by their past work with them (in some cases), and generally by their perceived value as resources. Selections are directed toward those for which the expected payoff is greatest. Filmmaker estimates are formed on the perceived utility of hiring one composer rather than another, based upon: (a) the perceived probability that the selected composer will show or continue to show the traits (skills, payoffs) for which he is hired; (b) the comparative utility which may be returned to the producer for acquiring the services of one freelancer rather than another; and (c) that the finished project will be a success *because* of the freelancer's score. Broadly based estimates such as these are simply a means for reducing worry—tinkering procedures for "calculating" the return on the film because of hiring certain craft/artistic specialists.

Composers know that producers' uncertainties are important, that their moods are volatile, and that their assessments of freelancers shift in the breezes of high-grossing productions. They know what business they are in.

"Imagine yourself a producer in charge of a very, very expensive film," said a top composer connected to a network of successful producers, a free-lancer who had worked with some of the biggest people on some of the most expensive films in the seventies. "You could shop around and see who's good but not expensive," he explained, "but if your picture goes down the drain, the people who are working with you, and the people in charge, say, of distribution at Disney, Universal, Fox—wherever—will scream, 'Idiot, why didn't you get the best?' So there's pressure to hire a name. If there's a 6-, 7-, or say $18-million budget, and the composer's fee is $25,000, why not get the best? Why not get the top guys?"

He then looked over my list of freelancers, ranked by volume of credits from 1964 to 1976. "Producers have *their* lists also. It makes it a lot easier for them to hire a name than to go with a composer with credits, but maybe not big credits, someone who hasn't done anything very big."

He then talked about the race to put together the financing and idea for the next very big budget and, hopefully, high-grossing film that he was being considered for. The producers wanted something on the order of *Jaws*. Those filmmakers only thought about a few freelancers, he noted. They do not, cannot, pay attention to every composer's name on every film released in the industry. Some names were clearly in their "frontal lobes," as one of his colleagues put it. In this sense, reputation and "name" become not simply the possession of industry resources; rather, reputation is itself a resource and a medium of exchange. No matter how good, a typical low-budget picture lacks the presold advantages of big stars, a best-selling literary title, a proven director, a line-up made from the list of quality people, and major talents from the screenwriter to the cameraman and composer. The capital advanced was big money too. These filmmakers now think that $14 million invested in one big project, combining the familiar elements and specialists is better than, say, $2 million placed in seven films of perhaps outstanding artistry. With this kind of money and these kinds of risks, certain liabilities are inevitable. To reduce those risks, he suggested, producers with the resources move directly to "the big list," the proven talents. Composers outside the top cut are at a distinct disadvantage when it comes to being considered and hired for these large-scale productions. "You can work in trendy little films," he continued, "but you won't draw the attention of these guys"—speaking about the filmmakers he knew facing compelling economic reasons for selecting the top composers in the industry. He then ticked off the names of several major cinematographers that would "automatically be considered" by the producers—people with credentials such as Laszlo Kovacs, Lucien Ballard, John Alonzo, and Fred Koenekamp, all with well over fifteen feature credits from 1964 to 1978. He named several directors also, such as Sidney Lumet, Arthur Hiller, and Martin Ritt. Composers John Williams, Jerry Goldsmith, and Alex North were then tagged as perfect for the project. Past performances are powerful predictors of future ones, he implied. And filmmakers, especially those with high-budget films and leverage, are trying to calculate what will work for them.

As suggested in my interviews with agents and composers, budgets and music expenditures are important pieces of the commercial work world—important for the life blood of producers, directors, agents, and freelancers. Negotiations about whom to hire, at what cost, scoring what kind of music, at what length, using what size orchestra, and with how much time to write and orchestrate the score are little work worlds which reflect the larger industry. The same pressures are evident in conservatively mounted, modest film productions, with a relatively moderate budget for the composer and his music. But these projects cannot successfully compete for the services of the highly visible, acclaimed, and expensive Hollywood figures. Thus, the choices of a producer on the periphery are restricted by small budgets and, similarly, the choices of central figures are restricted by the risks of large budgets. The moderately budgeted projects (and their controllers) must choose among the small army of composers in the middle ranks and the third tier; they have their choice of literally hundreds of talented freelancers. Peripheral filmmakers and freelancers are more or less tightly coupled in the freelance hiring market. In contrast, the center of the film business, a $10-, $20-, or $30-million production, is constrained to seek out the highly valued major figures, those who have built up their film *credentials* and their proven ability to contribute to money-making ventures. The greater the uncertainty a film producer sees himself facing in production, advertising, distribution, and marketing deals, the more constrained the locus of attention, and the more focused or centered his range of preferred choices. A filmmaker at this top level of the business is obliged to cast his choices of specialists into a small circle of proven talents to secure and protect the big investment in an unstable and unpredictable mass market.

While the major figures in Hollywood's filmmaking circles may lack a wide range of options, they nevertheless possess the resources and clout to ensure that their needs will be accommodated by Hollywood's agents, directors, cinematographers, screenwriters, composers, and others before the needs of those with fewer means. Their power permits them to sanction and potentially control others by withholding film projects, attempting to persuade and forcefully give advice, giving or withdrawing acclaim, respect, and the like. Since freelance specialists as employees depend heavily on these market and honorific resources, powerful filmmakers can impose a wide range of sanctions.

If only the best will do, then a concentration of ties, direction of resources, and commercial success is inevitable. Networks of collective action between filmmakers and freelancers may be seen as a stabilizing force for profit-seeking enterprises, particularly where a product is assembled for national distribution and is subject to extraordinary levels of demand uncertainty.

A freelancer's location in this division of attention, ties, and status honor may be thought of as the relative advantage he has vis-à-vis others with respect to industry resources. These resources include all the variables to which value attaches in the business of film, from the positive evaluations and perceptions of others to the bundles of existing relations in networks of transactions. As filmmakers' alternatives narrow with an increase in budgets and resources, the options of freelancers expand: composers' range of alternatives and choices grow as they are asked to do more by more powerful filmmakers.[7] The concentration of transactions, success, and acclaim reinforces the centrality of the chosen few, giving them a firm center to integrate themselves with their labor.

Composers and other Hollywood specialists talk about this combination of centrality, "strength," and status attainment. Hal Ashby, a top film director, speaking of *Being There* and his own work in adapting Jerzy Kozinski's novel, said, "It's something I've wanted to do for years and now that I've become stronger in the business I find I'm in a position to bring my own ideas to fruition."[8]

Screenwriter Robert Towne, long respected as a script "doctor" in the film industry but unknown outside of the business, struck it big with his work on *Chinatown* (1974). He won the Oscar for best screenplay. Success leads to alternatives as well as tight networks of relations. He said, "Commercial success is what gives you power. Everybody meets everybody, but part of the reason you continue to know people is because you've worked with them, and it's gone well. Your friends almost inevitably become the people with whom you work."[9]

The mutual effects of a favorable demand situation, increased alternatives, recurrent work with filmmakers, and growing opportunities to integrate the business and aesthetic sides of commercial work, widen the gap between those in the center of the business and those on the semiperiphery and periphery. This injures freelancers outside the inner circle; they must chase the leftovers, losing out in a race for better projects on which to display their talents, and fighting to keep their skills and motivation alive as they see the big names hired time and again in the top tiers for the big film projects. Since the work of some is singled out and seen as worthy while the work of others is ignored and given less attention, it is important to study the process of definition and evaluation. Freelance centrality is not only a location in a social structure, but also the product of a process which involves the mutual dependence of employers and employees.

First let us consider the processes by which social networks become more effective as the freelancer moves into the inner circles or, the other side of the same process, the way networks and ties prevent a composer from holding a central position. Success as centrality in Big Hollywood depends on organizing activities through building connections with multiple filmmakers, being associated with commercially successful film productions, working with major film producers and directors, and on positive status attainment in the wider circles of the business which confer credentials, reputation, and prestige. Organizing through selectivity as well as through networks and connections will be taken up in the next chapter.

The most visible and measurable features are continuity in the freelance market and the consistency with which a composer appears among the top film projects produced by the top filmmakers in Hollywood. There are four features which will allow us to evaluate the top 40 freelance composers in the networks they form with the 62 most productive filmmakers:

1. The breadth and diversity of ties a freelancer maintains reflect his dominance and strength in networks of collective activity.
2. Freelancers and film producers who are tied to each other by recurring work transactions are more closely coordinated and interlocked than those who have only a single work point or nonrecurrent tie.
3. Freelancers who are tied to important filmmakers are themselves more important than those tied to an equal number of filmmakers on the periphery of network activity.
4. Freelancers who are associated with successful films are themselves more visible than those associated with an equal number of less successful projects.

I will argue that network location and centrality display orderly patterns and conventional—but highly turbulent—dynamics. Networks of freelancers and filmmakers in the top tier are linked by chains of work points of varying length. Individual composers vary greatly in the span of their recurrent and nonrecurrent ties. They vary in their ability to dominate a network. I will start with "the best," as judged by their competitive advantages: their visibility, perceived importance as employees, and career resources.

Prompt and Delayed Effects of Centrality

In many ways, filmmakers' selections of personnel seem to be little more than strategies for getting movies financed, filmed, and into postproduction— battle plans, as it were, with the principal energies of the filmmakers being expended on a kind of cinema logistics. Given the conditions of information impactedness, or encapsulation of the score inside the total project, the risks of this entrepreneurial activity may be decreased by developing a means of promptly monitoring the market success (or failure) and the critical reception of each Hollywood film project as an "experiment" directed at a public of consumers. One of the dominant composers at the top of "the list" said this about his career line from 1973 to 1980:

> The more things you do, the more people either get to like your stuff or hate it. And in my case I've been lucky enough that the more things I do, the more work I seem to be offered, or the better work I seem to be offered. I'm now at the stage where I turn down a number of pictures and a number of television shows because the question *now* isn't getting work—I can now work 52 weeks a year if I wanted to—the question is getting work that will make me grow, work that I enjoy doing. Just to work and grind it out is not good for one's psyche, one's talent. And there's a danger; you can get written out and get repetitious very fast.

> Just in this last year, I'm starting to get more opportunities to do really good stuff. My last film was a watershed score for me in the sense that it was the first picture score I did that was on a movie that had some attention paid to it. In a way it was my best score, although it was my strangest one. It appealed to a lot of directors who like to hear an original approach to music. It was a very "un-Hollywood" score, it was much more European. It was on the strength of that score that I got the last two projects. I'm moving into a better class of films and a better class of producers.

His recent films were with major filmmakers. One producer with an impressive track record and industry reputation saw the film with the "un-Hollywood" score. Within a few weeks he was hired to this filmmaker's big-budget project, with proven ingredients, major actors, an important screen-writer, and with technological whiz-bangery at which Hollywood excels. As for the career impact of this company and the assignment with, as he put it, "major production values," he was clear:

> I'm sure that score and that assignment moved me up to a new plateau in terms of being considered for first-class pictures. I know that a lot of people noticed the score because I got a prenomination for an Academy Award. The music branch of the Academy cuts the field down to ten scores and then they pick their five from that list, and I made the cut out of ten. It was a turning point for me. The recognition is important. Then I was up from consideration for one of the biggest pictures of the year. So, I think as you do more work, better work, your reputation generally increases. Sometimes it isn't that you do one particular film and then you get another film; rather, it's that people have seen your name on a number of projects. They like the music or they like the projects. So you become more of a contender.

He spoke of ranking, of an inner circle of sellers of evenly matched musical ability and of a market defined by demand for the appearance of signs of success. As an entrepreneur on this market, he was competing for acclaim and for the choices of certain filmmakers with a "higher class of product": "If you score a better picture, then that tends to put you in a better league. Of course, you work on better films because of what you've done in the past," he explained listing several of his recent credits in four years. "Producers look closely at what you've done, your credits. Some producers will take a chance and hire a composer who doesn't have the *big credits,* but that is *rare* on a major film, it's *very* rare. They're under pressure to hire a name composer."

The same respondent expressed satisfaction with his current situation of more credits, better credits, better employers, and better credentials. The consistency of his ties to a small circle of filmmakers meant that he had indirect links to some highly visible composers. He liked the company. He was in the running with three colleagues with whom he already shared a common filmmaker. "I'm up right now for a film," he said speaking of a producer in his network, "and I think it's going to be, if *I* get it, the *best* film next year. All the best people in town are working in it and I've never done a film that has this much prestige associated with it: the producer, the director, the actors, all the way down the line."

A large part of Hollywood life, as lived in the top tiers of the market, resembles a tournament for the major film productions. Such intense competition provides a very direct measure of the prestige and comparative standing of the central figures to each other. A lot is riding on who gets what assignments. As a freelancer gains access to these projects, his peers take note of his increasing power and prestige. Films are ranked the same way— in terms of importance, money, prestige, and market value, and through such competition the film and all participants validate their bids for a central position in Hollywood.

"There are three of us who are up for the project," he continued. Each big and expensive project like this is a kind of tournament, and thus the structure of connections and power become more clearly visible in this area of freelance life than in any other. "This is the *first time* I've been in consideration with those other composers. They are all number one guys, big league guys; and up until now I've been in the league with number two people. This is the big one for me. I don't know if I'm going to get it or not, but I suppose that this is one of those opportunities a composer waits for, that magical, important film that comes along infrequently, one maybe every couple of years."

He was restless and energetic. He was also nervous. With one foot already out of his current circle of producers, he was moving into a different network and this not only meant an expansion in the range of connections, but also a change in his calculus of risks and career uncertainties. He appreciated how completely his new status and power depended on the climate of opinion and the way he was seen by certain film producers with resources to back up their preferences. He saw the precariousness of the market. Indeed, the only certainty, no matter how huge the project, is uncertainty.

> This whole business is a risk, especially for me right now. There aren't that many good pictures being made, and for the big ones the number one guys are almost always chosen. Like actors, directors, screenwriters, or anyone in this business, you have your vogue—it may last for a long time or it may not, and that's it. You have to be ready for anything. I'm glad that right now I'm supposed to be *"hot."* But that doesn't make you feel that you're going to be in there forever. While it is happening it's very nice, and I'm trying to take advantage of it, be careful about what I choose, and do the very best work I can, but who knows what will happen? You're in favor, but the people you're in favor with change, and they change in their ideas about who they want for their pictures.

At times, Big Hollywood appears to be a market of a few dozen film producers looking for a very select, and acclaimed and successful, group of "major league" composers. The networks of cooperative action appear to be more or less sturdy mechanisms for bringing employers' needs together with the currently preferred and available supplies of composers. On the seller side of this market, each freelancer becomes alert to his rank vis-à-vis colleague competitors and employers. The preferences, pressures, and opinions of employers are quickly acquired through the details of agreements and other tangible market signals and "trade terms."

"Hot," "in vogue," "in fashion," "in demand," "cachet"—all these words we use, as we must, for there are few others by means of which we can describe how volatile climates of opinion are in Hollywood. As suggested by many respondents, coming into fashion with work continuity and a box-office hit beams an image of the freelancer and his work deeper into the culture of the industry. More work does not automatically lead to better work, as the case materials suggest. But it does appear that continuously active freelancers contribute more than their share of talent into the work community and receive more than their share of recognition, visibility, and ties to commercially successful projects. This assumes a relation between quantity and quality, an assumption not always justified. Still, the correlation coefficients between productivity (number of film credits) and nominations for an Oscar, winning Oscars for best score, and box-office successes are .62, .37, and .44 respectively. In terms of explained variance, increasing credits account for 36 percent of the chances of being nominated by one's peers for best original score, song score, or adaptation; credits also account for 16 percent of the chances for winning the Oscar and the credentials that honor draws; and 16 percent of the chances of working on a feature that becomes a respectable box-office draw are accounted for by volume of films scored, as shown in Table 8.1.

It is surprising how few individuals can dominate an occupational specialty; over 600 out of 1,355 films scored in the twelve years—40 percent—were composed by the productive and successful 10 percent of composers. These central figures speak of experiencing "the greatest award: being asked to work again." They also speak about working with "big" producers on "big" pictures. The composers in Tier 1 scored 156 out of 344 films (45 percent) with producers who had their names on five or more feature films during the twelve years. The composers in Tier 2 scored 144 out of 282 films (51 percent) with the same tier of filmmakers.

Resources and connections are useful in identifying the center: they give us a picture of a small circle of freelancers responsible for most of the work and who attain most of the recognition in the field, surrounded by a much larger group of relatively minor figures. By virtue of their combined films scored and their nominations and Oscars (and other festival awards), these composers spiral upward toward the status of central figures. They have accumulated staying power and a visible track record while being tied into the range of producers who distribute these resources.

"Cycles." That is the word that every top composer with some edge and bargaining strength came up with as a partial explanation of his present

TABLE 8.1

Correlation Coefficients for Productivity, Industry Recognition, and Film Rentals

	COSCAR	CNOMIN	FOSCAR	FNOMIN	FILM RENTALS
PRODUCTIVITY	.37	.62	.29	.49	.44
COSCAR		.66	.60	.53	.33
CNOMIN			.40	.65	.41
FOSCAR				.50	.24
FNOMIN					.37

a Pearson r for 442 freelancers scoring films from 1964-65 to 1975-76 production seasons.

PRODUCTIVITY = number of films scored; COSCAR = composer wins the Academy Award Oscar for his score; CNOMIN = composer is nominated for his score; FNOMIN = film project on which the composer works is nominated for best film; FOSCAR = film project wins the Academy Award Oscar. Film Rentals are income paid by the exhibitors to the film distributors for the project, standardized to 1972 income.

position in the movie business. "You are always aware of how the wind is blowing in the industry," said one of the most active and celebrated composers. He cautioned against any easy formulas. "The people who cast composers for feature films," he explained in a cautious manner, "whoever they are, and I suppose they are producers, directors—they really own the town in that respect—they get in the habit of using certain people during a certain period. Certain names are on their minds. I know how they get there or get off there. It runs in cycles. They see a picture they admire, perhaps, and they like the score and therefore they want to hire the fellow to do *their score, their film*. And there's a kind of *in vogue* thing that composers enjoy when they somehow get into the frontal lobes of producers."

Judging from the phenomenal grosses of this composer's films in recent years—topped off by several films with nominations and Oscars—those cycles of fashion can be highly advantageous. Getting into the frontal lobes of employers occurs in several ways. As suggested above, producers assess the performance abilities of a composer by seeing the project and listening to the film's score. This presumes an ability to discriminate between the film and the score, and further assumes evaluation of the composer's contribution to the total project, independent of the commercial success or failure of the project. Another means for assessing the performance capacity of a freelancer is labeling, typically stereotyping the composer by the type of film and its dramatic genre. Typically, the film and its score blend into one another; the employer may have very little real sense of music and the composer's contribution. One of the mischievous consequences of scoring "major," "important," and "big" projects is the bizarre labels attached to the composer identifying him with the genre of the movie, the scale or scope of the film. As I have shown earlier, composers then discover they have been typecast according to the content of the films they work on. They find themselves committed to a line of activity that confirms this very definition of themselves. Typecasting can have competitive advantages early in the career line. But as the following dominant composer notes, it has disadvantages too.

"When I first entered this business I was fighting *inexperience*. Now I'm fighting *experience*. Producers endow you with qualities you might not prefer to be endowed with . . . forever." This was a man with several nominations for best dramatic score, one Oscar, a gold record, and over thirty feature film credits. He is tied to one very influential producer/director, and his competitive edge in the market was dulled somewhat in 1970 to 1975. He explained: "When it [his Oscar-winning film score] hit and hit it *big*, for about two years afterwards it seemed that all I was considered for were large, epic-type pictures, or at least features which would use large orchestras. The feeling was that I couldn't work unless I had a large canvas, a lot of music, a big orchestra, and so on. Producers don't call you for other things. They think you can't do them. It's the nature of the beast. The people with the money who finance and produce pictures go with what is current, and if you have had some success and made some money for them doing one style, they assume that's all you *can* do.''

The observation by this central figure suggests another, related, means for assessing performance capacity: the imprimatur of money. Box-office grosses are carefully monitored in Hollywood, as suggested throughout. Phenomenal profits and film rentals mean something—they may mean everything. Producers who have little or no insight into the real place and value of a composer's contribution to the film frequently judge and hire a scorer for the superficial impressiveness and the amount of publicity and hoped for cash his participation will bring to their projects. Here is one of the top composers. He spoke of an ''alliance'' between box-office success and climate of opinion:

> The picture business is a big risk. I mean you can do a marvelous score for a lousy picture, and then you can be badly hurt by that. I think if the film doesn't succeed, however good the music, there's a stigma attached to the music by its *alliance* [to the film]. At least this is what happens with the nonmusical people in the business. People will not and cannot make the lines of differentiation between the quality of the music and the picture for which it was written. As people outside the music business, some of our favorite scores may be from some picture that has died a death. But from the point of view of career, I think it's more important to have a box-office success in the minds of most of the directors and producers I know. There are people who will say, ''Yes, so-and-so did a great score and the picture failed, and maybe I'll hire him.'' That person is exceptional.

The big-budget film can drawn an enormous amount of attention to the composer. Composer John Williams is in that position. He scored films for Irwin Allen, beginning with their association in television leading to their $42-million money maker *Poseidon Adventure* (1972), a film that received two Oscars and seven nominations, then *Towering Inferno* (1974), a film that made well over $50 million, along with three Oscars and five nominations, one of the nominations for Williams. Composer Williams has also recurrently worked with filmmaker Jennings Lang. He scored Walter Mirisch's *Fitzwilly* (1967), *Midway* (1975), and the Universal release *Dracula* directed by John Badham (1979). He also teamed up with Elliott Kastner's *Missouri Breaks* (1975) and the earlier *The Long Goodbye* (1972). His other associations include work for director Steven Spielberg and producers Richard Zanuck and David Brown on *Sugarland Express* (1973), and then one of the most successful films of all time: *Jaws* (1974), winner of three Oscars, one of them going to Williams for his powerful dramatic scoring. The budget on this film was $10 million and MCA-Universal was absolutely astounded that *Jaws* might glean $200 million. As of January 1980, the U.S.-Canada market alone had film rentals over $133 million. There is only one other film that made more money than *Jaws*. That is *Star Wars,* and John Williams scored this $175,849,000 money maker for George Lucas and Gary Kurtz in 1977 along with Steven Speilberg and Julia and Michael Phillips's *Close Encounters of the Third Kind*—a film with rental pegged at around $77 million.

In Hollywood, the supergrosser has become what the jackpot is in Las Vegas, and the avalanche of cash it can bring creates a shower of offers and advantages to composer Williams. The 47-year-old native of New York City has collected two Emmys, seven Grammys (a recent award for his score to *Superman*), fifteen Academy Award nominations, and Oscars for *Fiddler on the Roof* (1971) and *Star Wars*. He was busy working in London completing the score to *The Empire Strikes Back,* a sequel to *Star Wars,* when he signed a three-year contract to succeed Arthur Fiedler as music director and conductor of the Boston Pops.

"I certainly won't be giving up my film work," he said in a telephone interview.[10] He planned to continue working with Steven Spielberg on *Raiders of the Lost Ark*. The film was released by Paramount in 1981; it was a commercial and artistic success. Williams is an exemplary case of high visibility, a combination of recurrent and one-shot ties to many producers, and continued association with a string of blockbusters and heavy money-making films. It was his turn on the cycle of success in the 1970s. One thing he shares with Jerry Goldsmith, Jerry Fielding, Henry Mancini, David Grusin, Lalo Schifrin, and other centrally located composers is that he is a veteran of the business who bumped around in a lot of hits and misses before fortune turned in his favor.

Given Big Hollywood's tendency for the "think big" mentality and the supergrosser, many of the industry's current productions are highly expensive projects which push the top filmmakers toward the security offered by free-lancers with proven credentials and impressive track records. What is intended as a tactic to reduce uncertainty at the level of personnel selection results in the centrality of producers, directors, screenwriters, cinematographers, composers, and other artistic and craft specialists in networks of collective action.

If worry is the prevailing state of mind in this business, the huge investments poured into many of Hollywood's films result in recurrent and routine modes of hiring. These work relations may be seen as links between producers and composers which ultimately become networks. The small numbers of central figures come to work together on a large variety of projects; and judging from the film rental and Academy Award data, those projects are likely to be commercially successful. Thus, the center of Hollywood as a web of transactions and career outcomes offers three major areas of analysis: the clustering of links themselves into blocks of networks; the pattern of dominance and success within these networks; and the pattern of ties which any individual freelancer has.

Centrality as Social Structure

What is now needed is detailed knowledge of the linkages among the top tiers—that is, ties between the most active filmmakers and the most productive composers. What ties composers and producers together to become concrete social structures is the recurrent pattern of (a) the producers' choices of certain composers for their films and (b) the composers' selections of certain producers with whom to work. Numerous choices and offers *sent out to* composers in the elite and composers' own selections *sent back to* top filmmakers result in a complex combination of ties, interests, and choices. This organization is the means for inferring a structure of freelance social organization. It is the complex interweaving of hundreds of pair relationships among the top tiers of composers (the inner circle of 40) and the upper tier of active film producers (the top 62 with five or more credits between 1964–65 and 1975–76) that guides us in a search for the observed patterns.

Deciphering a Network of Transactions

I start with the composers. I look for freelancers who are similar or equivalent in their work ties to producers. The major assumption is that two or more composers can be placed in the same configuration of transactions if they have worked for similar sets of producers. The basic step is computing the pattern of ties across all composers to distinctive sets of employers. The criterion for placing composers in the same configuration or "block" is one of consistency, not connectivity. Existing techniques for clustering relational data provide guidance in discovering a pattern of relationships among multiple sellers of their skill and multiple buyers of those skills.[11]

Hollywood is a craft mode of production in which people are bound in tangible interaction on a project-to-project basis. I describe this structure as a network in which the points or nodes of the network are individuals and the links or "events" in the network are business relationships. The business event is the film project for which a music score is composed. Thus we have craft organization of activity whose elements are two sets of actors—producers and composers. We also have sets of projects in the form of films. And we have two types of relations between these units: freelancers, for instance, are interested in various subsets of events and getting the chance to work on those films; and the events are controlled by various filmmakers. These are the defining elements of a freelance system of craft organization.

Now, consider the events. The film project connects both sides of the market. Hundreds of events flow between the top composers and the employers. Consider how the work is allocated. Freelance work projects are not allocated by some master decision maker, but by a market mechanism in which producers compete for the most desirable composers. The composers compete for the most desirable projects and producers. Three steps are involved: freelancers decide which jobs to go after in this market, producers choose candidates for their films, and composers select among the offers they receive. Composers play an active selective role and it would be misleading to interpret observed ties and resultant blocks of networks as indicative only of the filmmakers' "tastes," preferences, and hiring resources. To the extent that two or more freelance composers work for the same set of producers, their lines of work will intersect. The freelancers will be tied together in a matrix of market action by the different events for which they have been chosen. They will also be tied by the projects they have themselves selected.

An example will make this clear. Fred Karlin and Michael Small are both major, central figures in Hollywood. They scored feature films for the same producer over the twelve years. The work points in their career lines converge. To the extent they "share" subsets of filmmakers, they are likely to appear close together in this matrix of Big Hollywood. Composers Karlin and Small worked for producer and director Alan J. Pakula, whose credits include *The Sterile Cuckoo* (1969), *Klute* (1971), *The Parallax View* (1974), *All the President's Men* (1976), and earlier, *Up the Down Staircase* (1967), *The Stalking Moon* (1968), and *Love with the Proper Stranger* (1963). If composer David Shire joins Karlin and Small, as he did when he scored the successful *All the President's Men*, he is likely to show a pattern of equivalence in his ties to this one part of the market, the part or niche made by Alan Pakula's films and his selections of composers for those films.

Similarly, when John Williams is hired by filmmaker Walter Mirisch, and Jerry Fielding and John Mandel are also hired by Mirisch, there is a pattern of common ties between the three to this one, highly productive filmmaker. All three are consistently linked to a common employer. All three have been subject to the control of Mirisch as an employer and as a "client" for their services.

As multiple sets of film producers, like Pakula and Mirisch, hire the services of freelancers like Shire, Karlin, Williams, Fielding, Mandel, and Small, a pattern of equivalence begins to emerge. Projects connect employers and employees to one another. To the extent that sets of film producers send their choices out to a subset of composers, different networks of action emerge, and the work relationships and ties—as points in any one composer's career line—can be inspected for their diversity, the pattern of recurrent and non-recurrent ties, and the eventual outcomes of the film (e.g., commercial success, accolades, reviews, Oscars, nominations).

The data points are straightforward. They have been introduced earlier. I use film credits from 1964–65 to 1975–76 for these top two tiers of composers and top tier of producers. The advantages of using credits as events are (a) the nonreactivity of recorded industry information of actual projects and their outcomes (compared to self-reports) and (b) the inclusion of all participants in the highly active center of the industry. In this matrix of Big Hollywood, the (i,j)th entry is the number of films worked on by composer j with film producer i during the twelve years.[12] These work ties are the connecting lines in a matrix of 300 films. The matrix is a 62 x 40 array (62 producers and 40 composers). The idea is to permute this m x n matrix so that rows and columns can be separately partitioned into relatively homogeneous clusters of collective action.[13] The location or boundaries of the resulting clusters or network blocks are inferred from the overall distribution of ties linking named producers to specific freelancers.

Figure 8.1 shows the results of the partitioning and permutation of the 40 composers. The partitioning proceeds "from the top down," moving in a tree-like fashion. It starts with all 40 and then divides them into exclusive blocks or networks on the basis of the consistency of their ties to Hollywood's top film producers. These blocks will yield configurations with relatively high density—they are likely to be relatively "packed" with ties between composers and producers. In this way, the partitions reorder the information of all the ties in this top tier market so as to reveal an underlying pattern as a whole. A complete list of the four blocks and the names of the figures (displayed in Table 8.2) indicates that producer selections are channeled toward composers such as Jerry Goldsmith, Lalo Schifrin, David Grusin, Henry Mancini, John Williams, Elmer Bernstein, and a few others. These freelancers tend to dominate the action in their respective networks and work with a variety of film producers.

The underlying pattern will be easier to see if we go a step further. Focus on the employers in the matrix. Take the top 62 filmmakers and apply the clustering technique to the *rows*—the producers. The aim is to identify employers whose patterns of ties are consistent or structurally equivalent to that of the composers. Thus, if John Foreman and Howard Koch, both active and recognized contributors to the film business, exhibit a similarity in their hiring of the top 40 composers, they will appear close together in the matrix. They are likely to be in the same block or network. Foreman and Koch, as a matter of record, do share some of the same freelancers. They hire many composers for their projects, but during the twelve years three composers exerted a potent impact on the market position of Foreman and Koch. Henry Mancini scored Foreman's *Sometimes a Great Notion* (1970) and Koch's *Once Is Not Enough* (1975). Schifrin worked on the Foreman and Paul Newman film, *WUSA*, and on Koch's *The President's Analyst* (1967). Composer Maurice Jarre scored Foreman's *The Life and Times of Judge Roy Bean* (1972) and *The Effect of*

FIGURE 8.1

Partitions of the Top Two Tiers of Hollywood Composers: Blockmodel
"Tree" of Top Forty

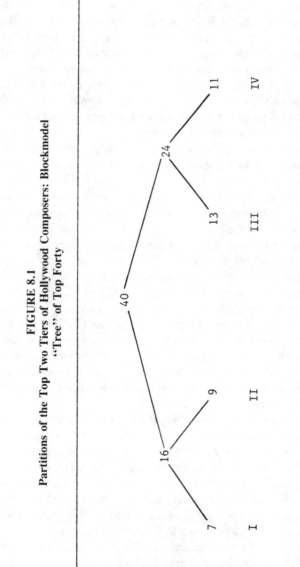

CONCOR applied to M x N (Filmmaker x Freelancer) matrix of work transactions for the most productive filmmakers (Tier A, N = 62) and composers (Tiers 1 and 2, N = 40). Roman numerals designate block "names" in a 4-block partition of the composers. See Table 6 for a listing of the composers located in each block. See Figure 2 for the composite matrix of filmmakers and freelancers.

TABLE 8.2

Listing of Freelance Composers in Each Block: Four-Network Blockmodel

Block	Composers
I.........	J. Goldsmith,* L. Rosenman, R. and R. Sherman, F. Myrow, G. Bruns, B. Baker, R. Brunner.
II........	D. Frontiere, P. Williams, L. Baxter, C. Bernstein, F. DeVol, J. Fried, J. Haskell, F. Karger, R. LaSalle.
III.......	L. Schifrin,* D. Grusin,* H. Mancini,* M. Jarre, J. Barry, W. Scharf, A. North, N. Riddle, E. Bernstein, L. Rosenthal, C. Fox, H. Hefti, V. Mizzy.
IV........	J. Williams,* M. Legrand, Q. Jones, J. Fielding, J. Mandel, F. Karlin, D. Shire, M. Small, M. Hamlisch, A. Previn, S. Phillips.

Starred names are the freelance composer (n=5) who are the dominants in both time periods, 1964–69 and 1970–75. They captured 1.5 or more percent of the market in the two periods.

FIGURE 8.2
Work Transactions in the Top Two Tiers: Matrix of Producers and Freelance Composers

COMPOSERS

I   II   III   IV

FILM PRODUCERS

1. ROSENBERG, A.
2. CHARTOFF-WINKLER
3. WISE, R.
4. SCHWARTZ, M.
5. ARTHUR, R.
6. DEHAVEN, C.
7. FRYER-CRESSON
8. MONTAGNE, E.
9. EDWARDS, B.
10. LEWIS, E.
11. HIBLER, W.
12. DAVID, S.
13. JACOBS, A.
14. PREMINGER, O.
15. SELTZER, W.
16. CONRAD, W.
17. DORFMAN, R.
18. TOWERS, I
19. ANDERSON, B.
20. MILLER, R.
21. WALSH, B.

22. TURMAN-FOSTER
23. RADNITZ, R.

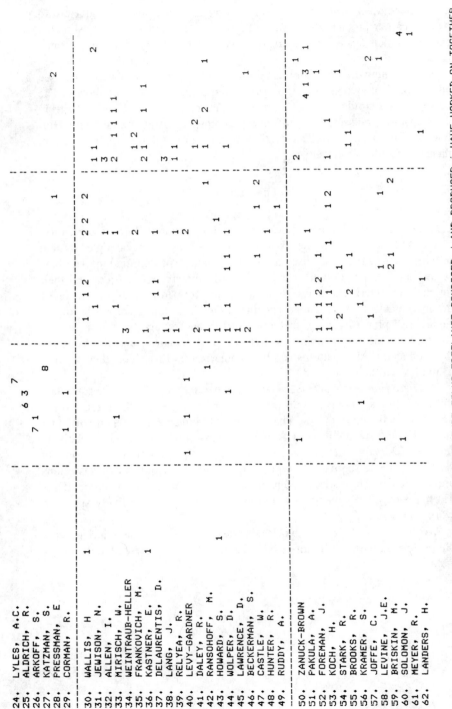

[THE NUMBER IN CELL i,j IS THE NUMBER OF FEATURE FILMS FREELANCE COMPOSER j AND PRODUCER i HAVE WORKED ON TOGETHER IN THE 1964-65 TO 1975-76 PRODUCTION PERIODS]
[300 FILMS]

Gamma Rays on Man in the Moon Marigolds. Jarre also scored Howard Koch's earlier project, *Plaza Suite* (1970). These filmmakers are "similar" enough in their ties to composers to belong in the same network, to the same niche.

Forming networks of action is an observable matter. An observer can see all of Big Hollywood as partitioned into specific networks or niches. The networks and similarities among film producers are inferred *indirectly* from their specific transactions with the top composers. And centrality for Hollywood's most productive and visible composers is inferred *indirectly* from their ties to film producers.

The Matrix

Figure 8.2 is the pattern of collective action. It is a picture of Big Hollywood. At first glance the matrix seems a diverse and loosely coupled system in which it is difficult to discern any sharp pattern of domination. The horizontal and vertical dotted lines help identify the sixteen matrices and their internal characteristics. These submatrices are formed by the intersection of the four blocks of film composers (the *columns*—running across the top of Figure 8.2, plus a listing of the names of freelancers) and the four blocks of filmmakers (the *rows*—along the left side of this matrix, and the names of the producers). Five patterns can be summarized at this point, then specific examples will be developed.

1. *There is a center-periphery pattern of transactions*. The more consistent the transactions among certain producers and composers, the more closely knit their total pattern of ties. The more closely knit, the more their particular submatrix will stand out—it will emerge against the background of relatively few ties. The *contrasts* between submatrices with a predominance of empty spaces and those submatrices with a predominance of points of transactions are very clear. Networks of joint performances appear in six submatrices. The remaining ten submatrices are either empty or comparatively sparse in work transactions.

A comparison of ties and block densities in the sixteen submatrices (displayed in Figure 8.2) is summarized in Table 8.3 and represented in the *image matrices*[14]

$$
\begin{array}{cccc}
1 & 0 & 0 & 0 \\
0 & 1 & 0 & 0 \\
0 & 0 & 1 & 1 \\
0 & 0 & 1 & 1
\end{array}
$$

or its verbal generalization, which is that Big Hollywood is a tangible social structure linking specific producers and composers, and the collective action crystallizes into six distinct networks, especially concentrated in the "double-decker" span of ties located in the lower right-hand corner.[15]

2. *An echelon social structure emerges.* This market can further be described by what I call an *echelon organization of activities.*[16] The image is one of multiple networks populated with loosely coupled ties in which each clique or configuration is located to the right and below the network above it. This is the resultant summary "picture," found in the image matrices. It is the morphology of Big Hollywood. The revealing contrasts between blocks of high and low density show a clearly segmented echelon market, a structure of action defined by the specific decisions and ties of a dozen or few score particular film producers with resources who settle into a schedule of work transactions with a subset of employees.[17]

3. *Loosely coupled networks differ in their volume and demand patterns.* Each niche in this market is unique. Networks of composers can be viewed as opportunity sets either favored by more stable demand patterns or hindered by a decline in the number of filmmakers seeking their services. The partitions at the four-block network level suggest that block II's standing vis-à-vis blocks I, III, and IV is one of comparative weakness. The latter three networks dominate the scene in terms of volume (as shown in Table 8.3), transactions with filmmakers (Table 8.4), and career performances of network participants (Table 8.5). The matrix shows inequalities in the distribution of credits, span of accounts across multiple producers, and visibility. High risk and attendant uncertainties about profits and awards exist all the way down the line in this matrix, but some submatrices are clearly more favored in terms of stable demand and career performances than others.

4. *A few dominate.* The matrix gives an image of the position and relatively long span of connections enjoyed by a small number of leading film composers. These composers have persisted and contributed heavily to the total volume of work in each of their respective networks. They are directly tied into projects with highly productive and visible filmmakers, and, because of this tie-in, they are more important and valuable to other producers than a composer who is only weakly connected to a few of Hollywood's top filmmakers. Moreover, a freelancer who is well connected across numerous producers has career continuity, an advantage often denied the composer who is isolated, tied to a single producer on multiple projects, and typically poorly integrated within composer and producer subsets of commercial action.

In the echelon pattern, note block I's position and how composer Jerry Goldsmith, along with Leonard Rosenman and a few others, dominate the productivity of this block. They capture many of the ties to the producer side of the market, just as Lalo Schifrin and Henry Mancini exhibit a relatively

TABLE 8.3
Matrix of Producers and Composers: (A) Number of Ties, (B) Densities of
Submatrices, and (C) Volume of Projects in the Top Tiers,
1964–65 to 1975–76

	Ties[a]				Densities[b]				Volume			
	composers				composers				composers			
p	34	2	11	8	.23	.01	.04	.03	66	2	18	12
r	2	8	2	5	.04	.11	.02	.06	2	34	2	6
o	3	6	39	25	.02	.03	.15	.11	3	6	50	35
d	0	4	26	17	.00	.03	.15	.12	0	4	33	27
u												
c		Total Ties = 192				Overall Density = .08[c]				Total Films = 300		
e												
r												
s												

[a] Binary ties: The presence of a work tie equals "1," the absence equals "0."

[b] "Density" is the number of "1's" within a submatrix divided by the number of possible entries, the row and column partitions are multiplied for the possible entries. There are, for example, 17 ties in the lower-right corner submatrix. Divide 17 ties by 11 X 13 or 143, the 11 freelancers in Block IV times the 13 producers in the fourth row.

[c] The cutoff criterion used to obtain the image used in the text is .08 = 192 binary ties/ 2480. Each of the 16 (4 X 4) submatrices is coded as a "zeroblock" or a "bond."

FIGURE 8.3

Matrix of Producers and Composers: Number of Ties, Volume of Projects in
the Top Tiers, 1964–65 to 1975–76

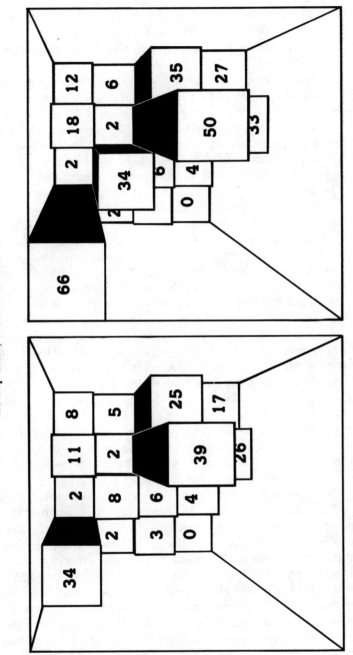

wide span of ties in their network (block III), and just as John Williams and Michel Legrand, for example, tend to dominate the available work in their network (block IV). All these persistent patterns of productivity and depth of client accounts sum up the essential ingredients of network location, centrality, and career survival.

5. *There is strength in diversity.* A solid business mix helps. In the matrix 70 percent of ties (134 of 192) are nonrecurrent—the composer and producer worked together only once in the twelve years. Only 19 percent (N = 37) of the transactions in the top tiers are between partners who worked twice during these production years. The percentages of freelancers and filmmakers who worked together on three, four, and five or more projects during this time drop dramatically to 4, 3, and 4 percent respectively.

The patterns of differentiation between the networks are clear. Networks I and III display a relatively wide span of transactions across the top 62 film producers (see Table 8.4). Some of those ties are one-shot, others are recurrent. Their relatively large volume of film credits from 1964 to 1976 shows these composers connected to filmmakers located both in the top productivity tier as well as other tiers of the industry. Blocks I and III have a higher mean volume of credits from 1964 to 1976 than freelancers in network II. Comparing block II and blocks I and II we see the difficulties of career lines where composers are recurrently tied to one filmmaker but lacking breadth in their connections to other employers. Integration into employer or client networks is thereby reduced, and so, it would appear, are the probabilities of continually staying in the market as actively as one's better connected colleagues.

The composers in the third network (block III) show the highest volume of projects scored during the 1964–69 period (10.0) with a modest decline relative to the work that those in networks I and IV acquire during the 1970–75 period. Block IV is clearly on the move. As a group or subset these composers boost their mean number of films scored from 6.7 in the first six years to 10.8 in the next six years. Individually they emerge as some of the most prolific and visible freelancers.

Dominance and diversification go together in a segmented, freelance market. Ten freelancers capture a large share of this market from 1970 to 1976, and most of them remain in positions of centrality in networks. The composers are Jerry Goldsmith, Lalo Schifrin, David Grusin, and Henry Mancini. The other central figures in Hollywood are all tied together in the fourth network (column four). They are John Williams, Jerry Fielding, David Shire, Michael Small, Fred Karlin, and Michel Legrand. A wide span *alone* does not account for their productivity. Contrary to a "straight" linear relationship between wide span of ties and productivity, the network in column four stands midpoint between the relatively wide span of Goldsmith and a few of his colleagues (5.7), Lalo Schifrin and his colleagues (5.8), and the "sparse" network found

TABLE 8.4
Work Transactions for the Top Tiers of Composers: Four-Block Level

| Block | Transactions with Top Producers | Visibility of Employers | | Combined Kudos for Composer |
	Span of Accounts mean	mean/(sum)[a]	Success Together[b]	mean/(sum)[c]
I	5.71	2.4 (17)	(5)	4.71 (33)
II	2.33	.9 (8)	(0)	1.33 (12)
III	5.85	3.8 (49)	(8)	6.23 (81)
IV	4.90	3.8 (42)	(13)	9.54 (83)
Sig. value*	(10.93)	(9.63)	(12.23)	(13.20)
p <	.02	.03	.007	.005

*Significance values are Kruskal-Wallis with 3 d. f.

[a] Composer has worked for a producer/director who has won or been nominated for an Academy Award, has won a Golden Globe Award, or has been a winner at the Cannes Film Festival.

[b] Composer and producer/director worked together where the film(s) has been nominated or received an Oscar, won the Golden Globe Award, or was winner at the Cannes Film Festival.

[c] Composers and their combined nominations or Oscars, Golden Globe Award, Cannes Festival; in addition the composer has worked for producers and directors with similar nominations and awards.

TABLE 8.5
Career Attributes for the Top Two Tiers of Composers: Four-Block Level

Block	Volume of Film Credits mean		Film Rentals$ mean/(sum)		Industry Visibility mean/(sum)	
	60s	70s	60s	70s	Films	Scores
I = 7	7.7	8.1	43.9 (307)	26.7 (188)	.71 (5)	1.42 (10)
II = 9	6.6	4.0	11.7 (105)	6.6 (59)	.11 (1)	.33 (3)
III = 13	10.0	7.8	38.4 (499)	20.9 (272)	.61 (8)	1.46 (19)
IV = 11	6.7	10.8	20.0 (220)	51.8 (570)	1.09 (12)	2.00 (22)
Sig. value*	(3.46)	(9.10)	(7.43)	(11.29)	(7.48)	(7.14)
p <	n.s.	.03	.06	.01	.06	.07

*For the first six columns, significance values are Kruskal-Wallis H with 3 df. Chi-square, 9 df for Rank.

$ Rentals in millions of dollars standardized to 1972 GNP implicit price deflator.

among composers Fried, DeVol, Haskell, and their productive but narrowly linked (2.3) relationships with only eight filmmakers. A moderate range (4.9) rather than a relatively wider span of ties to the producers characterizes block IV.

Among the networks on the main diagonal, those freelancers with both one-shot alliances and long-run partnerships outperform their colleague competitors, enjoy greater influence among producers and directors, and experience increased career resources. Their successes produce more successes and they are associated with filmmakers on films which have a greater chance of being commercially successful.

Market successes socially validate employers' decisions. The business skews heavily toward the hits, and a handful of top hits only. The data on film rentals suggest that visible results such as top-grossing films are unevenly distributed among the blocks. The top few projects can corner 15 to 20 percent of the market; the second-ranked films will likely attract 12 to 15 percent; the third-ranked films, 10 to 12 percent; the fourth-ranked projects, 7 to 8 percent; the fifth, 5 to 6 percent; and the sixth-ranked films in a peak season will capture 5 percent of the market. From that point on the market share of additional films tapers off quickly. By the tenth most popular film, the market share is no more than around 3 percent. These percentages are not absolute, but they reflect current trends in the motion picture business.[18] Producers' decisions are made within this market, and they are made in terms of visible results. They pay attention to each other's hiring preferences and to each other's results. Thus the business skews heavily toward the hits and, more important for our purposes, the few hit-making freelancers, as shown in the success of blocks I and IV in the 1970s (mean film rentals and industry visibility combined).

From the viewpoint of the composers, diversification, a mix of connections to these changing producers and their changing preferences, ensures some baseline for their own participation and market continuity. Visibility helps. Industry accolades and a comparatively strong demand situation backed by box-office performance have concrete payoffs, again as shown in the emergence of dominance among networks I and IV during the 1970s. Judged from the continued strength of composers Goldsmith, Schifrin, Grusin, Mancini, Williams, Shire, Small, Fielding, Karlin, Bernstein, Legrand, Rosenman, Jarre, and others, the social organization of the industry shows that network centrality is a function of an underlying *allocation and validation process* through which networks of ties and tangible market signals interact to produce distinctive advantages for a dozen or score of freelancers and filmmakers.

Central Figures

In this section I will present six examples of the way these principles—centrality, resources, and career development—work in the market. The first few examples are primarily quantitative and the remainder are principally qualitative. The quantitative comparisons have lessons beyond their specific findings. To make the strongest possible case that film productions are market facts with effects on filmmakers and freelancers, we should have details on the names of films and their outcomes. The nature of budgets, type of film, and other support personnel (screenwriters, cinematographers, etc.) are tangible signals with crucial effects on the distribution of work and resources. The examples show that "who works on what kind of projects with whom" reveals much about the power structure of the film industry.

The first example, a quantitative one, shows how the span of connections with visible and important employers on major film projects contributes to increased success in networks IV, III, and I respectively. Another quantitative example shows how small numbers dominate a network. The third example, a qualitative one, illustrates the importance of commercial success and box-office performance on the interdependence of *pairs*. The fourth, fifth, and sixth examples also illustrate the ways in which diversity of film credits, breadth and span of connections contribute to resources, recognition, and career success.

First Example

Networks III and IV contain some of the busiest and most successful composers. These freelancers in the "double-decker" image matrices draw their major sets of filmmaker associations from the producers in the lower part of the matrix—producer blocks III and IV. The size of this producer subset is 33 (Hal Wallis to Albert S. Ruddy, 20 filmmakers; Richard Zanuck and David Brown team to Hal Landers, 13). The observed number of ties connecting the composers in block III to the filmmakers is 39 and 26 ties, yielding a network density of .15 for each submatrix. The composers in block IV are similarly connected and exhibit a consistency of ties to the two sets of producers. In this case, the 11 freelancers such as John Williams, Quincy Jones, Jerry Fielding, Marvin Hamlisch, John Mandel, André Prévin, and others, have 25 ties to filmmakers in row three and 17 ties connecting them to the Zanuck-Brown partition along the lower right-hand corner of the matrix. The network densities in the two spanning sets are .11 and .12 respectively.

It would be extravagant to say that these interconnections form densely knit networks of collective action. But neither are these ties a loose and open aggregate of associations randomly distributed in the top tiers. Rather, the networks in the matrix show patterns of action that are loosely knit and a wide span of connections among many film composers and producers. The density matrix indicates that the composers in these two networks scored a large number of films, and also that they worked with filmmakers outside the network (in the upper-right corner, as previously stated—see Table 8.3).

At the other extreme, the nine composers in the middle submatrix (block II) are with minor exceptions integrated into the structure only through their strong ties to a small set of employers. The mean span of accounts in block II is less than three film producers (2.3) as shown in Table 8.3. This can be interpreted as a concrete instance of dependence on a narrow range of clients, and such a pattern of tightly coupled ties in sparse networks indicates something of a peripheral location in the top tier. Three producers are highly prolific in the number of films they send into the composer sector, but Arkoff, Corman, and Katzman typically depended upon peripheral freelancers with only one credit to work on their films. These filmmakers are responsible for most of the films connecting the top filmmaker tier to the lower tier of composers, the tier where work is scarce.

In contrast, there is an abundance of work for Lalo Schifrin, David Grusin, Elmer Bernstein, Henry Mancini, and others in block III. From 1964 to 1976 their connections with producer blocks III and IV total 145 films. Nearly half the films scored in the top tier are scored by members of these networks, and with few exceptions, these freelancers exhibit a relatively wide span of connections. Participation in the projects of several producers helps generate informal contacts with other filmmakers, as well as other craft specialists, and these contacts contribute to the interdependent web of connections at the center of Hollywood. Connections such as these make them highly productive contributors to the industry as shown in the volume by networks (see Table 8.5). From a producer's point of view such connections make them more attractive candidates than others still trying to break out of the middle area into the top tiers. All this suggests that integration into the center of this business gives these composers (block III) visibility and a competitive edge.

It is particularly characteristic of the political structure of freelancing that the central figures are network builders. They have many accounts and a diversity of ties. Table 8.4 indicates the mean span of accounts for the network dominated by Jerry Goldsmith, Leonard Rosenman, Richard and Robert Sherman, and the Disney three. The mean is 5.7 and Goldsmith's wide linkages contribute heavily. He is visible and highly connected. In another network, Lalo Schifrin is equally well connected with ties to 14 filmmakers in the top 62, with 15 films for those producers, and with 46 credits total over the twelve years. Elmer Bernstein has a span of more than 10 ties to producers in the matrix. Bernstein has a total of nearly 30 credits on feature films across all four tiers of film producers. The average number of accounts spanning the Schifrin and Bernstein network is similar to the Goldsmith block. The means are the highest we observe, 5.8 and 5.7. By contrast, John Williams, Michel Legrand, Fred Karlin, Michael Small, and the composers in their network (block IV) exhibit multiple connections with a mean of 4.9, suggesting something of a mid-position between the sparsely knit Fried and DeVol network (block II) and the wide mean range of the Goldsmith and Schifrin networks. Williams, for example, is tied to eight producers on a total of 15 films in this matrix. He is also very productive with a total of 28 films in the twelve years. Legrand, Karlin, Michael Small, and others are similarly linked with 6 to 8 productive filmmakers in this matrix, but they also work with filmmakers in producer tiers 2, 3, and 4. The important point is that there is not a straight, linear relation between span size and career success. A diversity of nonrecurrent *and* recurrent employer ties is a key ingredient of career continuity. It is conceivable that diversity of ties in a loosely coupled work system helps preserve more adaptability in responding to changing fads and fashions than either a wide span of one-shot connections or, on the other hand, a narrow range of recurrent ties with one or two employers. Composers with a moderate span of ties can therefore adapt to a considerably wider range of changes in their work environment than would be true for their colleagues.

Apparently, a composer's ability to survive and prosper grows out of his success at achieving integration across film producers at the center of this industry; his continuity in the labor market is related to his ability to secure a combination of recurrent partnerships and nonrecurrent collaborators. Accumulating credits is of course crucial but it is advantageous to accumulate those credits through a multiplicity of ties.

Quantitative data show us there is advantage in strong and weak ties, and the structure of success is partially defined by that. Numbers in the matrix cannot tell us why that is the case, though we can speculate, and speculation is supported by the interviews. First, a *career portfolio* mixed with one-shot and recurrent ties renders freelancers less vulnerable to the downswings in the fortunes of their producer-employers, let alone the liability of dependence on a strong tie to a single filmmaker. Second, visibility and multiple connections combined reassure other film producers. They see their colleagues placing their ''bets'' and resources on certain film composers. This commitment is a kind of ''cultural insurance,'' drawn upon and imitated by producers when they are deciding which composers they are going to try to hire for their own films. Third, a diversity of film work increases the chances that a composer will face challenges and perhaps arrive at novel solutions for dramatic problems. As one of the composers in the third network expressed it, ''If you are going to work more than once in Hollywood, you have to be able to work in more than one idiom.'' A range of styles decreases the probability of narrow typecasting. A mix of business relationships also forces the composer to adapt to various filmmakers and their films, budgets, and personalities. A freelancer in the same network (block III) said, ''Basically, I've carved out a world in which I operate most comfortably. I work with a variety of people. Some of my business associates are close friends and we've known one another and worked successfully with one another for years. Others are young film producers and directors coming into this business. I've been lucky because of the challenges from these different personalities and their projects.''

Integration into networks, diversification of ties and projects, and adaptability are in the career interests of freelance composers. Indeed, they *are* their career interests, as I have illustrated in the case materials and interviews.

Second Example

Seven freelancers in the upper left-hand corner of the matrix draw their ties principally from 21 filmmakers. Thirty-four ties connect them to the producers, yielding the highest observed density for any of the networks. (The density is .23 [34/147], as shown in Table 8.3.) From 1964–65 to 1975–76, this highly productive network did 66 films. A very high percentage of the work done by members of this network is, of course, done within the network, but not quite all of it, and it is interesting to note the pattern of "extra-network" ties. When the producers hired other composers in the top tiers, there are 22 ties (across row one) and 32 projects. When the composers, by contrast, are hired by other filmmakers in the top 62, there are only 5 ties and 5 films, and they were all picked up by Jerry Goldsmith and Leonard Rosenman. In other words, the composers are considerably more dependent upon the producers than vice versa. These extra network transactions present in extreme form a tendency within the network less obviously. The transactions within block I are evidence in miniature of freelancing as a set of interdependent ties where events of career interest to each freelancer are, to a considerable extent, under the control of participants other than himself. Freelancers are "controlled" by particular subsets of producers on whom they rely for their work, while each film producer is materially "interested" in a wide subset of composers.

Some composers are highly sought after, but they are a very small subset, barely a handful. Goldsmith, Williams, Schifrin, Mancini, and Legrand are sought after by many producers, and in such positions of strength and centrality, they pull the market together producing almost a visual focus in the matrix itself. Look at the string of multiple ties and tightly coupled linkages between Schifrin, Elmer Bernstein, John Williams, Fred Karlin, and Michel Legrand with the producers in rows 3 and 4. This "stacking" of connections across producers illustrates the enormous advantages to a composer of a combination of tightly coupled ties together with a series of one-shot business connections. Such a structure is unusual but noteworthy because it allows a composer to maximize his interests and control over conditions of work.

This is exactly what Jerry Goldsmith has managed to do. He moved into the 1964–65 season with an impressive string of credits. Already one of the central figures in the business, he was known for his contributions to such films as *Freud, Lonely Are the Brave, A Gathering of Eagles, Lilies of the Field,* and *Take Her, She's Mine.* He followed with a string of 20th Century-Fox releases produced by Aaron Rosenberg: *Shock Treatment, Fate Is the Hunter, Morituri,* and *The Detective.* Producers Chartoff and Winkler hired him for two of their films; both made some money: *Spys,* directed by I. Kershner made $5 million, *Breakout,* directed by Tom Gries and filmed by veteran Lucien Ballard, made $8 million.

Composer Goldsmith's career continuity is related to his long-term partnership with director Franklin Shaffner. They worked together with producer Arthur Jacobs on the original *Planet of the Apes* (1967), and the composeer was hired for the sequel a few years later, *Escape from Planet of the Apes.* (Producer Jacobs put three more *Planet* movies into production; for *Beneath the Planet of the Apes* [1969] and the final *Battle for the Planet of the Apes* [1972] he hired Leonard Rosenman.) Director Schaffner and composer Goldsmith also worked on the successful *Patton* (1970), produced by Frank McCarthy, with screenplay by Francis Coppola and Edmund H. North. This film won a nomination for the composer and seven Oscars while making over $28 million in domestic rentals. They then did *Papillon* (1973) with producer Robert Dorfman, a single tie for the composer—one of the numerous single ties in Goldsmith's career line (see matrix). Schaffner and George C. Scott teamed up together after *Patton* on *Island in the Stream* (1977), Peter Bart and Max Palevsky producing, Goldsmith writing the music. *Boys from Brazil* (1978), with executive producer Robert Fryer, matched director and composer for the fifth time in over a decade of film work.

There are other tightly coupled relations during the 1964–65 to 1975–76 period. Goldsmith worked with producer Saul David on the 1964 production *Von Ryan's Express,* and then again with two of Saul David's productions: *Our Man Flint* (1965) and *In Like Flint* (1966). They worked next a few years later on the lavish *Logan's Run* (1975). Producer Edward Lewis and director John Frankenheimer worked together with Goldsmith on *Seven Days in May* (1964) followed by *Seconds* a couple of years later. *The Impossible Object* (1974) was a Frankenheimer-directed project that received a premature and disastrous screening at the Cannes Festival.

Goldsmith averaged 4 or 5 pictures a year, just as the big composers had done in the bright days of the big studios. He is fast, dependable, and versatile. In a 1976 interview he said:

> I tackle every assignment just as seriously as if I were aiming it at a concert hall audience. Somewhere over 100 features are made every year. The odds are against every one of them becoming a masterpiece or even a minor classic. But I'd be cheating the audience and myself if I tried to judge a film's place in history before I decided whether to

give it my best effort, or only half an effort. If a film story is less than inspiring, I find something in it to challenge me. I create a musical problem and then try to solve it. My work is successful if it adds a special dimension to the movie, even though I know right from the beginning my contribution is certainly not the single most important element.[19]

Among his recent films are *One Little Indian* (1973) for Winston Hibler at Walt Disney productions, *The Don Is Dead* (1973) for Hal Wallis, and *The Wind and the Lion* (1974). With producer Robert Evans and director Roman Polanski, he scored the highly successful *Chinatown* (1974). Another project with Evans, *Players* (1979) with Ali MacGraw and Dean-Paul Martin, was a flop, but several reviewers noted that his score, in the words of one reviewer, "is one of the few subtle and effective touches in the film." *The Omen* (1976) had already brought him an Oscar. *MacArthur* and *Damnation Alley* were scored in 1977 followed by the sequel to *The Omen—Damien–Omen II* (1978) produced by Harvey Bernhard. Goldsmith teamed on *The Swarm* (1978) with Irwin Allen, the disaster filmmaker who usually worked with composer John Williams. In 1979 he scored the music for the science fiction horror *The Alien*.

Goldsmith achieved his extraordinary success through a fruitful combination of recurrent and nonrecurrent ties, but the matrix shows that it is also possible to develop a successful career almost wholly within the orbit of one set of film producers. The single genre and high-volume matching of filmmaker and composer, though different in structure, can lead to less spectacular but still substantial success. Three busy freelancers maintained a solid local base and simultaneously turned out a high volume of scores. Significantly, all three worked out of Walt Disney Productions. Bill Anderson's production credits include *The Biscuit Eater* (1971), *The Barefoot Executive* (1971), *The Million Dollar Duck* (1971), *The Computer Wore Tennis Shoes* (1969), and *The One and Only Genuine, Original Family Band*. Most of Anderson's films were scored by in-house composers Buddy Baker and Robert Brunner. However, one of his productions was scored by the Academy Award-winning composer-lyricist team of Richard W. and Robert B. Sherman, who won two Oscars in 1964 for best song and best music score with their music and lyrics for *Mary Poppins*. The Shermans also worked at Disney on *Tom Sawyer*, along with the commercially successful *Bedknobs and Broomsticks* ($8.2 million) and the Arthur Jacobs-produced *Huckleberry Finn* (1974).

Buddy Baker and Bill Anderson teamed together on the $7-million money maker *Superdad* (1974) and the commercially sluggish *Treasure of Matecumbe* (1975). Baker scored over 13 films in this studio from 1964 to 1975. Robert Brunner turned out 14 films working for Disney producer Ron Miller on such projects as *Snowball Express* (1972), *Castaway Cowboy* (1973), *Gus* (1975), and the highly successful *North Avenue Irregulars* (1979).

Another Disney regular, George Bruns, worked with Winston Hibler on such projects as *The Horse in the Gray Flannel Suit* directed by Norman Tokar (1968), *The Aristocats* (1970), and with producer Bill Walsh who wrote the $17-million success *Herbie Rides Again* (1974).

These are tightly knit associations. Together these three composers contribute heavily to the aggregate volume of films scored in Hollywood. If we add composer Jerry Goldsmith, whose output is slightly under 25 films scored with the 16 producers in this network (and over 25 with filmmakers out of the top tiers), we arrive at a total well over 50 projects. If we add composer Leonard Rosenman, who worked for producer A. P. Jacobs on the *Planet of the Apes* sequels, and who also did a 12-tone score for *Fantastic Voyage,* produced by Saul David, and the music for Robert Arthur's *Hellfighters* (1968), then they do more than three-quarters of all the work done within the network and around 17 percent of all the work scored within the top tiers. Clearly, these are all major contributors to the Hollywood scene, despite the differences in their career performances.

Third Example

As suggested above, recurrent ties among partners and recurrent box-office hits are necessary but not sufficient for centrality. Furthermore, the two do not always go together. In the previous example we saw successful long-term collaboration in blocks I and II, but the story behind the numbers in block II also suggests some of the problems with recurrent ties. The center of those ties in block II is producer and director Robert Aldrich, and so I will describe his ties to various composers to exemplify the problems such recurrent ties can pose for composers. During the years he was putting together his own production company, Robert Aldrich worked with composer Gerald Fried. Fried had broken into the film business through director Stanley Kubrick and the visibility earned on Fried's imaginative score for *Paths of Glory* (1957). Fried began his work with Aldrich on *Whatever Happened to Aunt Alice?* (1968) with Geraldine Page and Ruth Gordon. (Aldrich had directed the powerful *Whatever Happened to Baby Jane?* six years earlier with Bette Davis and Joan Crawford.) Fried worked on *The Killing of Sister George* (1968), produced in England; *Too Late the Hero* (1969); and the action adventure *The Grissom Gang* (1970). Aldrich then turned his attention to the work of Frank DeVol, and composer DeVol scored four films in succession for Aldrich.

Composer Frank DeVol has a long list of credits. He has worked with producers and directors with various track records, men such as Aaron Rosenberg, Stanley Kramer, Martin Melcher, Norman Jewison, and others. He keeps busy. Among his credits are *Send Me No Flowers* (1964) directed by

Norman Jewison, produced by Martin Melcher, with Rock Hudson and Doris Day. He wrote the score for the popular and Academy-nominated film *Cat Ballou* (1964) starring Lee Marvin, Jane Fonda, and Nat King Cole; the songs were by Mack David and Jerry Livingston. Another film followed in 1966, *The Glass Bottom Boat,* then another with Melcher and Aaron Rosenberg, *Caprice* (1967). He scored *The Happening* (1966) and the critical and commercial success *Guess Who's Coming to Dinner* (1967) directed by Stanley Kramer; the film won two Oscars, was nominated in six categories, and made over $25 million in film rentals.

The association between Aldrich and DeVol reaches back to the Bette Davis, Olivia de Havilland, Agnes Moorehead, and Joseph Cotten macabre drama *Hush, Hush, Sweet Charlotte* (1964), winner of six nominations, including DeVol's score. This was followed by joint efforts on *Flight of the Phoenix* (1965) and the immensely successful wartime adventure *The Dirty Dozen* (1967), winner of three nominations, one Oscar, and over $20 million in domestic rentals. Aldrich had hit it big. It was not until five years later that the two teamed up again. This time it was *The Emperor of the North* (1972) with Lee Marvin and Ernest Borgnine. This film failed to find an audience. The alliance between DeVol and Aldrich still held because Aldrich kept coming up with projects, coaxing several projects along at the same time, hoping that some would finally become films and then projects to be scored. *Ulzana's Raid* (1972) made it to the screen. It was a dismal flop. With a string of films that had cost millions of dollars fading at the box office, producer Aldrich, by his own admission, was in "terrible trouble." He came up with the popular and very profitable vehicle for actor Burt Reynolds, *The Longest Yard* (1973). This project was a carefully produced and clever reworking of the plot of *The Dirty Dozen.* Directed by Aldrich, with Eddie Albert, Ed Lauter, and with plenty of gridiron-prison action, it received one nomination and made over $25 million in rentals.

Speaking of *Ulzana's Raid* and *The Emperor of the North,* filmmaker Aldrich is explicit about the risks producers and directors run when they start producing expensive film projects. "You can make three or four of those in a row," he said referring to the sequential failures at the box office of *Ulzana's Raid* and then *Emperor,* "and you'll be back doing television. No way you're going to make $3- or $4-million pictures that die. I don't care how well they do critically; nobody wants to know you. We misjudged the audience, or misjudged the application of those stories. We misjudged something. Fortunately, I got lucky with *The Longest Yard.* People who are in my business— and I'm not in the Bergman/Fellini business, that's another business, I don't know how to do that—people who are in my business have to have a commercial success every two or three years . . . certainly every third picture, fourth at the most, or you're in terrible, terrible trouble."[20]

Several themes are important. First, Aldrich is very clear on what business he is in. He is very clear about what market he is in. Survivors who stay at the top continue the flow of projects into the market of movie buyers, the audience. Aldrich specializes in the medium- to high-budget adventure melodrama package, with production costs usually near $4 million. As noted earlier, men like Aldrich are private entrepreneurs and key individuals on the business side of filmmaking. These independent producers put all the financial and creative ingredients together, and unless they take a renegade route, they deal ultimately with one of the big distributors: Columbia, Paramount, 20th Century-Fox, United Artists, Universal, Orion, or Warner Brothers. The first stages of filmmaking—raising the money and shooting the picture within a reasonable cost—are of course tied into the majors, which function as both producers and directors. They usually become deeply involved in the financing, production, and sale of the independent producer's film, and the producer knows he will pay nicely for the studio's service in each area. Financing costs, and the costs of prints, advertising, interest, and other expenses are so great that they can never be far from his mind. Considering a project or a string of projects he must constantly be aware of market pressures and particularly the buyer side of this market. Each producer and distributor is poised and alert to buyer (audience) preferences and behavior. They are alert to details of gross receipts. They all pay attention to assets earned relative to liabilities incurred in the production, advertising, distribution, and exhibition of the project(s).

Second, the producer gambles for high stakes. A movie, if it is a blockbuster, can return a fortune. Most producers get a set fee plus a percentage of the profits for their efforts and it is in that percentage that fortunes can be made. There are concrete pressures to earn at least three times the initial expenses of producing the film. On a $4-million film, as Aldrich notes, the payoffs can be easily calculated. Start by counting gross receipts, net profits, and break-even points for the participants. On a string of projects, and here we get to the real gambling, a producer in the medium- to high-budget league has to hit it big in one out of four to avoid a softening of interest in him and his films. To stay in, to put it bluntly, he needs visible successes, just like everyone else in Hollywood. Without those market payoffs, potential backers with money will turn to other filmmakers; distributors will stop returning calls. Each producer feels the urgent pressure, and the nature of his business is to respond to such pressure.

The implications for freelancers are very clear. The inability of a producer to establish and then sustain a solid economic base during a sequence of projects results in sudden slackening in aggregate demand for freelancers. Whether caused by bad luck or poorly judged material, commercial failure can lead to the sudden severance of long-standing and tight bonds between a filmmaker and "his" composers, cinematographers, editors, art directors, screenwriters, and other specialists.

Aldrich and Frank DeVol continued their association in the Burt Reynolds and Catherine Deneuve film *Hustle* (1975) written by Steve Shagan. The dollars did not exactly roll back in from the theaters on this project either. The association between filmmaker and composer held together into the police melodrama *The Choirboys* (1977). The outcome was a disappointment for Aldrich made more difficult by the publicly acrimonious work relation with writer Joseph Wambaugh. The film was not the hit Aldrich and producer Merve Adelson hoped it would be. The next production was the big-budgeted and carefully advertised *Twilight's Last Gleaning* (1977). Jerry Goldsmith, rather than Frank DeVol, was chosen to score this film, an adventure in missiles, the military, and mighty politicians. Frank DeVol was passed over in favor of Goldsmith—probably the single most sought after composer in Hollywood. Despite all these precautions, the box-office figures were disappointing.

Fourth Example

In an interview, one composer noted the key role of strong ties: "The main thing is associations—that's the key. I sat down the other day with another composer, and we figured out that every successful composer has a producer who's his 'father.' You go right down the list." The list was composed of Henry Mancini, John Williams, Jerry Goldsmith, and Frank DeVol. They all enjoyed what could be called "steady associations." These associations had also paid off; the producer's projects were successful commercially and the freelancer's contribution was a part of that success. Their success together solidified their work relationship. He named one of the above composers. "For him, the producer will say, 'Nobody does my films except so-and-so.' That association has lasted for a while, and basically what it did was establish the composer. And if the producer is powerful, and has clout, and can get his way, then when he wants him, he gets him. 'Those are the conditions,' the producer says, and they get passed all the way down the line. The idea is to have contacts, success, and these kinds of steady associations." Tightly coupled ties with important filmmakers provide continuity and stability of credits as careers are launched, as both the composer and filmmaker *move together* from periphery to the center.

Access to a "better class" of producers and directors is in the career interest of composers, as noted by one of the top composers in the network (blocks III and IV) of Schifrin, Williams, Fielding, Jones, Legrand, and Shire. This freelancer compared himself to one of his favorite actors.

> I guess you'd have to classify me. I'm not a star but I'm in the same category as, I guess you'd say Robert Ryan. He's kind of *there,* and you know he's there, and you know he's good, and he's working all the time, and if you want that kind of thing, he's it—which is really

kind of a nice place to be. I have really not had any protracted period
of unemployment at all for a long, long time. I kind of like it the way
it is. The only thing that I don't like is now having to do auditions for
new people, new filmmakers who say, 'Well, what have you done?'—
to me! Or having to explain why I do what I do to younger producers,
to people who have no idea how it's done or what it's supposed to be.
That's why I try not to change groups so often. Everyone I've worked
with, the association has been a long-lasting one. I haven't had any of
that short, chaotic thing. I have a lot of good friends, and we kind of
appreciate one another and it's not all that bad.

It was not all that bad, given an impressive string of film credits, several
Academy Award nominations, and a handful of producers and directors who
always thought of him first for their projects. Their success together helped
both producer and composer in the business. Though this person disliked the
prima donnas and the plus-music boys, he also recognized the value of working
with talent just coming into the business. It was in his interest to spread
accounts and he did so in films and television. Moreover, a record of visible
accomplishments does not impart lasting prestige; if such a record is not
renewed continually by a composer it will lapse. As this person says of
himself, like the career line of Robert Ryan, "he's *there*." Presence. Because
there is no rational way of predicting which ties will pay off, the freelancer
spreads accounts, placing dependence on the collaborative partnerships while
minimizing the investment in a span of loosely coupled or nonrenewable
business associations. The tension between strong ties in the form of partnership and weak ties in the form of one-shot ties of convenience predisposes
the commercial composer to certain interdependencies, propensities, tendencies, and liabilities. The tension, indeed, shapes his character, one which is
both a response to and cause of the shifting quality of work transactions in
Hollywood.

Composer Jerry Fielding's career was one of alliances and visible accomplishments; he made incalculable contributions to the Hollywood music scene.
Until his death in February 1980, he was a Robert Ryan type of contributor.
He was always "*there*." He had presence. He was one of the more esteemed
and celebrated colleagues. With a combination of close working ties and a
modest span of nonrecurrent ties with filmmakers, Fielding had continually
stayed active in the market, and one factor in that continuity was his strong
ties. Particularly visible in his line are the relationships with director and
writer Sam Peckenpah and producers Martin Baum and Joe Wizan. Peckenpah
and Fielding worked on the following films: *The Wild Bunch* (1968), *Junior
Bonner* (1971), *Straw Dogs* (1971), *Bring Me the Head of Alfredo García*
(1973), and *Killer Elite* (1975). Fielding received Academy nominations for
The Wild Bunch and *Straw Dogs*. At the same time he worked for a variety

of producers in television, as well as scoring films for his associate Michael Winner—*Scorpio* (1978) and *The Big Sleep* (1978).

Fielding's association with producer Robert Daley and actor Clint Eastwood's Malpaso Productions was also important to his career. Daley preferred using the same crew on these Eastwood projects and specifically preferred the services of Fielding for these assignments.[21] Some of the composer's credits were his outstanding score for *Outlaw Josey Wales* (1975), another nomination for best score, *The Enforcer* (1976), Eastwood's third "Dirty Harry Callahan" film. These projects were followed by *The Gauntlet* (1977) and *Escape from Alcatraz* (1979), directed by Don Siegel.

In similar fashion, the career portfolio of Henry Mancini is simultaneously mixed with tightly and loosely coupled work associations. He scored several projects for Stanley Donen—*Two for the Road* (1967) and *Arabesque* (1966); for producer Mel Ferrer—*Wait until Dark* (1967) and *The Night Visitor* (1971); for Martin Ransohoff—*The White Dawn* (1974), *Silver Streak* (1976), and Arthur Hiller's *Nightwing* (1979); for producer Walter Mirisch—*The Hawaiians* (1969) and again, a decade later, *The Prisoner of Zenda* (1979). Along the way are credits for Stanley Kramer—*Oklahoma Crude* (1973); David Wolper—*Visions of Eight* (1973); John Foreman—*Sometimes a Great Notion* (1971); the musically knowledgeable producer and director George Roy Hill—*The Great Waldo Pepper* (1975); the productive filmmaker Howard W. Koch—*Once Is Not Enough* (1975); and *W. C. Fields and Me* (1976) produced by Jay Weston, a film that brought director Arthur Hiller and Mancini together for another project. Strings of connections such as these run through the *mutual* career biographies of some of the major figures producing and composing in Hollywood today. Diversity of ties also pays off. Asked if he has been typecast, Mancini said the following in a 1978 interview:

> Well, I was tied-in very closely, especially in the first five years, with Blake Edwards. Fortunately, we started with *Peter Gunn*. That was the big one. Then *Mr. Lucky* came on and that was a success. The next thing we did was *High Time*, which didn't make much of an impression on anybody. *Experiment in Terror*, however, was completely different from *Peter Gunn* and *Mr. Lucky* and that was a good thing for me to do at that time because it set up a whole different frame of reference. Then came *Breakfast at Tiffany's*, which was a romantic comedy, something I hadn't done before. Then *The Days of Wine and Roses* which was a very heavy drama. In the meantime, I'd done *Hatari* for Howard Hawks. So I didn't stay in one place long enough to get typed. As a result, I've had a pretty good cross-section of projects.[22]

David Grusin, also in block III, has had a good cross-section of projects and mix of business associations. He has strong ties to one of the most important film producers, Ray Stark: in 1970 with *The Owl and the Pussycat;* in 1975 with *Murder by Death;* in 1977 with *The Goodbye Girl;* and in 1979 with the Jane Fonda and Robert Redford film *Electric Horseman.* He has scored 30 or more features and has a diversity of styles in his career such as the score for Lawrence Turman's *The Graduate* (1967), Norman Lear's *Divorce American Style* (1967), Martin Melcher's *Where Were You When the Lights Went Out* (1968), and Hal Wallis's *Shootout* (1970).

Grusin's career has been tightly connected to the career of producer and director Sydney Pollack. They have worked together on *The Yakuza* (1975) with Robert Mitchum; *Three Days of the Condor* (1975); and *Bobby Deerfield* (1977) produced by John Foreman, with whom Grusin worked in 1968. He also scored Charles Joffe's *The Front* (1976), produced and directed by Martin Ritt. His other credits are also diverse. He scored television comedy and dramatic shows during the 1960s, scored feature films for some of the newer directors and producers breaking in, and during the mid-1970s, Grusin became a record producer, as well as recording artist, making one of the first direct-to-disk jazz albums released. He has scored films for Peter Yates, such as *The Friends of Eddie Coyle* (1973), worked for Franco Zeffirelli on *The Champ* (1979), and for director Norman Jewison in the Al Pacino film . . . *and Justice for All* (1979). Like colleagues Henry Mancini, Jerry Fielding, John Mandel, Fred Karlin, David Shire, Lawrence Rosenthal, and others he has a few stable, long-term ties and has not stayed in one place long enough to be typecast. He moves across projects and across "product lines"—such as comedy, drama, adventure. With these strong and long-term associations he moves along with filmmakers who keep active and visible in the Hollywood market.

Next to Grusin in the matrix is Boris (Lalo) Schifrin. Here is a composer with credits, credibility, and industry recognition. He began writing for films in his native Buenos Aires, soon went on the road with Dizzy Gillespie's Quintet (1960–63), got a start in Hollywood at Wolper Productions, and then did some substantial television work. He won several Grammys—couple for his breakthrough television show *Mission Impossible,* one for *Jazz Mass* with Paul Horn, and one for an album, *The Cat.* Oscar nominations include *The Amityville Horror* (1979) with director Stuart Rosenberg and producers Ronald Saland and Samuel Arkoff, *The Fox* (1968) directed by friend and collaborator Mark Rydell, and *Cool Hand Luke* (his score was a major contribution to that 1967 Rosenberg project). He worked with Rosenberg again on *Voyage of the Damned* (1977), produced by Robert Fryer and written by Steven Shagan.

Schifrin has over 70 movie credits, nearly 50 of them during the 1964–77 period. Among those credits are *Golden Needles* (1974) and *Enter the Dragon* (1973) with producers Fred Weintraub and Paul Heller; *The Beguiled* (1970) with producer and director Don Siegel, executive producer Jennings Lang, and star Clint Eastwood; *Carley Varrick* (1973) with Siegel as filmmaker again; the highly innovative and successful *Bullitt* (1968) produced by Robert Relyea and directed by Peter Yates, a film that made over $19 million. Schifrin then scored *Dirty Harry* (1971) produced by Robert Daley and directed by Don Siegel. The sequel, *Magnum Force,* was released two years later by Daley and Eastwood's Malpaso Company, this time directed by Ted Post. This film also neared the $20 million plateau. He also teamed up with director Siegel again on the political thriller *Telefon* (1977), scored the British released *Escape to Athena* (1979), and worked with producer Jennings Lang for two Universal releases: *Nunzio* and *Rollercoaster.*

On the surface at least, interdependent alliances between composers and producers and directors resemble our usual image of "coalitions." In a freelance work world in which loosely coupled ties predominate, recurrent work associations stand out. Here is a partial list:

- Henry Mancini and Blake Edwards.
- Jerry Fielding and the Robert Daley and Clint Eastwood group.
- Fred Karlin and Alan J. Pakula: *Up the Down Staircase* (1967), *Stalking Moon* (1968), and *The Sterile Cuckoo* (1969).
- Michael Small and Alan J. Pakula: *Klute* (1971), *The Parallax View* (1974), and *Comes a Horseman* (1978).
- Bernard Herrmann and Alfred Hitchcock: *The Trouble with Harry* (1955), *The Man Who Knew Too Much* (1956), *The Wrong Man* (1957), *Vertigo* (1958), *North by Northwest* (1959), and *Psycho* (1960).
- Miklos Rozsa and Billy Wilder: *The Private Life of Sherlock Holmes* (1970), *Fedora* (1979), and others.
- Ernest Gold and Stanley Kramer: *On the Beach* (1960), *Judgement at Nuremberg* (1961), *It's a Mad Mad Mad Mad World* (1963), *Ship of Fools* (1965), and *The Runner Stumbles* (1979).
- John Mandel and Hal Ashby: *The Last Detail* (1973) and *Being There* (1980).
- Stu Phillips and Glen Larson: *Buck Rogers* (1979) and numerous television productions in the late 1970s.
- John Morris and Mel Brooks: *Blazing Saddles* (1974), *Silent Movie* (1976), and *High Anxiety* (1977).
- John Barry and producer Albert R. Broccoli: The *James Bond* films.
- Carmine Coppola and Francis Coppola: *Apocalypse Now* (1979) and *The Godfather Part II* (1974) with Nino Rota.
- John Williams and Irwin Allen: *Poseidon Adventure* (1972) and *Towering Inferno* (1974).

Fifth Example

The middle submatrix indicates eight ties connecting freelancers Frank DeVol, Gerald Fried, Jimmy Haskell, Charles Bernstein, and Fred Karger to producers in the second block or row. As noted in the third example the alliances between Robert Aldrich and Fried and DeVol are a dominant feature of network II. The network has a relatively open structure, not as closely knit as blocks III and IV. The volume of credits among these associates in block II is robust with eight ties producing over thirty films, due to the recurrent work relationships among these filmmakers and freelancers. Here are some of those projects, described in terms of their genre, production values, and Hollywood participants.

Composer Jimmy Haskell and producer A. C. Lyles have a work relationship extending back to a couple of Rory Calhoun westerns, *Black Spurs* (1964) and *Apache Uprising* (1965) directed by R. G. Springsteen. These films were followed by *Fort Utah* (1967); Springsteen's *Red Tomahawk* (1967) with Howard Keel, Joan Caulfield, and Broderick Crawford; *Hostile Guns* (1967); and another Howard Keel vehicle *Arizona Bushwhacker* (1968) with a good veteran cast, a weak plot, and the voice of James Cagney as narrator. Haskell and Lyles also worked on the Rory Calhoun and Janet Leigh film, *Night of the Lepus* (1972), in which an Arizona ranch is overrun with dangerous rabbits.

Composer Haskell scored the Arthur Gardner and Jules Levy production *The Honkers* (1971), a James Coburn and Slim Pickens saga about wild bulls and rodeo performers. Haskell later scored *Joyride* and *Deathgame* in the late 1970s. Gardner and Levy went on to the highly successful *White Lightning* (1973) with Burt Reynolds and Ned Beatty, directed by Joseph Sargent. Composer Charles Bernstein scored that film and then received several other assignments in this genre. Bernstein's credits include *Hex* (1973), *That Man Bolt* (1973), *Mr. Majestyk* (1974), *Gator* (1975), *A Small Town in Texas* (1975), *Trackdown* (1975), *Outlaw Blues* (1977) with producers Fred Weintraub and Paul Heller, *Viva Knievel* (1977), and his successful score for producer Mel Simon's *Love at First Bite* (1979). He scored *Foolin' Around* in 1980.

In another tightly coupled association, composer Fred Karger worked for Elvis Presley and Colonel Parker at one point, and then for the prolific producer of low-budget films, Sam Katzman. Katzman's money makers range from *Rock around the Clock,* to *Hootnanny Hoot,* to a gangster musical, *Calypso Heat Wave* (1957), and *Don't Knock the Twist.*[23] Karger scored these films and worked almost exclusively for Katzman during the twelve years. He also scored the Presley feature *Harum Scarum* (1965) as well as the Katzman remake of Judy Garland-Mickey Rooney musical *Girl Crazy* (1965). *The Fastest Guitar Alive* (1967) came next, with *Riot on Sunset Strip* (1967) and *The Love-Ins* and *Hot Rods to Hell* in the same year. Karger also scored *For Singles Only* and *Angel, Angel Down We Go* (1969). Producer Katzman turned them out quickly depending on ties to a relatively small core of art directors, directors, cameramen, and song writers.[24] Once a working relationship was strongly established, his loyalty was as tight as the music budget, a quality he shares with other Kings of the Budget features. When Katzman left the filming scene, Karger's productivity faded somewhat, an indication of the effect of strong or recurrent work ties on careers. This also indicates the effect, particularly the possible negative effect, a composer must always consider in developing strong ties to the exclusion of diversified ties. Film-makers' careers are, after all, precarious too.

When American International Pictures' Samuel Z. Arkoff sensed a trend, he moved in fast, often with several films. During the sixties to roughly the mid-seventies, Arkoff and his associate James H. Nicholson, and until 1970 Roger Corman, churned out numerous formula productions on medium budgets. They captured the youth market and developed a formula, a standardized recipe, for combining the ingredients of action, horror, sex, and social message. From about 1964 to 1965 a sort of cottage industry flourished around the "bikini" youth sagas. A line of movies starring Frankie Avalon, Annette Funicello, and Dwayne Hickman, with supporting roles occasionally played by Fabian and Connie Stevens, rolled off the American International assembly line. William Asher was the screenwriter and director for many of these movies, including the prototype *Bikini Beach* (1964). Songs and arrangements were often written by Jerry Styner, and the composer was Les Baxter. Free-lancer Baxter, like his colleague Fred Karger, piled up a string of credits in a very short time; all the films and scores were within a single genre and most were done for the same producer. Baxter kept busy with *Pajama Party* (1964), *Beach Blanket Bingo* (1964), *How to Stuff a Wild Bikini* (1965), and *The Ghost in the Invisible Bikini* (1965). Arkoff followed up with *Fireball 500* (1969), in which the beach kids end up at the stock-car races, and then the *Dunwich Horror* (1970), in which Sandra Dee and Dean Stockwell move through "black masses" and "demonic rituals." The *Dunwich Horror* was directed by Daniel Haller, Roger Corman's art director on many AIP and New World pictures, a company Corman founded in 1970. Both Corman and Arkoff typically hired directors, composers, and other craft personnel with no previous film credits. Most of these associations were one-shot and non-recurrent. Several young directors said Corman gave them the chance to make their movies. And while Corman did not pay them much money, they admit, no one else was going to give them the chance to make a film.[25]

"We really don't have a great deal of money to spend," Corman said recently speaking about his new production company, "although currently we're spending more money than we did a while ago. Now if we were to hire a veteran director at the money we have to get a director, the chances are we would not get a top director. But we can go with a new director, gamble on his talent and on my ability to recognize his talent and to work with him, and I have the chance of having another Peter Bogdanovich, Francis Coppola, Marty Scorsese, whatever. So I have more of a chance for a break-through picture."[26]

Asked how he maintains the quality of his productions given budget resources and time constraints, Corman said he picks the best writers, the best directors, and the best actors available under the given circumstances, and in low-budget films, this selection has often led to new directors. He believes that a veteran filmmaker should be doing more important work if he's really good. ''A veteran who is working on B pictures after thirty years might be very competent, and probably is—otherwise he wouldn't be working at all— but what he will give you will be a competent B picture.'' Corman has always looked for the B picture, but one that is better than run-of-the-mill B films: ''One with some spark that will lift it out of its bracket. And that's why . . . the Coppolas . . . and so forth.''[27]

The implications are clear. First, the track record for beginners or first-time directors has been very good to producer Corman. Second, strong producers with relatively modest budgets prefer working with pliable and talented tyros than with central figures. Third, that material pitched to the teen market, as many of these films are, demands younger, in-tune directors. And finally, the ''top 10,'' most sought-after directors are usually tied up with their own projects and cost a fortune as well, which forces people like Corman to look elsewhere. As one producer said in an interview, ''You go through the ritual of checking with the top directors in town, and you discover that they're deeply committed to fifteen projects in development, so you're forced by the situation of the marketplace to look at the new kids on the block.''

Producer Arkoff has explained the ties to young talent. He believes that his enterprise took more chances on young, smart, and tasteful filmmakers than any other company in Hollywood, and Arkoff did it to some degree, not simply because these directors were less expensive, but because his company felt they had something to say. He claims that it was important for a company like his to have something to say to the young people who were going to the pictures.[28] Bike films, psychedelic films, the Poe thrillers, and teen market material appear across a wide span of projects developed by Arkoff and Corman. Singly or together, their volume of work is impressive, and it projects for new talent: *Tales of Terror, The Pit and the Pendulum, Comedy of Terrors, The Raven, Mask of the Red Death,* and the successful Corman-directed *Bucket of Blood,* along with *The Wild Angels, Wild in the Streets,* the Jack Nicholson-written *The Trip,* and Corman's New World Pictures such as *Caged Heat, Night Call Nurses, The Student Teachers,* and the hit *Deathsport* (1978), earlier titled *Death Race* starring David Carradine, with music by Andrew Stein. This futuristic science-fiction gladiator picture ran only 83 minutes, cost approximately half a million dollars, and has grossed worldwide about $7 million.

A striking feature of this network is the very small proportion of ties to the most productive film composers. Arkoff has over a dozen films during the twelve years and Corman about the same number, but the majority of work goes to composers who earn their first credit in Hollywood or an AIP or New World Picture projects. This is in keeping with the structured interests of producers with relatively modest resources and many alternatives. Obviously, these producers get the talent they want without going to the services of the central figures of the composing world. Corman advises his directors to ask the following questions of their cinematographers when setting up a scene: "How long will it take to make it excellent? How long will it take to make it good? How long will it take to get an image?" The third option is highly preferred. The same principle might apply to the selection of the composer and it is certainly the imperative under which he works—"How long will it take to get some music on the sound track?"

Sixth Example

To survive, a freelancer must be urgently concerned about his position within Hollywood as a network of connections, and experience teaches him to envision that scene as a configuration of specific people joined to one another by working relationships and the products that are the result of those relationships. With time and more points in a line of activity, composers, directors, and other freelancers trying to make intelligent choices about possible career options will discriminate several types of ties linking them to others. They develop a sophisticated sense of long- and short-term success for they know that freelancers linked with successful films are themselves more valuable than those associated with an equal or even greater number of less successful projects. They also know that it is important to be tied to important film producers and directors, and that not all filmmakers and projects will endure in the long run.

We mentioned film director and producer Don Siegel in connection with his ties to composer Lalo Schifrin, and a final example illustrates his thoughts and those of another filmmaker about the long run and the short run. There are no formulas for success, Siegel implies, but the outlines of a career strategy are clear.

"There's a game involved in being successful in Hollywood," Siegel said in an interview, "but I never learned how to play it."[29] This will come as a surprise to fans of his cult classics, such as the 1956 *Invasion of the Body Snatchers, Riot In Cell Block 11,* and the sensational *Dirty Harry.* He talked about gambling on people and the importance of building alliances and connections in Hollywood's networks. "I never even knew what the game was. I was and still am naive. Around 1957–58, a young actor sent me a script that he wanted to star in and could arrange the financing for. His name was Robert Evans. How could I know that in a few years he would become one of the most powerful moguls in the industry? But if you're going to spend your life in this town and have a successful career," he said, "you should have instincts about such things. You should know them intuitively. It can help you play the angles, and not only save you years of your career, but even give you the career."

Whether one arrives at it intuitively or by a shrewd assessment of the odds, the conclusion is the same: a little gambling spirit is necessary to survive in Hollywood. Also, you never know who is going to make it and become a high roller. This keeps everyone attuned to how others are doing in the race for access and success. And the behavior a freelancer adopts in order to adjust consists in behavior meant to secure diverse connections to secure leverage. In Hollywood the long run is a succession of short runs. As one composer on the move puts it, "Recently I've worked with some of the younger people, some of the young filmmakers. Now some of those projects have been small projects, intimate films with a not too terribly large budget. But I believe in those films. I've enjoyed *that kind* of work also in addition to the larger films. After all, these young filmmakers may become the Stanley Kramers, the Francis Coppolas, and the Irwin Allens of tomorrow."

Diversity and Uniformity

The six examples and supportive data on career attributes by network in Table 8.4 suggest that the film industry was bullish for some and bearish for others in the 1970s and 1980s. A few central figures are at the top of the list for the more costly film productions; some composers are further down the list, and others totally "zeroed out." What I have called the "skewing" of business toward the hits—and the people who worked on those commercial successes—pushes some freelancers into central consideration, into positions of leverage, onto career plateaus which provide recognition and resources.

The six examples and matrix suggest patterned differences between networks but also individual differences even among composers within the same network. Those in the "big leagues" are in a different position compared to those who may indeed be productive in terms of credits but only narrowly tied to others. Composers with a relatively wide span of accounts acquire valuable experience working with a variety of producers and directors in different environments under different sources of financing, and on different types of films, from the offbeat to the conventional. A growing span of accounts may appear to increase career risk, but it also builds potentially useful associations for the long run, for the future. The freelancer knows Hollywood is dynamic and that it creates uncertainties on a project-to-project basis. Since new faces and work opportunities continually arise, there is pressure for composers to stabilize these uncertainties to protect what they have and increase their advantages. The attempts of these people to build long-run stable coalitions is one mark of careerism and "playing the game" (as seen in examples 4 and 6). Ties to a wide range of employers present other, usually short-run advantages. Formal and informal contact with a range of current "moguls," rising stars, and "might have beens," offers an equal range of information, and this allows the composer to know his work environment better than more narrowly linked freelancers do. The liability is this: if a freelancer knows the shifts in fads and preferences among a variety of employers, he may chase after this information and frequently change his activity in response to the demands of these potential and actual employers. The composer may then find himself buried in the "Hollywood game," working too much on projects that eat away at his distinctive abilities. The behavior he adopts in order to adjust may consist entirely in behavior meant to secure recognition. This is why careerism, Hollywood style, has its source entirely in other people. When a composer fits into the temporary judgments of others, and does so with success, this adaptation can be costly. It can be costly because connections and recognition in the short run might deteriorate or disappear leaving the composer stranded with loyalties that are liabilities and a reputation that is narrow and outmoded.

Like everything else in the film business, centrality depends on the co-existence of diametrically opposed features. At best, increasing work moves the freelancer deeper into a diversified market. At worst, more credits push the composer into a string of successive, nonrecurrent ties. The freelancer's ability to keep active on the market and accumulate credentials in a hurry is related to his ability to keep his performances fresh, to generate renewed energy and enthusiasm, and avoid the rut that can be formed by several years of writing the same kinds of film scores for the same kinds of films with the same kinds of film producers. He needs to keep moving. The composers need some choice and the chance to be associated with a variety of films, but such choice and opportunity always carry the risk that the string of films may flop, the projects may not be intrinsically challenging, and the support personnel may be less than first-rate (as suggested by example 5).

A wide span of ties may appear to offer some career insurance, but it can equally easily dissolve into an indiscriminate mix of films and undistinguished filmmakers in a kind of promiscuous careerism. But the obvious advantages of recurrent work ties are also balanced by liabilities. The composer may fit into a niche and experience success, and this can be costly. The most obvious liability for the composer is the likelihood of being typecast and trapped in a limited range of work. The pairing itself may also be dangerous. Such a stable relationship may be unable to survive a line of commercial flops; it may even prevent the individuals from coming up with novel solutions to both commercial and artistic challenges (as suggested in example 3). Such limitations may have more than artistic implications. As the freelancer works more and more with fewer and fewer producers, people with whom he is comfortable, he quite naturally works less and less with employers he may find difficult, indeed nearly impossible to deal with. But in the long run they might well turn out to be profitable and successful business associates or partners.

By comparing the career attributes in Table 8.5 and by looking at examples 1 and 5, I have shown that only some sets of employers and employees enjoy a solid business mix of recurrent and nonrecurrent ties across important films and successful film producers. It is such a mix of ties that pays off in reputation, recognition, and resources, as shown in the profile of network III and IV and examples 1 and 2. Freelancers do not develop such a mix at their leisure; each composer has an urgent and immediate need for recognition and rewards. The earlier qualitative materials suggest that such centrality in Hollywood is subjectively important for many freelancers and that the anxiety and pressured feelings of these people can be attributed to the distinct pressures of commercialism. But that is only part of the story. Freelancers have to keep moving both in terms of artistic development and *relative* market position. The whole scene moves quickly and composers know that they have to attain visible credentials in a very short period of time or else they will lose position in relation to their colleague competitors. Thus freelance employees may be ambitious and envious not merely to get to the top, but also because they know that continued access to producers and preferred projects is the only route to status attainment and career centrality, which is the only sort of security available to them. Diversification, they report in interviews, tends to reduce some career risks by spreading work investments through chains of filmmakers (as illustrated in examples 2 and 6). Composers know that fluctuations in the economic fortunes of filmmakers can affect their own promotion chances and recognize that diversification of accounts helps them ride out the cycles and changing preferences for freelancers. Multiple ties protect a composer's career portfolio, because at any given time it is unlikely that all the employers he works for will be affected by such sudden shifts of fortune.

The problems of career continuity and network centrality are compounded by the fact that it is not only the freelance market—an internal labor market—which is turbulent but the entire industry environment. The more dynamic the movie maker, and the more the film industry turns toward the big-budget production, the more a handful of top films and filmmakers capture the audience market, and the more narrow filmmakers' choice of freelancers is likely to become. As producers' resources increase, their alternatives decrease. As their alternatives narrow with box-office munificence and financial success, they will hire only a select subset of composers. Successful careers are forged out of a combination of strong and recurrent ties with successful and prestigious filmmakers leading to industry dominance and centrality. Career success is at least momentarily enjoyed by a small number of favored freelancers. The market and hiring situation, however, are never static. Career or status attainment presents a paradox of very active individual struggle and surprisingly uniform and persistent results. Freelancers struggle and social organization endures. This is possible because, while each freelancer actively comes to terms with the changing hiring situation before him, employers provide the schedule and volume of options (job opportunities), connections, and market choices upon which to draw just in order to realize one's self-interest. Each person is affected by the resources and alternatives of others. Careers are interdependent. Each absorbs these experiences as part of his career socialization; and each person crafts these market events and personal experiences in a way that suits his particular style and ambitions. From an inside perspective, this gives the impression of diversity and selectivity.

Only some sets of buyers (film producers) and sellers (composers) occupy positions of centrality in Hollywood. The correlates of success are clear. Where strong ties are highly concentrated, freelancers have low to moderate success. Where weak ties are widely spread across filmmakers, freelancers are likely to have moderate to high resources, continuity, and status attainment. Where both strong and weak ties are moderately dispersed across networks of filmmakers, those freelancers will dominate their networks and the industry. From an outside perspective, this gives the impression of network uniformity and persistence.

Both inside and outside perspectives are right. Diversity and uniformity occur together. Freelancing is a loosely organized structure of work activities.[30] An unchanging social structure, with a highly skewed distribution of resources, may well be essential to a loosely organized and changing population of freelancers and employers. Big Hollywood's distinct networks crystallize out of a persistent pattern of hiring when particular buyers of expertise and talent (filmmakers), with given schedules of resources and alternatives, settle into self-reproducing business transactions with distinct (and small) sets of sellers (film composers).

Notes

1. More generally, "client choices are a form of social control. They determine the survival of a profession or a specialty, as well as the *career success of particular professionals*" (my italics). William J. Goode, "Community within a Community: The Professions" *American Sociological Review* 23 (1957): 194–200. See also James Coleman, "Notes on the Study of Power" in Roland J. Leibert and Allen W. Immershein (eds.), *Power, Paradigms, and Community Research* (Beverly Hills: Sage, 1977).

2. Freelance hiring is loosely organized in these three respects so that it can adapt to continuous change in a turbulent mass market for movies. This is a structural accomodation much like that of the construction industry and other lines of work

222   MUSIC ON DEMAND

as described by Arthur L. Stinchcombe. See his "Bureaucratic and Craft Administration of Production," *Administrative Science Quarterly* 4 (1959): 168–87; and id., *Constructing Social Theories* (Harcourt, Brace, & World, 1968), pp. 258–64.

3. Charles A. Barrett, "Agent Says Music Writers Should Get Needed Pay Boost," *The Hollywood Reporter* (June 1, 1979).
4. Paul Baratta, "A Closeup on Film Scoring," *Songwriter* (December 1977).
5. "Verna Fields: Dialogue on Film," *American Film* 1 (1976): 47–48.
6. Paul M. Hirsch, "Processing Fads and Fashions: An Organization-Set Analysis of Cultural Industry Systems," *American Journal of Sociology* 77 (1972): 639–59.
7. Demand for top-tier composers is likely to be inelastic where (1) a project's outlay for music is relatively small, in comparision to the overall budget; (2) where want for valued and qualified candidates is urgent; (3) where equivalent substitutes are unavailable and/or undesirable; and (4) where the freelancer and producer are jointly linked to the success of the total film. Thus there are advantages to hiring selected professionals in the technical and artistic subsystems. Inelasticity of demand is influenced by uncertainty in market outcomes, information impactedness, and ignorance of the relations of cause (film score) and effect (success of film).
8. Greg Kilday, "A New Direction for Hal Ashby," *Los Angeles Times* (May 8, 1978).
9. "Robert Towne: Dialogue on Film: *American Film* 1 (1975): 33–48.
10. n.a., "Williams Takes Over as Boston Pops Conductor," *Daily Variety* (January 11, 1980).
11. The general logic, concrete procedures, and substantive importance of block-models are well established and need no extended discussion here. See the useful "Constructing Blockmodels: How and Why," by Phipps Arabie, Scott A. Boorman, and Paul R. Levitt in *Journal of Mathematical Psychology* 17 (1978): 21–63. Another article that stresses that the criterion for lumping individuals into the same block is a consistency idea, not a connectivity idea, is Ronald L. Breiger and Scott A. Boorman's "An Algorithm for Clustering Relational Data with Applications to Social Network Analysis and Comparison with Multidimensional Scaling," *Journal of Mathematical Psychology* 12 (1975): 328–83.
12. In applying the CONCOR hierarchical clustering algorithm, we use just the presence of a tie (one or more projects) to locate the clustering of points. Recurrent work (two or more film projects) between the *pair* (producer and composer) is simply entered into the matrix after the technique has been run on the raw or unordered array of ties. Thus, one or more projects are designated "1" in the appropriate cell; this prepares the raw matrix for partitioning.
13. The idea of permuting the rows and columns of a $m \times n$ matrix to reveal a desired structure or hidden pattern—a kind of rendering order from chaos—has a long history in archaeology (incidence matrices for hundreds of objects found in hundreds of prehistoric graves), in ecology (incidence matrices of the presence or absence of particular species at a particular site), and in political economy and elite networks (incidence matrices of interlocking boards of directors of major American banks and corporations). The freelance system of Hollywood, like other craft modes of production, is ripe for this kind of partitioning: (1) the active population of the industry is built up from project to project; and (2) the matrix facilitates

direct inferences concerning the coupling of ties (recurrent or nonrecurrent), the span of ties across employers (narrow or wide), and the connectedness of networks (close-knit or loose-knit).

14. Contrast between the networks or blocks of action is directly inferred from the overall distribution of the "O's" and "1's" denoting the absence or presence of ties. An image matrix can be constructed where an "O" in the image corresponds to a zeroblock and a "1" corresponds to a submatrix containing a mean number of ties above the grand mean. The grand mean for the entire m x n matrix is .08.

15. Density is defined as the number of ties within a submatrix divided by the number of possible entries in that submatrix. The upper-left corner of Figure 8.2, dominated by composer Jerry Goldsmith, has a density of .23 = 34/147. There are 34 binary ties and 7 composers x 21 producers. Ten of the submatrices with a predominance of empty spaces—and few connections between producers and composers—are off the "stacked" and relatively active main diagonal. The five submatrices in the lower-left and left-hand side of the matrix show a total of only 13 connections between filmmakers and freelancers. The sum total of film projects is only 13. This is a lean set of work associations.

16. This does not mean that I have revealed a hierarchy of networks, only that the majority of transactions are loosely knit along the principal diagonal. I call the structure "loosely knit" because less than all possible interconnections in the submatrix actually appear. Without comparative studies of other industries and their occupations, we have no firm empirical grounds for expecting higher densities among employers and employees in craft modes of production. The transactions are nevertheless loosely coupled, for ties are characterized by nonrecurrence, or "impermanence" and "dissolvability." See Karl Weick's "Education Organizations as Loosely Coupled Systems," *Administrative Science Quarterly* 21 (1976): 1–19. Moreover, most intuitive notions of the strength of ties between freelancer and filmmaker should be satisfied by the following definition: The strength of a tie is a combination of the frequency of interaction, the level of trust, the emotional intensity, and the reciprocal resources and services which characterize the tie. See Mark S. Granovetter, "The Strength of Weak Ties," *American Journal of Sociology* 78 (1973): 1360–80. Weaker ties have limits on the claims that can be made on them, but they also tend to provide indirect access to a greater diversity of resources than do strong ties.

17. Harrison C. White, "Markets as Stages for Producers," Structural Analysis Programme, Working Paper Series No. 11 (University of Toronto, 1980).

18. A. D. Murphy, "Showbiz' Optimism Must Yield to Hard Evidence of Experience," *Daily Variety* (June 27, 1980).

19. Marshall Berges, "Carol and Jerry Goldsmith," *Los Angeles Times Home Magazine* (September 19, 1976). See also Tony Thomas, *Music for the Movies* (New York: A. S. Barnes, 1973), pp. 208–14; and Irwin Bazelon, *Knowing the Score: Notes on Film Music* (New York: Van Nostrand Reinhold, 1975), pp. 188–92.

20. Robert Aldrich, "I can't get Jimmy Carter to see my movie," *Film Comment* (March-April 1977): 46–52.

21. Frank Barron, "Malpaso Prods. Mulling Next Production Projects," *Hollywood Reporter* (June 16, 1979).

22. Chuck Berg, "Henry Mancini: Sounds in the Dark," *Downbeat* (December 7, 1978).

23. Todd McCarthy and Charles Flynn (eds.), *Kings of the Bs: Working within the*

Hollywood System (New York: E. P. Dutton, 1975). See especially R. Staehling, "From *Rock around the Clock* to *The Trip:* The Truth about Teen Movies"; and Linda Strawn, "Samuel Arkoff."

24. Richard Thompson, "Sam Katzman: Jungle Sam, or, The Return of 'Poetic Justice, I'd Say,'" in McCarthy and Flynn.
25. *Robert Corman: Hollywood's Wild Angel* (documentary), Christian Blackwood, Blackwood Productions, New York.
26. Ibid. Marshall Berges, "Julie and Robert Corman," *Los Angeles Times Home Magazine* (October22, 1978).
27. Charles Flynn and Todd McCarthy, "Roger Corman," in McCarthy and Flynn, pp. 309–10.
28. Interview with Samuel Arkoff, "The New Hollywood," National Public Radio (Fall 1979); Marshall Berges, "Hilda and Samuel Arkoff," *Los Angeles Home Magazine* (July 22, 1979).
29. Bernard Drew, "The Man Who Paid His Dues," *American Film* 3 (1978): 22–27.
30. The organizational structure of work activities is inversely associated with market turbulence. Paul R. Lawrence and Jay W. Lorsch, *Organization and Environment* (Cambridge: Harvard University Press, 1967); Richard A. Peterson and David G. Berger, "Entrepreneurship in Organizations: Evidence from the Popular Music Industry," *Administrative Science Quarterly* 16 (1971): 97–106.

9.
THE CHOSEN FEW
Selectivity and Career as Retrospective Success

Being in demand means that I can be just a little more choosy about what I will do and what I will not do. I've had the good fortune to be associated with a couple of very successful projects and to be asked to work by some very productive and talented filmmakers.

—Inner-circle freelancer

A career in this town? You have to go past it before you can understand it.

—Inner-circle freelancer

Settling for More

Resources circle in on a chosen few. Those few are in a competitive demand position because they have the connections, knowledge, skills, and experience to capture top dollar. This track record makes them valuable to producers but the composers do not regard all producers and projects offered them of equal value. They can make choices. They can be selective.

These selections continue to be difficult, despite the fact that their increased visibility and market worth draws employers to them. Cause and effect relations are uncertain. A busy freelancer cannot know beforehand what will bring off a successful result, because there is no simple set of invariant means that can insure a desired effect on his career line.[1] He draws upon a residue of past experience, intuition, or relies upon chance and guesswork. Facing a market full of uncertainty, the freelancer will try to hedge his bets. He will select projects he feels comfortable and "at home" with, and so tend to choose filmmakers he defines as good collaborators or partners. He also knows it is wise to work on a variety of projects and accept new and different challenges.

To strengthen his comparative advantage over colleague competitors, there are market reasons and symbolic rewards in working with someone who is powerful and well connected. Thus the problem of which work to take and which to turn down becomes a luxury and a key problem. Choice is highly contextual, depending on the dramatic values of the film, the blend of personalities between himself and the filmmakers, the money he can squeeze out of the producer, the terms his agent reaches, time allotted for composing and recording, and so forth. The relevance of getting access to better films and filmmakers tests the composer's judgment about whether anything at the end of the project promises to alter those circumstances for the better. Having more projects to choose from broadens prospects for both success and failure—that is the luxury and complexity of being in demand.

Film work is not a situation of clearly anticipated outcomes. Provision has to be made for the circumstances under which a man's hopes for a film fail. We should distinguish what a freelancer does from the conventional view wherein an option or choice point arises, is noted by the person on the market, analyzed for its properties, and then a decision is made and implemented with some clear expectancies about the outcome. But in the Hollywood market competing options arise simultaneously, clear prediction of market success is impossible, the properties of the project are rarely apparent until the work is completed, and future reactions of others can transform the composer and his circumstances.

Control over work is conditional, is not an either/or phenomenon. It is made up of more-or-lesses, of degrees, generally small degrees at that. Whether one can successfully forecast these beforehand becomes something of an art in Hollywood—all wish they had the touch, many claim they have it under some conditions, but only a few seem to be in a position to successfully exercise it. At best, increased demand by filmmakers gives one some flexibility to avoid certain activities. Hollywood culture is full of proverbs, jokes, and partially formulated plans of ideal action centering around the importance of saying "No." The occasions of their use draw attention to what freelancers desire, what they are having to deal with on a day-to-day basis, and the frequent gap between the two.

As we have seen, freelancers vary greatly in their power to be selective. Those just starting out in episodic television have to take anything and everything they are offered just to get a toehold in the industry's work. Peers often provide that opening shot and contact with important others. They alert him to the nuances of his occupation, teach him his duties, and give him the opportunities to learn his craft. In return for his willingness and commitment to the job, they must protect him from his own mistakes, run interference between him and the studio brass, assume responsibility for his work if he errs in good faith, and, if things go well, actively recommend him to television filmmakers, heads of music, and other colleagues. Of all the freelancers, these entrants into the system exercise the least selectivity of all because they are in the weakest competitive position. Not only are they open to any kind of assignment, but they are often the recipients of busier composers' requests to "ghost" for them. They are delegated the dirty work left behind as budgets run out, time runs short, or as their busier colleagues find themselves committed to doing too much work. It is this unselected influx of work and demands that a new composer in town receives. He is asked to help, and being new at the business, is happy to do anything he can get his hands on. Cues from television episodes that are infra dig to those at the top are prized assignments.

As newcomers move from the periphery deeper into the network of colleagues, peers, and clients, they still have to endure projects and people they have no hand in selecting. They have little selective power. At the next career stage they are known personally by filmmakers and move from the protective wing of their sponsors. They work one-on-one with producers, try to develop long-term or repeated relationships with them so that they can move up in the allocation of work. But compared to those composers sought by major producers for high budget and prestige films, they still have very limited power of selection and must resign themselves to dealing with many television producers while paying their dues on episodes in hopes of getting their own pilot or show.

In the inner circle colleagues are highly visible not only to one another but to their prospective clientele, and are therefore capable of attracting clients by establishing a reputation in the film industry as competent practitioners, as men with proven "track records." Because they are in demand their perspectives on selectivity are most important. Their inside perspectives are suggestively different from conventional outside views. To the outsider, those who are winning in film composer circles are winning big. They seem to have the pick of the best films available. The top thirteen freelancers seem to do everything right. They are in demand. Their films make money, their record albums sell, and they have magic. Seen from afar, say from the stance of a newcomer in the industry, those in demand have abundant choices. One might even construct a theory about how they got there. Many do. In so doing it might appear that what has happened was intended, even inevitable, and at all times planned. It is this career selectivity—as against the "take it as it comes" of the less fortunate—that "explains" to the outsider why one composer gets a shot at a film that costs $11 million to make and grosses nearly $200 million; why that freelancer then goes on to work for the same producer on yet another blockbuster, and, why, out of the last five releases scored by a top-league composer, two have been nominated for Academy Awards.

But from the inside looking out, what appear as abundant choices and selections are, to the composer experiencing it, difficult and complex choices. Seen from the perspective of those who are winning, the chance of projecting into a definite future is problematic. Some have better judgment than others; but there is no surefire method. Luck, chance, determination, saying "yes" at the right time, avoiding saying "no" at the wrong time—all these are offered, at times reluctantly, as keys to the top. Living on the edge of the business is one thing, making it work for you at the top is another. But whether one is breaking in, languishing in the middle levels, or thriving in the "big leagues," the freelancer is still obliged to expend resources and choices on maintaining himself from project to project. There is no formula. "I can be sort of selective now," is ultimately a statement about the complexity and ambiguity of his own circumstances.

"When you're hot, you're hot," goes the old saying. The next composer is hot. He is the fastest riser into the top ranks with twelve films in four years and an impressive string of work with three of the best filmmakers in Hollywood. My interviews with him over a period of years give us his perspective. In the summer of 1972, when he was in his mid-thirties and had been moving up the television ladder for about three years, he saw himself then as consolidating his efforts to get out of episodic television and into feature films. He was well connected, a close friend of a powerful young producer, and well acquainted with several other talented men who had come of age with him in the business. By the end of 1973 he had done some choice Movies of the Week, but more importantly for him, had completed two features. By 1975 his first hopes had come true. In that year he took on what he called "a special, little film" produced and directed by his close friend and associate. They worked well together and arrived at a brilliant film score. The project was a critical success bringing the composer directly to the attention of some knowledgeable film producers, one a former music editor and acknowledged "music nut." Thus, his third film was with a filmmaker who appreciated, understood, and could talk music. That project led to something of a close association and finally in 1976 he was tapped to do the score for the filmmaker's multi–million dollar project. We had lunch at the studio during a break in the final dubbing stage of that film. Asked if there had been any turning points or "breaks" in his career, he said:

> I think you could say I've moved into another league since the last time we talked. I did a film [A] that received a lot of attention . . . and it was a very difficult film to score and I guess because the solution I reached was an interesting one, you know, people noticed it. Frankly, I thought the score wouldn't be noticed at all because it was so much a part of the fabric of the picture. It's not something with a big theme where everyone says, "Isn't that pretty?" It had the opposite effect. A lot of people, espeacially some of the younger people, seem to be turned off by the formula, big lush approach to scoring, or the standard solutions to detective pictures or pictures with violence such as the big

orchestra sound with a pretty theme. Whereas, in that film [A] we took an approach that the score was not going to be about what was happening outside but what was happening inside, and it was an approach to the character. And with certain sensitive directors that approach is appealing; the score then becomes more of a service to the picture than of service to itself. As I said, after that I think I got the next film which was a very good film with a good director. I think I got it through him.

The more things you've done, the more things you've got a chance of being considered for, and I want to avoid being typecast. I like to work on totally different things, so I'd perfer not to be known as someone who writes one kind of thing because I'd hate to just keep getting called for the same kind of picture. And if you do only a certain type of scoring, that restricts what you can be up for, the things you can do. If people think you can only write one kind of thing, you're only going to be offered those kinds of things. If you keep them guessing . . . like a jazz-oriented film score [A] is totally different from an orchestra score [B] and [C] is totally different from those two, and [D] is completely different from all of those. Hopefully people begin to get the idea that you can handle almost anything, so that you can become potentially considered for almost anything. So . . . I don't think there's a type I fall into. One of the reasons I took [A] is because right after [B], when I realized that it was going to get a lot of attention, I thought that my name was going to come to prominence with a lot of people with a very specialized score . . . the instrumentation was special . . . and they're going to think, " Well, it's a wonderful score, for what it is, but can he write for orchestra, can he do something that is much more up front?" And I went after [B] because I knew it would be New York, up front, violence, big orchestra, and a totally different kind of picture. And I was happy to get it at *that* point in my career. So as soft a score as [D] was, [B] was as loud, probably the loudest score I've ever written. So in that case it was a project that I specifically *went after*. I called the writer, I knew him, I had read the book and asked him to put my name in the hopper. And I knew the producer from other work I had done for him, so . . . that was it.

He tried to tackle a variety of genres to escape being typecast. The producer he is working with is at the top, as he notes, was impressed by the range demonstrated in his previous films, and decided to take a chance on him. Apparently that range of talent provided security against the risk the producer was taking by hiring aspiring, unproven talent. He continued:

[H] is a big jump for me. It's a big, stereo, panavision, $10 million picture with a big orchestral sound. I haven't done anything like this before. Television, now I'm being more and more selective about.

That's a position you want to work yourself into, that's important to do because generally television is not that rewarding, there aren't that many opportunities to grow, also you have to work much faster and I like to take my time, so it's nice with a feature. With a feature, on the order of [E], the schedule is more relaxed and you have more time to think about it, do research and get yourself . . . ready. But, you know, I'm up for television all the time, I just turned down a Movie of the Week because I've been doing so much work the last three months I wanted to catch my breath for a few weeks. I didn't want to run off two pictures in a row into a television project that has to be ready in two weeks, I don't want to do that.

It is a business of contacts and a film composer needs a business sense as good as his artistic sense. One of the above composer's colleagues, who was clearly hot at the moment, talked about staying power and being careful about what he decided to do. The opportunity to be selective was a luxury, he insisted. Not many had it. This colleague was a man of no little refinement artistically, of wide experience in record, musicals, and film, and of great judgment of filmmakers and their projects which he used carefully to satisfy his own goals for predominance as a film composer. He was kind and soft spoken, but also determined and, if need be, calculating. I got the impression that he immediately thought about a situation in terms of how much time he should allow it—and how much effort. He loved to talk about his work. In discussing the producers he had worked with, this freelancer laid out a series of career stages. He had an impressive rise into the inner circles. I asked if there were any big breaks, any turning points in his career. He reflected on the question. Until one of his latest films he was considered a good writer— but with the winning of the Oscar for the song his reputation and the demand for his services grew.

Sure. There's a word going around right now, it's called "survival." A lot of people do one film and that's it. The biggest award in this town is the next film, the next assignment. Your sixth, seventh, eighth film, that's the one. At first you struggle just to work, then you get an important credit. Then people start asking for you. And hopefully, you can then pick and choose the properties you want to work on. This is unlike the studio staff days, where you'd get the assignment and you'd have to do it—it was your assignment. So you would see some delicious and active properties, and then you'd see some dud.

"So you have some choice?" I was asking for details.

"Some. You're approached by a company or a producer. They say, 'Would you like to do this project?' You'll take a look at where the project is. You'll say, 'No, this is not what I want to do,' or 'I want to get away from this kind of thing.' There are times when you have to diplomatically bow out of something which you know is destined to be wrong." You can always say "no," but there are contingencies.

> There are two things I just want to add to this. A, when you're in the position of saying "no," it's because you're busy. I mean you really are at a point where you don't need that. But if there are long fallow periods you might take something. It sounds almost too good to be true to say "no" to something, even though nothing is happening. Unless it's a really dreadful thing that's offensive to you or really in bad taste or vulgar—to me, that would be impossible. I'd say "no." But for the most part, I've turned down things because I felt they were not going to succeed, no matter, because of the way they were put together. So you look ahead at the end of the tunnel and say, "Is it worth the effort? Is it worth the dollars they will pay us? Is it worth all the effort and all the dreams that are going to go into this thing?" And you know it's not going to happen.

> [He looked back to one point in his career and noted the danger of working on a poor film:] I hate to use the expression, but I was *fat* enough at the time and said I didn't need it, so I could afford to turn it down. I'd be a liar to say I just turn things down, that's not true. There are times when you say, "*If* I did this, with all integrity, it would be awful." And I don't want an awful credit after my name, because your next job is harder to get.

> Producers all look down their lists [pointing to the list of composers I had before me]. They have a list like yours, with the top guys in town, how much money the films they've been on have made, the grosses. So do the backers. And the question is: "What have you done *lately?*" Fortunately for those who succeed—but unfortunately for a lot of very, very, very gifted people, they do very good work on *bombs. Bombs.* They don't have it so easy getting that next one. How many people are sensitive enough to say, "But listen to the score of this dreadful movie, forget the fact that somebody's cutting off somebody's head with a hacksaw, listen to this contrapuntal thing that's going on up there"? How many people are going to stop and do that? How many people have the sensitivity to do that? And then when the picture comes out with a zero box-office return, that guy could be the greatest, he could be the next big-name composer, but he'll be sitting on his duff, because nobody's going to hire him. You never know whether you are making the right choice or not, of course.

This was the overwhelming theme. From the inside view there is a clear awareness of the restrictions upon their power to predict and create futures for themselves. They go with gut reactions to a filmmaker and his film. They often muddle through because of the complexity of cause-effect relations. They never know if the project they are working on will be a smash or commercial flop. There are gaps between the way they would like to see things done and the way things are done.

Being selective is a strategy composers use to try to get access to better material because the better the material the more the work satisfaction. A composer expects and desires to see himself in terms of working in better projects, with more important budgets and filmmakers. Here he has the control to create an integration of career and self. The work of choosing is complex. Everyone wants to be connected with a success. Every composer wants to be on a project which will transform his circumstances for the better. But the composer must wait to see what happens once the film is released and reviewed to learn whether it was the "right" or "wrong" choice. For those who were winning big it looked as if all their choices were right as well as predetermined.

One composer talked about the difficulty of picking and choosing projects: "It's important to be in a position to be able to pick and choose, of course. You can pick something from a career point of view and you can be wrong. How can you judge, how do you know what it's going to do?" While composers would like to get to the position to be selective about their work, they never know what the consequences of those selections will be: "I don't consider myself an overall expert, you know, I might like something and it might be a flop," said another man I had interviewed in 1973 and 1977. "Choices are the crux of the whole business." The first time we talked he had completed three movies in two years, and had some picks of what he wanted at the television studio from which he had "graduated." He hit the jackpot in 1975 with a very effective score.

We talked about "building accounts" and trying to improve one's position in the network of referrals, the importance of accumulating fewer but better credits, and the ways in which the "luxury" of selectivity is continually hemmed in. "The way the industry works, I think, is you try to move to a place, judging from people who have been in my position, and I've been fortunate, where you can get *choosey*, that's important."

"You get choosey over what you will do? What you won't do?" I asked. The question carried both ends of the continuum of choice at the same time, and he responded to both.

> People who would be in my position, judging from the way they have behaved, get rather selective and insist, as best they can, that they do pictures that they *think* will enhance their career and they will actually turn down pictures, yes, to answer your question. You get to a point where you don't grab everything, you want to be associated with films

that have some quality. That's important for me. It takes time. I'd say in retrospect that over the past three years . . . I've moved into a position of being able to be more selective, to take the things I'm particularly interested in and try to stay away from other kinds of work. You have to be careful about so many things, for instance, *volume* and *money*. Both are important. There's a lot that is valuable. I know for *me, right now*, I make a lot of choices. It's a prime time for me. I'll consider anything, almost, as long as I feel it's interesting, and I see that I can probably work with the producer, the director, or whoever.

This demand position is "the place to be." Getting there is difficult and not every film is of high quality. In some cases the freelancer continues to work for a producer because he worked for him in the past; he will take less than desirable projects in the hope that the person producing or directing them will move into a secure place in the industry, or will have a successful film, or perhaps work on a "small, special project" that the composer would like to be associated with. "Hopefully you pick right, you never know, it could be a big flop, as I said, or it could be a project that leads everyone associated with it to something bigger, then the phone doesn't stop ringing." The phones continued to ring for our next composer. Over the past twelve years he has worked on thirty films, some of which have been top money makers. His latest completed project was working with a close associate and film producer on the smash hit of the year. The film broke all box office records and was well on its way to becoming one of the all-time money makers in Hollywood history. He was at the top—at the moment. I interviewed him in his studio at one of the major film companies early one morning. He is in his forties, cooperative, subdued, and careful about how he uses words dealing with his career development. He insisted that much of what happens to a career occurs as a result of those indispensable ingredients—luck, timing, personal relationships, and, of course, a viable film property where the composer feels stylistically "at home."

"Seen from the outside," I said, "you're in a postion right now to be *very selective*. Are you more careful now than earlier in your career, say eight years ago, about what you work on because of your place at the top?"

Well, I've always tried. I think there's something erroneous in what you've been saying. It may seem as if I have the choice of everything I want and it may seem to other people that's how it works. It doesn't work that way. If I could choose *every* picture I wanted, I would choose—always—the five successful pictures of the year. But you can't do that. Nobody can really do that. It seems as though I have my choice, but I don't. First of all, it's very, very, hard to wait till a picture is finished to see if you like it and *then* try to guess if it's going to be successful and *then* try to guess if you can write a good score for it. By that time, it's usually too late: the producers are already so nervous that they can't or won't wait. These days the postproduction schedules are incredibly tight. It's very difficult. What's happening now is that a composer is chosen while the film is *being shot,* or even before or just after they've shot and are going to edit—so you really can't see a prime cut or a cut that's even in good enough shape to tell how solid that film is going to be.

There are time limitations in choosing the work and also in the work itself. A composer decides to work on one particular film for a particular period of time. "There comes a time where you have to make a commitment to a film, so having made a commitment to it you've eliminated other things that you maybe rather have had." To underscore the point, he noted a common observation made by these freelancers. "There are just not that many good films, quality films made in any one year. And I mean you can't go around the town screening all the *ten* pictures available and pick one of them. They don't come ripe for assignment in that kind of progression." At best, a composer can accept the two or three films that may be available in the next three-month "time frame." He may get a chance to look at two of them and pick the best one, but even that takes some luck.

Any one decision is made at *a given time.* Certain films become available and ready for the composers. Agents start making their claims and their pitch. Spotting sessions and interviews are arranged. Negotiations are undertaken. A composer is signed to do the film. He has committed himself to it in a series of gradually restricting business decisions and artistic judgments. Others depend on the freelancer's commitment and determine their lines of action on the basis of it. The filmmakers expect his full attention—that he will not split his efforts by working on another film or television project at the same time. They want a full commitment. After all, that is what they are paying for. If another, possibly more interesting and even lucrative film deal comes along, the composer is still tied by his earlier decision. Options are limited by choices already made. In retrospect his original choice may be seen as working with the "wrong" people on the "wrong" project at the "wrong" time. Actions constitute commitments. And commitment bounds selectivity as surely as limited opportunity does.

Finally personal relationships influence choices. The highly sought after composer may get caught in the middle of filmmakers' demands: "You may not be able to take advantage of a choice you are given. You don't want to insult the producer who has done the *one* film or the *other* fellow may be someone that you've done five pictures with and you feel a kind of personal attachment to his work in the sense that there's a *relationship* there. These things act as well to limit your choices of what to do."

Resources, Alternatives, and Bounded Selectivity

Selectivity is aimed in two directions. First, as an expression of desired expertise and professional skills it is geared principally to control over the content: (a) the degree to which one feels stylistically compatible with the dramatic action; (b) the extent to which the musical problems can be worked out given bounded rationality and the filmmaker; and (c) the tightness of fit between one's craft "instincts" and the perceived demands of the film project. Second, selection as an expression of future prestige and commercial success demands diversification of the ties, increased volume, and advantage in the volatile and unpredictable market outcomes of commercial work. Commercial success is a major element of control and exerts pressures to tie in with particular producers, on particular films, and produce scores in certain directions.

The "resource-alternative theory" suggests that the relationship between filmmakers' and freelancers' power and selectivity is asymmetrical. On the one hand, filmmakers have control over the conditions of freelancers' work because composers do not have access to many producers and their projects. On the other hand, composers' power depends on their market strength. Thus, resources, alternatives, and selectivity covary. This theory qualifies the conventional wisdom about client control, for an employer's power is usually believed to originate in the fact that he can take the business elsewhere and hence "punish" freelancers who do not meet employer demands. Here we see there is a countervailing market strength in the inner circle of freelancers, because employers with big-budgeted projects need high-profile "names" to (a) reduce the internal complexities of bounded rationality, (b) reduce as far as possible the uncertainty of audience reaction, and (c) develop ties with the select few with proven track records. Through this winnowing process, successful Hollywood composers accumulate rewards that lead to even greater productivity, network connections, and further selective power.

The ambiguity and complexity of freelancers' decisions are magnified by the cooperative nature of filmmaking. Different members of a project contribute different portions to a larger product, but each member's contribution is evaluated only in terms of the group product and its market outcomes. Individual members have no way of determining the effect of their contributions to that outcome. Encapsulation of the score within the film, and the vulnerability of the film to audiences in a turbulent market, distort the relationship between cause (the composer and his score) and effect (the success of the commercial project).[2] A composer's work is sequential. With luck, the sequences of film projects improve in the combination of assurances he seeks— whom he is working with, production values, budget, dramatic excitement, reduction of equivocality, and stylistic compatibility. Each top composer I talked to stressed that a man has to, or tries to, pursue his own artistic instinct. To feel "at home" with a film in a spotting session is to reduce uncertainty, to be sure; more importantly, it affects the relation of the composer to himself and helps him create a definition of himself as a writer.

> No one deliberately sets out to make a flop. You do a film and, of course, you try to do your very best. So much is out of your hands after a certain point anyway, but you set that aside and hopefully you're working on something where you feel comfortable—artistically, stylistically. Many people think that someone sits around and just takes those things which will be big successes. You can't do that. My own viewpoint is that it is very precarious, that's a good word, it's very precarious to be happy, to be at home with the assignments that you're able to get. It's very difficult and extremely hard to keep the continuity of that. If you do, you might be lucky enough to all of a sudden look back and see that you've had a successful career and, hopefully, are going to have one in the future.

The closing remark suggests that a career line is lived forward and understood backwards, as suggested in the phrase, "You have to go past it to understand it." The creation of meaning is always directed to that which has already occurred in a line of work. A Hollywood career is always retrospective.[3]

Not everyone in this line of work is in a position to accumulate more than their share of retrospective munificence through competent performance, visible projects, and box office bonanzas. Dominants with hot track records command more attention from employers, have more projects offered to them, and have more chances to pick those which will match their tastes and talents. They look like they can bring something valuable to the project—a name, powerful credentials, an impressive past, a future hope. They reduce the fears that producers and directors have about their own careers. Such composers have "good fortune" and credibility. "Good fortune" is their term for competence plus visibility plus luck and commercial success—the past ability to get results.

Risk-Bearing Selections: Precariousness in Being Particular

The precariousness of commercial work dictates that freelancers become involved in lines of work in order to see the wisdom of their choices. The gap between their actions and responses in the climate of opinion are oftentimes quite loose. This independence of action and response is accentuated by the uncertainties introduced by the mass-audience market for films and television work. Composers act within constrained and shifting boundaries. The range of choices and work activity is narrowed by conventions, budgets, and past work alliances. Composers may attempt to act in a proactive rather than reactive manner, making the best strategic selections they can, but typically they are only moderately effective, and when they are, very little of the variation in opinion or success of the film project is attributable to variations in what the composer does. Thus they see plans modified, projects twisted, and careers reshaped in this loosely linked relationship among themselves, their employers, and the popular culture consumers.

Most of the elements discussed below are present in the freelancers I talked to over the past seven years. Emphasis varies among dominants, mainliners, and contributors. Still, the most prominent elements in most responses are recognition of risk running, the importance of the fit between skills and preferred projects, and autonomy.

Many consequences of choices made are unforeseeable. Some may dramatically improve one's fortunes, others could freeze an otherwise brilliant climb to the top. There is widespread doubt, anxiety, and ambivalence about what to take and what to turn down. Many views, even quite strong ones, are prefaced or followed by expressions of puzzlement. There is constant awareness of lack of information, inability to forecast futures, and gaps between what one does at work and the response to that work by filmmakers, other industry personnel, and eventually the audience.

Second, and directly related to feelings of confusion, there are frequent expressions of annoyance and frustration with people who offer them their jobs. The trade-off between what the composer requires of his work and what the work requires of him is difficult to negotiate. The pressure of time, the fear of failure, the habit of doing what has "worked" before, the limits imposed by production companies—all these factors combine to make it difficult to do creative and innovative work in Hollywood. Being in demand gives a composer leverage; but it simply means a freelancer is able, within some limits, to reduce his "share" of potential troubles.

Third, if one cannot always be selective in a positive sense, one may still be selective in a negative sense. This is not the freedom to achieve access to the better work, but rather the freedom from work that is infra dig. At each stage a career involves choices of some rather than other activities.[4] In his economy of efforts, a freelancer knows that his work is in a producer's medium. Some producers have the most authority and power: they get the largest credits, the most money, and command large-budget productions. Access to those people is important and choices that will improve access are sought. But "good fortune" not only increases opportunity, it also decreases *dirty work*—more suited for some composer trying to break into the business who is willing to work with a producer whose film budget is questionable and whose tastes are objectionable.

Finally, for the composer who is fortunate to have power of selection, life is still ambiguous and difficult. Despite all attempts by composers to find projects that will define their images of themselves, and despite their efforts to select among filmmakers who are respectable, trustworthy, powerful, and have worthy projects to collaborate on, their accomplishments seldom last for long before they become outdated. The film world is a business of fast-moving assignments and connections. Potential clients come to a composer with a film and an idea; they are putting their ideas and themselves on the line. They do not relish rejection. They dislike a short-lived spotting session where the composer rises at the end of the film and suggests that the producer find someone else, insists that he does not understand what the film is trying to say, cautiously urges the producer to consider some ideas for music scoring that are explicitly intended to get him off the job. Employers in Hollywood do not like being turned down, especially if they are willing to pay his fee. Said a top composer in his early forties and currently popular among producers due to several Academy Award films from 1972 to 1980:

> You can't turn down too much that you feel, how shall I say it, "un-suited" for, that you would prefer not to do. I mean, if you're in demand you'll be getting asked to do feature films, maybe a theme for a television program, Movie of the Week, a wraparound title, but you'll get a shot at a lot of work, quality work. That's the plateau to be on. But I do think that filmmakers don't like to be rejected, and if you start making a habit of it, of being too particular, you might . . . I won't call it ostracism, but, in the meantime they'll find someone else to do their projects and if it works out they'll maybe use that person again, and then maybe again if the thing takes off. This is how you can lose work. There are plenty of hot, young talented composers in town. You con-stantly feel that heat.

Freelance work involves the running of risks because members are severely limited in their ability to formulate goals, to understand cause-effect relations, and to predict futures. Moreover, they are running against their colleague competitors, which only exacerbates the ambiguity of "lessons" from past events and experience. Ordinarily, a career is interpreted as simply onward and upward progress in a system of ranked positions or statuses. In Hollywood, and other lines of freelance labor, career progress is not through a stable hierarchy of positions but from one discrete event to another. These events tie employer to employee, client to expert, and the tie is made for the duration of the project. One moves from tie to tie, event to event. Since the occupation is practiced in an open framework, directly with clients, career progress means that a composer gets access to more and hopefully better films and their makers. Seen from the inside, the chance to work is the reward.The chances to work with those at the top networks, on quality projects, is a key to seeing why some times and activities are preferred over others. In Hollywood, for better or worse, both short-term coalitions and long-run alliances become a stabilizing force. A key ingredient of the dominant freelancer's career is an increase in resources which permit increased chances to make finer and finer decisions concerning with whom *not* to work. It is against something, then, that a career emerges, both as a concrete and public event as well as a private and meaningful satisfaction. Negative selective power is risky but it may well be the freelancer's most formidable weapon in this struggle for advantage and favor.

Notes

1. Peter McHugh, "Structural Uncertainty and Its Resolution: The Case of the Professional Actor," in S. N. Plog and R. B. Edgerton (eds.), *Changing Perspectives in Mental Illness* (New York: Holt, Rinehart, & Winston, 1969).
2. This suggests the following pernicious programmatic rule: to multiply the turbulence and instability of a set of freelance activities, deprive members of the means for controlling the conditions and evaluations of an outcome while holding them to account as causal agents of the outcome. That composers are often "blamed" for the commercial flops of their projects is a constant background feature of Hollywood's film community.
3. Karl E. Weick, *The Social Psychology of Organizing* (Reading, Mass.: Addison-Wesley, 1969), esp. pp. 59–71. Each successive point, project, or credit transforms the career as object so that the contingencies, the situation in which the freelancer interprets what is going on, and the kind of "theorizing" or thinking employed are altered, winnowed away, sharpened, eliminated, and reified, as a line of activity builds up. In each "state" the freelancer selects from available "facts" and interpretations about projects and their outcomes. I have shown how the organizing principles of networks, uncertainty, selectivity, and the dispersion of ties enable members to search for "valid" and "real" explanations of what happened in a successful career. In this way, if freelancers define the consequences and outcomes of their careers as real, they are real in their antecedent situations.
4. One cannot imagine an occupation in which action and response are more loosely linked. Such a career is, as Hughes has put it, "a sort of running adjustment between a man and the various facts of life and of his professional world. It involves the running of risks, for his career is his ultimate enterprise, his laying of his bets on his one and only life. It contains a set of projections of himself into the future, and a set of predictions about the course of events in [the] work world itself." Everett C. Hughes, *The Sociological Eye: Selected Papers* (Chicago: Aldine, Atherton, 1971), p. 406.

10.
BIG HOLLYWOOD, LITTLE HOLLYWOOD

It's nearly impossible to get a movie made in Hollywood today. There are seven actors, two actresses, and six major directors who run the business. If you don't get one of them, you can't do your picture . . . Easterners look at us with great disdain. They have a view of us sitting around the pool and phoning in scripts at $250,000 a page. The truth is there are only 12 of us who make a living at it. The studios made only about 40 films last year. The odds are awesome . . . . I grew up in Brooklyn during the 1940s, thinking of Hollywood as a magical place, and was determined to become part of it some day. It's still a magical place for me.
— Steven Shagan, screenwriter[1]

Johnny Williams blows me away. Lalo Schifrin is always into something new. Henry Mancini, a man who has worked on more pictures than I can imagine . . . . Just go down the list. They're all good, they really are. For me to even be approaching their circle is an honor that you can't imagine.
— Bill Conti, composer[2]

An elite of 36 among some 400 Hollywood stuntmen and stuntwomen do 75 percent of all the stunt work in motion pictures and television.
Will Tusher writing on Hal Needham, stunt-man-turned-director[3]

Passo a passo si va lontano (Italian proverb: ''Step by step, one goes a long way'')

In the foregoing chapters I tried to give a developmental perspective on freelancing and to link macrosociological levels to the working experiences and self-interest of participants. One purpose behind writing about composers was to develop some ideas and strategies for studying career lines and the social structures that sustain them. I wanted to understand the relationships between the commercial artist/craftsman in a culture-producing industry in terms of the networks of transactions in which he finds himself. I have argued that networks of collective action emerge out of the purposeful behavior of freelancers and filmmakers seeking their own self-interest.

The argument suggests that a career in a craft mode of organization is built upon productivity and continuity in the market, and that a career is a succession of joined work events. The market is an arena in which filmmakers and freelancers meet: the market is a means of organizing commercial activities. These activities involve recurrent contracting under conditions of bounded rationality and precarious certainty. Two things of interest are evident from the data. It is clear that this community, like most work communities, is dominated by an elite. The community manifests severe inequalities in the distribution and control over events and resources. As events, the projects and connections of individual freelancers influence the total configuration of relationships in the larger social organization of Hollywood. The location of top freelancers in networks of collective action with film producers affects composers' subsequent behavior and outlook. Second, and related, it is clear that number of projects and their continuity are linked to career success. A chosen few dominate. They have superior staying power and chains of influence. They have diverse work ties which are often dispersed within sparsely connected networks of filmmakers. These networks, by their very nature, are not organizationally bound up with any particular studio arrangements. Freelancers are not salaried employees; they work in an open, changing, internal-market system. They are employed on a project-to-project basis rather than being contained under the contractual obligations of major film production companies. Their sparsely knit, ramifying networks provide a broad range of direct and indirect ties to the producers, directors, and other support personnel of their work community. In fact, the networks *are* the building blocks of that community.   The impact of commercialism and connections is particularly pronounced because of the lopsided dependence of freelancers on producers and directors. Composers, screenwriters, cinematographers, directors (as well as stuntmen, sound mixers, and other support personnel) have to involve themselves in industry presentation of self, which involves actively selling their abilities to perform contradictory tasks (under conditions of bounded rationality), to obtain credits, experience, connections, and images essential for gaining leverage in a contractual system dominated by a powerful few. Any attempt to fight the irrationalities of art and commerce simply results in other, equally hungry colleague competitors receiving assignments. By paying close attention to the crises and dilemmas of commercial roles which arise as one gains (or loses) resources and alternatives, we can see how a Hollywood-made career looks and feels to those experiencing it.[4]

The business looks very different depending upon whether a freelancer is on the way up or has already arrived. It looks different at every middle stage too. I tried to show that experiential career concerns and self-interests vary depending upon whether a person is securing a foothold in television, fighting it out for a second film credit, moving through the small army of colleagues standing on the plateaus just below the chosen few, or accumulating resources and visibility at the very top of this industry. I've tried to lay out the tracks along which these career lines run, as well as the way self-interests change as the career line develops.

It takes sizable chunks of time and movie credits to determine patterns of distribution of projects and their personnel. With these distributions at hand, I have tried to articulate a version of freelancing as an organized relational activity, as a concrete network of tightly and loosely coupled ties among named people on real movie assignments. This reflects my interests in deciphering social organization through the combined use of distributional and relational data. Taking the most active freelancers in the film industry from the mid-1960s to roughly 1980, I have indicated how prominent participants respond to their industry's tendency to assess their ability through typecasting. Freelancers are also judged by the market success of projects, a success in which the composer can never be sure of the degree of his contribution.

I have shown how resources and alternatives play a part in career success. Several distinct patterns appear. First, all else being equal, a high volume of credits is likely to be the result of diverse work with several producers and directors. This in turn helps generate informal contacts with other filmmakers, and an industry-wide network of ties is likely to grow.

Second, among freelancers with a similar number of credits, those working for major film producers on major commerical packages are in a better position to mobilize greater industry resources than are those associated with the same number of credits but from projects of lesser visibility, publicity, and commercial potential or payoff.

Third, the survivors, the central figures, become more likely candidates for consideration on a wider range of film productions than those not so favored. As a result, their selective power expands. When they are winning, they are more able to define the premises of action in the direction of their own talent and career.

Finally, the process described here suggests a means by which both sides of the labor market bring their very different interests and goals together. From the standpoint of filmmakers, the desirable freelancers possess chains of influence in the form of (a) track records and visible credentails which are reassuring to a producer facing risks; and (b) concrete transactions with prominent other filmmakers which are attractive to an employer because they increase his *confidence* in his own decisions. Hiring talent is "good taste," and also good business, since there are enough risks in the business without handing a project over to composers too unproven or nervous to come through under pressure. I have also tried in the later chapters to demonstrate that studying commercial activity requires more than ethnographic illustrations, informant anecdotes, and respondent self-reports or estimates. We must demonstrate that collective actions arrange themselves predictably and consistently in patterns which persist over a sufficient time span to make them socially and historically relevant. Hollywood may be a game of trends but there is a stable structure to its highly conventionalized hiring practices. By looking at the recurrent and routine intersection of people on various tiers of productivity, we can see how films themselves are key units shaping, competing, and selecting the preferred and available talent. The projects themselves pull the employer and employee sides of the market together. Specifically, we can easily see how credits and connections sharply bind *film projects (and their controllers) to subsets of freelancers; conversely, we can see how increases in credits and visibility further refine the selective matching of freelancers to subsets of desired projects and their producers and directors.*

In looking at Hollywood success, we can view success as a process governed primarily by the qualities of the freelancer himself or by the nature of the transactions of *dual entities.* I have used both views and treated career mobility as a movement through a succession of assignments, challenges, and work-based ties. The latter chapters have emphasized the importance of the transactions in the top tiers: a fitting together of the activities of prominent film-makers and freelancers so that they consistently link up on a large number of film events.

The idea of major and minor contributors in this community is of considerable value because it suggests the presence of a relation through which macrolevel tiers affect microorganizational processes.[5] The matrix of transactions and four blocks within the top tiers show this microorganizational level at work. These networks of collective action affect chances for career success, since tightly and loosely coupled ties generate opportunities for diversification, risk reduction, and connections across multiple, sparsely knit networks. The structure of ties provides the sinews of everyday functioning in Hollywood. Contrasts between top-tier blocks suggest that the particular network a composer is associated with will affect his chances of capturing a share of both success and continuity in today's major film scene.

I believe the microorganizational force suggested in the matrix extends to the larger structure; that the implications of that matrix reveal as much about the culture-producing industries generally as they do about the particular relation of composer to employer. Seen this way the matrix becomes central to the understanding of the social organization of a major sector of the American business-entertainment industry.

It is standard for anyone writing about this industry in general and Hollywood's specialists in particular to slip into the role of partisan. I suppose every occupational researcher becomes, after a long involvement with interviewing, observation, and record keeping, sympathetic and even sentimental about the people studied. You come, quite naturally, to understand them and side up with them in their struggles with their real and sometimes imaginary enemies. You pick up their vocabulary and the practiced ways in which they artfully talk about their motives, their interests, their selves. You develop a story but you have to keep enough distance to see how things really look and why things work the way they do in today's business—the first being an ethnographic and descriptive enterprise, the second an interpretive and theoretical activity.

Over the eight years I spent interviewing composers, I have armed myself with long lists of Hollywood's participants, kept track of who is doing what assignments in films and television, and kept an eye on the artistic and commercial success of those projects. I have talked to numerous heavyweights in the industry, picked up a lot of their jargon, developed distributions of projects and their personnel, collected run-downs of film revenues and gross rentals, gone out to watch composers at work in the recording studios, and at times followed them around for a day or so through dubbing sessions. I have been treated to lunch by these men, and naturally shared some of my hunches, leads, and tentative insights with a few of them. And I have laid out a matrix of the concrete ties among the prominent few. In so doing, I developed my own "list" of who counts—by credits—while attempting to push the idea of Hollywood as a network of activity from mere metaphor into loose measurement.

Writers about Hollywood tend to slip out of a comparative, and even pattern-seeking frame of mind. To begin with, a comparative study of several work specialties—like screenwriters, soundmen, cinematographers, and directors—is time-consuming and few sociologists are willing to invest the time it would take to enlarge their occupational case materials enough to provide a comparative basis. The attractions of writing anecdotal, narrow, and ultimately catchy case studies are very seductive. At the opposite extreme, many who study occupational communities believe that each tiny piece of the work world is a kind of society in miniature; that studies of any line of work in the film business, for example, illuminate on a reduced scale the broad outlines of Hollywood in general. In fact, some go farther and assume that any stripped down case study tells us something substantial about American society.

I have tried to avoid either extreme. My point in citing Steve Shagan, two-time Academy Award nominee for *Save the Tiger* (1973) and *Voyage of the Damned* (1976), Hal Needham, one of the top stuntmen-turned-director with credits such as *Smokey and the Bandit* (1977) followed by Burt Reynolds's vehicle *Hooper* (1979), and Bill Conti, experiencing a meteoric rise into the charmed circle by 1979,[6] is to suggest that their observations about "the lists," the "small numbers" running the film business, and hiring "the top ten" sum up the sentiments and interests of an extraordinarily wide range of specialists in various occupations within this business. Since information on these credit lists and small numbers has clearly played a part in the telling of this story, a brief note on the distribution of work among directors, screenwriters, and cinematographers might be useful at this point.

As any credit buff knows, a collection of filmographies—people by their films by year—immediately gives a very clear picture of the major contributors to the Hollywood scene. The major figures are those who work steadily and achieve wide recognition for their outstanding talents and their contributions to the craft and the industry. Table 10.1 indicates the number of credits for participants in each of the four specialties. There is, of course, some crossover as writers become directors, cinematographers turn into directors, directors produce their own projects, and so forth. Multiple credits also show up, as two writers craft the same screenplay, or the duties of filming a project are handled by two cinematographers. Multiple producer credits on films also extend the number of participants on single film projects.[7] None of this changes the overwhelming similarity of the pattern of distribution here to that already observed throughout the ranks of film composers.

Among directors of photography, 20 out of the 250 (8 percent) contributed to nearly 1 out of every 3 films from 1973-74 to 1977-78. A very active

TABLE 10.1
Volume of Film Work by Occupational Specialty: Hollywood
1973–74 to 1977–78

Volume	Producers	Directors	Screenwriters	Cinematographers
1	301	247	298	136
2	85	69	92	43
3	28	29	31	23
4	11	20	10	11
5	5	6	1	6
6	4	4	1	11
7	0	0	0	6
8	2	0	0	3
9	1	1	0	0
10	2	0	0	3
11	0	0	0	3
12	0	0	0	2
13	0	0	0	1
14	1	0	0	1
15	1	0	0	1
Totals	441	377	433	250

Source: Variety Anniversary Issues, Volumes 41 to 46, from October 1973–
September 1974 to October 1977–September 1978.

minority worked on nearly 200 of the more than 600 projects listed. And a central 5 dominated much of this credit market. These 5 cinematographers constituted only 2 percent of the cameramen but enjoyed a continuity of effort, doing 1 out of every 10 assignments produced and released. They were called to work by the best producers and directors on prestigious productions. The 8 percent were all called upon to produce the widest possible variety of moods, settings, and looks on a wide variety of films.

Especially striking, to one perusing the pages of *Variety* or *American Cinematograp her,* a magazine published by The American Society of Cinematographers, is the consistency of expertise and craftsmanship, showing up again and again in their films. The same names roll recurrently on the major credit crawls. Some of these men and their films are the following for the five years: Robert Surtees was busy working on *The Sting, The Hindenberg,* and *The Turning Point;* John Alonzo filmed *Chinatown,* among his other assignments; Harry Stradling, Jr. filmed *The Way We Were;* Owen Roizman, like his colleagues above, was an Academy Award nominee for his stunning work in *The Exorcist* and *Network;* Fred Koenekamp filmed *The Towering Inferno* for Irwin Allen; Haskell Wexler contributed to *One Flew over the Cuckoo's Nest* and *Bound for Glory* in 1976. Other cinematographers with major credits are: Vilmos Zsigmond and his *Close Encounters of the Third Kind* for director Steven Spielberg; William A. Fraker's *Looking for Mr. Goodbar;* and David Walsh with credits that indicate the demand for the talents of these cameramen—his work includes *The Other Side of the Mountian, Murder by Death, The Sunshine Boys, W. C. Fields and Me, Whiffs, Rollercoaster, Scott Joplin,* and *Silver Streak.* Walsh finished the five years with an active and representative season—with *Foul Play, The Goodbye Girl,* and *House Calls.* Other leaders with major credits are Laszlo Kovacs, Frank Phillips, and Victor Kemper. These are the names that surface again and again as the film industry selects its Academy Award contenders as the various specialties make their nominations.

Second, a small and equally prolific core appears within the ranks of the Hollywood scriptwriters. These are men who craft the original screenplays as well as screenplays adapted from other material. Table 10.1 again provides a sharp division of personnel by their film credit volume. If we use credits as a means of ranking, only 1 out of 10 screenwriters is a prominent figure. That is, of the 433 total listed 43 have written and received credit for about a quarter of the feature films in these five years. Their credits are impressive: Robert Towne's work, already noted in chapter 8, includes *The Last Detail, Chinatown,* and *Shampoo.* He is a winner of two nominations and an Oscar. Norman Wexler and Waldo Salt worked together on the script for the successful *Serpico,* and William Goldman's lengthy credit list includes *The Great Waldo Pepper, The Stepford Wives,* his Oscar-winning *All the President's*

Men, Marathon Man, and *A Bridge Too Far.* The prolific Neil Simon has credits for *The Prisoner of Second Avenue, The Sunshine Boys, Murder by Death,* and *The Goodbye Girl.* Other dominants are Paul Schrader, a writer and director with screenwriting credits on *The Yakuza* followed by *Taxi Driver, Blue Collar, Rolling Thunder,* and the project he both wrote and directed, *Hardcore.* Lorenzo Semple, Jr. worked on the Robert Dorfman and Franklin J. Schaffner film *Papillon,* Alan Pakula's *The Parallax View,* and then *The Super Cops, The Drowning Pool,* and the Sydney Pollack-directed *Three Days of the Condor.* Semple wrote the script update of the Dino De Laurentiis-John Guillermin version of *King Kong.*

Third, the major directors stand out starkly. Despite the crossover between specialties (writer-director; director-coproducer) and the looseness of multiple credits, the proportion of directors engaged in relatively high-volume activity is as strikingly small as that of the cinematographers and writers. Eight percent of the film directors capture one quarter of the market. Thirty-one out of 377 directed four or more productions over the five years; this small number of major contributors have their names on 143 of the 615 director-credited films. Sixteen percent of all the directors put their talents to work on 1 out of every 3 films, as shown in Table 10.1 (60 directors with a range of credits from 3 to 9 projects). Some of the leading figures in the credit count are the following: Herb Ross, whose films include the already mentioned *The Sunshine Boys, The Goodbye Girl, The Turning Point,* and *The Seven Per-Cent Solution;* Vincent McEveety of Buena Vista studios, with *Castaway Cowboy, Superdad, The Strongest Man in the World, Gus, Treasure of Matecumbe,* and *Herbie Goes to Monte Carlo;* and Robert Altman, Sidney Lumet, and Steven Spielberg, the latter with credits such as *The Sugarland Express,* screenplay by the busy Hal Barwood and Matthew Robbins from a story by Spielberg and produced by Richard C. Zanuck and David Brown with director-photographer Vilmos Zsigmond. Spielberg then teamed up with Zanuck and Brown on *Jaws,* with cinematographer Bill Butler and composer John Williams. Williams followed that success with *Close Encounters of the Third Kind,* the screenplay by Spielberg, photography credits including Zsigmond, William Fraker, Douglas Slocombe, John Alonzo, and Laszlo Kovacs. Martin Scorsese was also busy. He directed four films during the 1973–74 to 1977–78 period. They were *Mean Streets, Alice Doesn't Live Here Anymore, Taxi Driver* with producers Michael and Julia Phillips, and *New York, New York* with producers Irwin Winkler and Robert Chartoff, and photography by Laszlo Kovacs.

Finally, the numbers for producers and their credits reflect the pattern already described. The five years provide a miniature mosaic of the larger canvas already described. A few have their names on many productions. There are over 700 total projects with producer, executive producer, and associate producer credits for these individuals; nevertheless, only 6 percent of these producers make 23 percent of the films. Twenty-seven filmmakers have 4 or more credits during the five years on over 160 productions. The names are familiar; the team of Robert Chartoff and Irwin Winkler; Jennings Lang; Robert Daley; Elliot Kastner; Ron Miller; Ray Stark; and the teams of Zanuck and Brown, Weintraub and Heller, Michael and Julia Phillips.[8]

Those are some of the major contributors. Film credits and filmographics such as these immediately give an objective means of separating the major from the minor contributors. The differences are striking between the active few "in the industry" and the credit-starved many on the sidelines. As noted in chapter 2, there are few second acts to the majority of Hollywood careers in filmmaking. More than half of the film producers (68 percent, or 301 of 441), directors (65 percent, or 247 of 377), screenwriters (68 percent, or 298 of 433), and cinematographers (54 percent, or 136 of 250) worked on only one film from 1973–74 to 1977–78, as shown in Table 10.1. The gap between the active center and unproductive periphery is pronounced. There are no absolute standards that can be invoked to establish how pronounced is the social division of labor between the major and minor contributors. Whether the glass is half full or half empty depends on the observer's sympathies and perceptions of how Hollywood works and just how small is "a small number" of active producers, directors, screenwriters, cameramen, and composers. Some would suggest that the large number of people with the single credit is evidence of the openness of the film industry and the ease with which projects become financed, filmed, scored, and released—and then reviewed in *Daily Variety* and *The Hollywood Reporter*. Others would say that the industry rarely gives newcomers a chance, and that the entry barriers are well guarded and very formidable, since over half of the freelancers in these various specialties with a credit never set foot on the faster track. In such a view, my numbers would be plain evidence of the structure of inequality and the vulnerability of newness. One might conclude that one out of every two specialists with a single film fail to experience anything approximating a career line, if we define a career in films as "any set of two or more joined points of film assignments." Thus, while career mobility is a central life interest for many of Hollywood's participants, a large proportion fail to come with two or more joined points, as measured by the data on the volume of film work for five years.

Whether the overall distribution of these joined points within occupations is limited to a relatively few freelancers or, on the other hand, available to many, depends on what the observer expects to find. If one approaches the evidence offered here with expectations derived from some enthusiastic version of the American dream of success in movies, anything less than the discovery that almost every aspiring composer, director, writer, cameraperson, and film producer moving from two into three, four, five, and six credits will seem disappointing indeed. If, on the other hand, one begins with the suspicion that the four occupations have different productivity rates, given the difficulties of financing films and putting together the package of money and talent, then the business will seem obvious—obvious in the divisions splitting the industry and these specialties into three very separate businesses: a nonrecurrent and essentially one-shot enterprise on the periphery, a short string of joined points for a smaller number of people in the middle areas, and recurrent transactions enjoyed by a few capturing a large share of the work and linking up again and again with highly successful results. Those in the middle area, outside the inner circle, scurry around for connections, worry about the next assignment point, and are alternately hassled and bored to death by their projects and controllers. But insofar as these credits and ties appear to flow consistently to an exclusive but unstable minority of talented and lucky few, Big Hollywood will still smother the significance of these sectors of Little Hollywood under the glare of publicity, fancy maneuvering as reported in the trade papers and press, and the often hyped-up figures about production costs.

It does not seem to be much of an exaggeration to say that the minor contributors, as I have defined them here, become a microcosm of the larger world of work—a sort of reduced copy of many activities of production found in the worlds of jazz, sports, television broadcasting, and publishing—any line of activity in which real participants leave historical "traces" and "records" of their contributions. These contributions are the credit lists by which everyone keeps scores—whether they be participants by record albums, scholars by published papers, artists by gallery showings, etc. The film world is much like the academic world, the jazz world, and other settings, in being populated by highly qualified personnel who rarely contribute more than *one unit* to the publicly accessible cultural record of that business. This suggests that a most persistent feature of freelance work is nonrecurrent activity by large numbers of participants.

In *Little Science, Big Science* Price has shown that most scientists who publish actually publish very little and that a small number of eminent scientists are responsible for producing far more than their proportionate share of the scientific literature. Extrapolating from patterns in physics and chemistry, Price estimates that over 50 percent of the scientific population that publishes at all writes one paper or a fraction thereof per individual lifetime, that 10 percent of the population is responsible for over 30 percent of all the papers written, and that only 3 percent of the population are highly productive, major contributors.[9]

These estimates are strikingly similar to my own for the film business. Over 50 percent of the freelance composers who score movies at all score only one project in a five-, ten-, or fifteen-year period; slightly more than 10 percent of the composers are responsible for over 30 percent of all the scores written for films; and a bare 3 percent of the occupation are of highly productive, major contributors

Similarly, producers, scriptwriters, directors, and cinematographers at work from 1973-74 to 1977-78 parallel this division of Hollywood's specialists into major and minor figures. Some may object that the five-year period, as shown in Table 10.1, is too short a span of time to tap the accumulation of credits and career points, that my data may underestimate specialists in the top tiers as well as in the middle areas. Table 10.2 and the accompanying "J-shaped curve" track the volume of work for four occupations from 1964-65 to 1977-78 (see Figure 10.1) (where number of filmmakers and number of films are the same, only *one* "point" on the J curve is plotted). Table 10.3 supplements Table 10.2 by dividing each occupation into four tiers starting with single-credit members in tier 4 in the lower row and then allocating the remaining credits equally into three productivity tiers. This crude and conservative allocation avoids overlapping categories and simply illustrates the pyramid effect of more and more credits to fewer and fewer participants as we move from the periphery to the middle area of tier 3, and then into the very active and prominent tiers 1 and 2. The pattern for the fifteen-year period parallels the productivity distributions for the five years.

Two points of interest emerge from this analysis. It is clear that over 50 percent of the Hollywood film community that has the good fortune to work in movies at all works only once, as shown in Tables 10.2 (row 1) and 10.3 (tier 4). Over 65 percent of the producers, 60 percent of the movie writers, 56 percent of the directors, and 57 percent of the cinematographers have a single credit. Not only are the lower plateaus of the business heavily populated, but career movement to the adjacent volume or credit plateaus appears to be very difficult. Aspirants are winnowed away as 951 screenwriters have one credit but only 217 have the second point in their activity line; 114 moved to the third film but the attrition is sudden with only 46 with four credits over the fifteen years. Of course, only a cohort study of the successive paths taken by members of these occupations could reveal the organization of attrition. Insofar as these aggregate data yield information on "drop out" rates, I again suggest the following: this business is an activity which has a low degree of recurrent work for most of its members, a correspondingly high degree of career failure for many, and very low probabilities of moving from tiers 4 and 3 into the top tiers 2 and 1.

Second, the picture for Big Hollywood resembles Price's observations of scientific populations and their productivity. Approximately 15 percent of the members are likely to be responsible for over 40 percent of the credited work—that is, work that publicly counts on the cultural record.[10]

Among film directors, for instance, 17 percent—or 146 of a total of 835

TABLE 10.2
Volume of Film Work by Occupational Specialty: Hollywood
1964–65 to 1978–79

Volume	Producers	Directors	Screenwriters	Cinematographers
1	831	470	951	335
2	200	153	217	86
3	107	66	114	39
4	39	52	46	23
5	17	26	35	25
6	20	24	9	16
7	10	13	7	10
8	11	11	4	11
9	6	6	0	9
10	4	5	3	2
11	1	3	0	4
12	3	1	1	3
13	2	3	0	2
14	1	2	0	7
15	0	0	0	4
16	1	0	0	3
17	0	0	0	2
18	0	0	0	1
19	0	0	0	2
20	0	0	0	2
21	0	0	0	0
22	2	0	0	0
23	0	0	0	1
24	0	0	0	1
25	0	0	0	0
26	0	0	0	1
27	0	0	0	1
28	0	0	0	1
29	0	0	0	1
TOTALS	1255	835	1387	592

Source: Weekly Variety, October 1964 to September 1973; Variety Anniversary
Issues, Volumes 41 to 46, from October 1973 to September 1979.

(Table 10.3, tiers 1 and 2)—directed four or more projects for a total of 877
film credits or 47 percent of all the work in Hollywood during the fifteen
years. Based on productivity, some of the major figures in this occupation
are Sidney Lumet, Gordon Douglas, Arthur Hiller, Richard Fleischer, Robert
Altman, Jack Smight, Robert Aldrich, Blake Edwards, Martin Ritt, Lee
Thompson, Stuart Rosenberg, and Brian DePalma.

Similarly, only 14 percent of the tightly organized cinematographers in
Hollywood, or 84 of the 592 people with film credits, worked on 6 or more
projects during these years and captured over 950 assignments (50 percent).

FIGURE 10.1
Cinematographers, Directors, Screenwriters, Producers: Number of
Filmmakers and Films

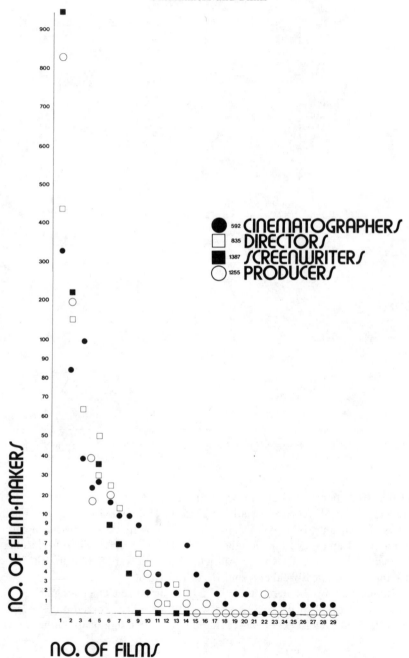

TABLE 10.3

Four Occupations and Four Tiers: 1964–65 to 1977–78

	1255 PRODUCERS	835 DIRECTORS	1387 SCREENWRITERS	592 CINEMATOGRAPHERS
TIER 1				
SPAN OF CREDITS*	6–22	7–14	5–12	14–36
N CREDITS TOTAL	519	395	352	502
% CREDITS	.22	.21	.16	.28
N PERSONS	61	44	59	27
% PERSONS	.05	.05	.04	.04
TIER 2				
SPAN OF CREDITS	3–5	4–6	3–4	6–13
N CREDITS TOTAL	562	482	526	461
% CREDITS	.24	.26	.23	.25
N PERSONS	163	102	160	57
% PERSONS	.13	.12	.11	.10
TIER 3				
SPAN OF CREDITS	2	2–3	2	2–5
N CREDITS TOTAL	400	504	429	506
% CREDITS	.17	.27	.19	.28
N PERSONS	200	219	217	173
% PERSONS	.16	.26	.16	.29
TIER 4				
SPAN OF CREDITS	1	1	1	1
N CREDITS TOTAL	831	470	951	335
% CREDITS	.36	.25	.42	.19
N PERSONS	381	470	951	335
% PERSONS	.66	.56	.69	.57

*"CREDITS" are defined as one individual working on a project; one project can have multiple credits for personnel in a single occupational category.

The big names in this line of activity are Fred Koenekamp, Joseph Biroc, Harry Stradling, Jr., Philip Lathrop, Laszlo Kovacs, Lucien Ballard, Victor Kemper, Robert Surtees, Richard Kline, Frank Phillips, John Alonzo, and Michel Hugo. All of these men are in the top tier, having worked on 15 or more films during these years; all are well connected to many major film producers and directors, and all are elected members of The American Society of Cinematographers.

The leading writers of Hollywood-made films are Lorenzo Semple Jr., Stirling Silliphant, Neil Simon, James Barrett, Peter Stone, Francis Coppola, Woody Allen, Bill Walsh, Alvin Sargent, Dalton Trumbo, and Blake Edwards, to mention some of the highly productive members of the top tier (tier 1) with five or more credits to their names.[11] These leading writers, some of whom are also directors, constitute 4 percent of all those with screenwriting credits; they did 16 percent of all the films made in Hollywood. Together with the adjacent tier 2, or those with three to four credits in fifteen years, they account for 40 percent of all the films written. Thus, a highly productive 15 percent wrote two out of every five projects.

For the producers of films, small numbers also dominate the Hollywood scene, as I have shown throughout. Five percent of the filmmakers have their names on 22 percent of the work; 60 individual producers or producer teams (such as Zanuck and Brown) are credited with over 500 projects from 1964-65 to 1977-78. Those with a shorter credit list of three to five projects (Table 10.3, tier 2) still capture a moderately large chunk of the production market: 163 filmmakers did 562 of the credits, or 13 percent of those just below the top tier put together approximately one out of every four films. The major names in the top tiers are familiar, as they should be. They are Elliott Kastner, Ray Stark, Jennings Lang, Blake Edwards, Robert Daley, Chartoff and Winkler, Zanuck and Brown, Hal Wallis, Joseph Levine, Ron Miller, Bill Anderson, and others.

Consider again that the distribution of people by projects in each line of work shown in Table 10.3 cannot be described independently of the composite transactions between specialists. Each occupation depends upon other occupations for various types of resources: personnel, capital, expertise, legitimacy, visibility, and so forth. The sum total of mutual interlocks of personnel by productivity tiers forms the composite transactions. The "composites" bridge the gap between individualistic and collectivistic explanation: for credits are experienced by the individual and measurable in the individual but cannot occur except by reference to ties and, generally, to questions of what specialists with what level of productivity are linking up, in some recurrent fashion, with other specialists to produce a large number of projects together.

Generally data on the composite transactions between directors and cinematographers, producers and directors, and producers and screenwriters sup-

TABLE 10.4
Composite Transactions: Four Tiers of Directors and Cinematographers,
1964–65 to 1978–79

Directors	Cinematographers				Ties
	Tier 1 (14–29)	Tier 2 (6–13)	Tier 3 (2–5)	Tier 4 (1)	
Tier 1[a] (7–14)	43%	29%	23%	5%	100% (395)
Tier 2 (4–6)	35%	29%	23%	13%	100% (474)
Tier 3 (2–3)	23%	24%	35%	18%	100% (486)
Tier 4 (1)	12%	21%	31%	36%	100% (438)
				TOTAL	1793[b]

[a] Productivity tiers are from Table 10-3.

[b] Total ties are less than total number of projects due to no listing of the personnel on the credits. There are 1881 films and in 88 cases the film director or cinematographer is not listed. The data are complete for 96 percent of the cases. Source: Variety October 1964 to September 1979.

port the view that the film industry is loose and small enough to be interlocked at the upper reaches of its commercial life. The tables suggest that a large number of productions are a result of transactions among the most active members of the film community. The data even suggest that the organization of work takes on the characteristics of a coordinated elite. For example, over 70 percent of the most active film directors work with the top two tiers of Hollywood's elite cinematographers. The second tier directors with four to six credits derive over 60 percent of their credits with the same active set of cinematographers, and together these central figures are credited with one-third of all film work in Hollywood (588 of the 1,793 credits, as underlined in Table 10.4).

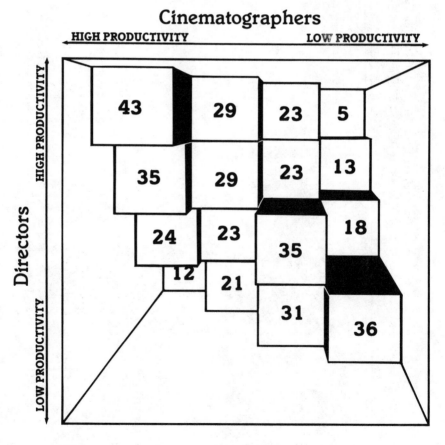

FIGURE 10.2
Composite Transactions: Four Tiers of Directors and Cinematographers,
1964–65 to 1978–79

Producers and directors are a special case. They are the key nodes of the freelance system because of the intersection of the business-entrepreneurial system and the artistic-craft system. Of the 61 film producers credited with six or more films from 1964-65 to 1978-79, 65 percent worked with directors in the top two tiers, as shown in Table 10.5. Over half of the ties of producers in the second tier are with the same set of active directors. These highly active film producers made one out of every two Hollywood feature films in this period—or 946 out of a total of 1,847 credits. Nearly one out of every three projects was directed by a freelancer in the top two tiers. By way of contrast, filmmakers with only a single credit contributed almost one-third to Hollywood's productivity—591 films; and about half of those projects were directed

FIGURE 10.3
Composite Transactions: Four Tiers of Producers and Directors,
1964–65 to 1978–79

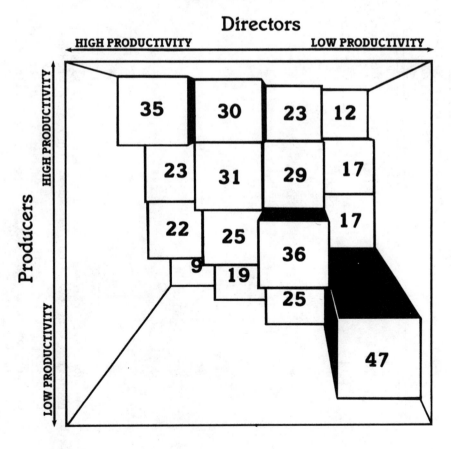

TABLE 10.5

**Composite Transactions: Four Tiers of Producers and Directors,
1964–65 to 1978–79**

	Directors				
	Tier 1 (7–14)	Tier 2 (4–6)	Tier 3 (2–3)	Tier 4 (1)	Ties
Producers					
Tier 1[a] (6–22)	35%	30%	23%	12%	100% (476)
Tier 2 (3–5)	23%	31%	29%	17%	100% (470)
Tier 3 (2)	22%	25%	36%	17%	100% (310)
Tier 4 (1)	9%	19%	25%	47%	100% (591)
				TOTAL	1847[b]

[a]Productivity tiers derived from Table 10.3 taking only the producer listed either first on the project's credits or the person with the most producer credits over the fifteen-year period.

[b]Total ties are less than total number of projects due to no listing of personnel as producer and/or director of the project. There are 1881 films and in 34 cases the producer and/or director is not listed. The data are complete for 98 percent of the cases. Source: Variety, 1964–65 to 1978–79.

by individuals with only a single credit. Thus it would appear that Big Hollywood is a recurrent set of interlocks among specialists and Little Hollywood is an isolated series of nonrecurrent ties among one-shot directors working with one-shot filmmakers.

I have suggested that the business is divided into center and periphery because there are (a) many employers but few with great market power or resources, and (b) few freelancers with the demand power enabling them to act as monopolists in the freelance sale of their particular types of talent and expertise. Perhaps a few of the stronger guilds such as the cinematographers can act to limit the number of new entrants into their occupation, but such power is rare in most lines of freelancing. The dearth of single credits for cinematographers, at least in comparison to screenwriters, probably reflects the entry barriers, task structure, and sponsorship activities among the much more restricted cinematographers' guild. Thus, screenwriters with one film credit in these fifteen years are tied into the Hollywood system at all levels through their work with producers. Not surprisingly, film producers with a single credit are jointly tied to single-credit screenwriters in over half of their transactions. But producers with only two credits also pick up the services of writers on their first film (44 percent) and second film (21 percent). The heavy hitters hire heavy hitters however, and the top two tiers of filmmakers and screenwriters are linked, as shown in Table 10.6. Producers with six or more career credits recurrently hire writers with three or more films on over half of their projects. Tier 2 producers spread their accounts over the range of screenwriters: nearly half are picked from the top two tiers, and approximately a third of their work is with writers who have only one feature credit in the fifteen-year period.

The disproportionate distribution of names on the credit crawls and the interlocking of major contributors with major contributors and minor figures with minor figures underlines the industry's deeply entrenched pattern of social and economic behavior. When we compare the brief five-year period of work (Table 10.1), the twelve-year period (Table 10.2), and then fifteen-year period (Tables 10.2-10.6), we see a stability of work distribution and composite transactions. While the identity of the high and low performers may shift due to either upward or downward career mobility, the distance between the top tiers and the periphery remains essentially constant.

It would take us too far afield to discuss even briefly the personnel, credits, and resultant networks of cooperation spanning Hollywood's other occupations, but we expect freelance social organization to produce remarkably similar work lines and experiences among art directors, film editors, sound editors, production managers, and production designers. It is safe to predict that the future of Hollywood will be decisively shaped by the forces discussed in this and preceding chapters and by the consistent manner in which multiple

TABLE 10.6
Composite Transactions: Four Tiers of Producers and Screenwriters, 1964–65 to 1978–79

	Screenwriters				
Producers	Tier 1 (5–12)	Tier 2 (3–4)	Tier 3 (2)	Tier 4 (1)	Ties
Tier 1[a] (6–22)	24%	30%	18%	28%	100% (475)
Tier 2 (3–5)	20%	28%	21%	31%	100% (457)
Tier 3 (2)	16%	19%	21%	44%	100% (311)
Tier 4 (1)	8%	17%	17%	58%	100% (554)
TOTAL					1797[b]

[a]Productivity tiers are from Table 10.3, also see footnote a., Table 10.5.

[b]Total ties are less than total number of projects due to no listing of the personnel on the credits. There are 1881 films and in 84 cases the film producer or screenwriter is not listed. The data are complete for 96 percent of the cases. Source: Variety 1964–65 to 1978–79.

FIGURE 10.4
Composite Transactions: Four Tiers of Producers and Screenwriters,
1964–65 to 1978–79

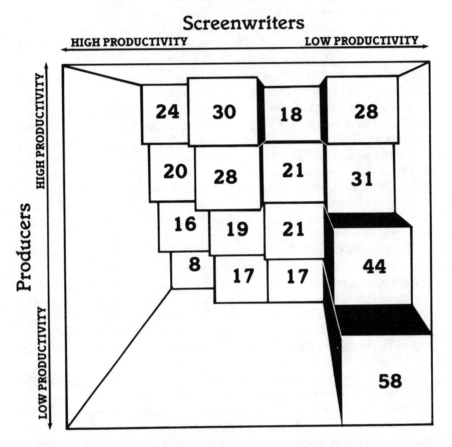

specialists react to these forces. These sketches of Big and Little Hollywood may produce different reactions in different observers, but what seems most important is the *relation* of several themes.

1. *Conspicuous Production.* Success is a whore to productivity. The industry's specialists are driven by both internally and externally generated pressures to produce visible evidence of their talent. In a glass house like the film industry, with its built-in glare of evaluation and publicity, conspicuous work is crucial to success. Because the ingredients that produce hit films are essentially ineffable and certainly impossible to define and measure, flimsy evidence and speculation become real data. Conventional judgments of a freelancer's current performances shape his behavior, because if a freelancer

wants to capitalize on his expertise, he is forced to comply with the conventional ways in which things are done in this work community. The pressures to produce are very real. So are pressures for self-promotion. The implied sanctions for failing to bend to either are equally real and can be seen everywhere. The interviews with film composers suggest that public "face" as well as private self-esteem are influenced by the continuity of demand for one's talent and skill. The reputation a person acquires, with himself, his self-definition, is a cumulative result of productivity and his own assessment of whether "his projects" are successful or not.

While my results confirm the importance of *positive* reinforcement among professionals in Hollywood, they provide a less complete picture of the possible consequences of failing to meet expectations. Still, the interviews suggest that anticipated or actual *negative* sanctions are powerful motivators for freelancers. Produce or perish. Insecurity as a motivating force varies with conditions in the job market as well as by location in the industry's tier structure. There is the fear of being perceived by others as a failure if their productivity declines. This creates the tension between being too selective on the one hand and "taking too much work" on the other.

2. *Conventionalization and Qualifications.* Hollywood's "social market" depends upon publicity and visibility-specific reward structures. In such a context, the uncertain and delayed recognition that commercial "hits" provide may be as important to a freelancer's productivity as the immediate recognition from employers and colleagues. Given the reward structure in the culture industries, being associated with a success may symbolize their qualifications and ties to the larger film enterprise for themselves and also boost their real market demand.

Three tendencies describe the process of identifying who is qualified to work. These tendencies influence how freelancers try to define themselves in a promotional marketplace. *Encapsulation* of work describes the tendency of the work community to focus on the film and its commercial fate, rather than the specialized skills and professional contributions the freelancer makes to the final product. Work is always embedded in the total project. It becomes difficult to assess the distinct contribution of one to the efforts of all. *Typecasting* designates the tendency of employers towards pigeonholing: the selective perception of a limited number of details about the freelancer, his identity, and his circumstances. Simplistic labels are attached to the person and his work; often his last film becomes his master identity for the time being—at least until his next hit or flop. For better or for worse the composer finds himself continually tagged as this or that kind of composer for this or that type of film assignment. Reshaping these reflected images is the hard work of trying to be selective and getting different projects, in different film genres, and with different artistic and compositional requirements. Diversity is a matter not only of craft perfection but deliberate behavior designed to improve and change the received labels that others will invariably apply to the freelancer. Finally, due to business pressures and bounded rationality, there is a tendency of producers toward what can be called *assimilation*. This improve and change the received labels that others will invariably apply to the freelancer. Finally, due to business pressures and bounded rationality, there is a tendency of producers toward what can be called *assimilation*. This happens when definitions of the freelancer become more coherent and consistent with the preoccupations or preconceptions of filmmakers eager to match only with equivalent personages.[12]

The notions of encapsulation, typecasting, and assimilation suggest how members of a work community seek short, concise, and easily understood conceptions of work and of one another. The tendency is to reduce to slogan, and such a reduction severely restricts the possibility of the freelancer promoting his own self-definitions. Getting the next job is the key and attrition quickly knocks off many directors, screenwriters, cinematographers, and composers from the very means by which they might be able to transform their circumstances and public identities. Goffman has noted that "defining situations as real certainly has consequences, but these may contribute very marginally to the events in progress . . . those who are in the situation ordinarily do not *create* this definition."[13] Ordinarily the freelancer must wait to see what happens to "his film" to learn what his previous situation really was. In this way, points of opportunity in a line of activity are known only in retrospect. Also the job definition may be firmly in place before the composer arrives on the scene. Thus, members differ in their power to influence the conspicuousness of their contributions.

The freelancer is also the carrier of messages into this prevailing climate of opinion. His job is not only to work but to convince others that they will be the beneficiaries of his expertise. Filmmakers perceive advantages from hiring one freelancer over another independently of the actual activities of the carrier. I have assumed more or less constant selection rules in employers' decisions. I have also assumed a ranking of freelancers for selection at any one point in time. They are ranked by filmmakers in terms of "track record," defined attributes, and perceived worth. Thus, filmmakers select the professionals from this ranking to fill the available projects. Since these productions are themselves ranked—by budget, production values, financial investment and risk—a freelancer's chances of getting hired reflect both his perceived work plus the estimated worth of specific film assignments.

Selection probabilities also change in response to the availability and kind of film being made in Hollywood. As more films are made on relatively similar budgets for instance, a much greater proportion of projects may go to the middle and even lower ranks. The evidence for 1964-65 to 1981-82 suggests that many qualified and talented freelancers may get a first chance, but few move from the fringes into the middle area, and fewer still get the credits that will send them into the top positions. Selection of many for nonrecurrent work in Little Hollywood can only occur if there is an accumulation of recurrent ties among the chosen few in Big Hollywood. It is the pattern of these expansive (and recurrent) and restrictive (and nonrecurrent) selections from filmmakers and freelancers that produces the overall pattern of rigidity and flexibility we observe. Attrition and disproportionate accumulation are the extremes of the market spectrum, as already sketched in the resource-alternative model.

On the restrictive side this means: (1) excluding freelancers who have produced little that is perceived as beneficial to Hollywood's "buyers" and employers of qualified talent; (2) excluding qualified freelancers who have had the opportunity to work with filmmakers but have produced few projects or visible accomplishments that have attracted the attention of significant others. On the expansive side this means: (1) favoring professionals in the technical subsystem who have produced work perceived as beneficial to entrepreneurs and others in the managerial system; (2) favoring those "sellers" of expertise and credentials who have worked within networks of "buyers" and who are associated with successes on these joint ventures.

3. *A Null Model of Status Attainment.* Calling any set of two or more joined points a "career" and the connecting lines "activities of selection" has allowed me to treat Hollywood's film industry as a population-transforming operation. Considering personnel by their television and feature film credits—their productivity during various periods—has allowed me to infer the existence of a primitive but effective sorting device by which both extremes of the freelance market are distributed. To all but the most pathologically romantic, it should be obvious that the effect of the transformation is a progressive attrition of candidates so that only a fraction of qualified and talented industry personnel get the chance for succeeding points in a line of activity and, as a final result, only a small number make it onto new and better plateaus of opportunity.

Throughout I've insisted that an accurate view of Hollywood must consider both sides of the market—*both* the supply of talent and expertise and the perceived demand for that talent. Since this framework comes close to advocating the "Matthew effect" identified by Robert Merton,[14] and since it sounds like a strategy for preserving the status of those who have already "arrived" in the inner circles, I would suggest a null model as follows: success or status attainment Hollywood-style is unrelated to productivity; it is unrelated to the dispersion of connections across multiple filmmakers; unrelated to the commercial success and visibility of the project in which one's work is embedded or encapsulated; unrelated to the strategy and tactics that a freelancer employs to influence others in this climate of opinion; and unrelated to the networks of collective action one forms and is, in turn, formed by. This weakness-of-everything model assumes that the process of "making it" into the top tiers is random. In any five-, ten-, fifteen-, or twenty-year period of filmmaking and hiring, every extant composer, for example, who scores a film has an equal, constant probability of success. In some lean years it may be a little harder to keep the continuity of activity going; in other years it may be a little easier, *but for everyone equally*. In sum, nothing that the freelancer does or undergoes really affects his chances in a population-transforming and resource-allocation process.

The irony is that the weakness-of-everything model is enthusiastically endorsed by many of Hollywood's participants simply to keep alive their estimations and hopes of hitting it big. The relative durability of such expectations in the face of inequality is a prominent feature of participants in the film industry specifically and the culture industries generally. The constant menace of not working combines with a nervous other-directedness, a looking for windfalls, and unreal expectations of the benefits of hustling. These expectations are a symptom of the instability of freelance structure. Someone always has a chance for making a name for himself in a hurry, as "films that can't miss" miss, as "losers" win, and as newcomers "break through" television work into the top tiers. From the point of view of the freelancers, a weakness-of-everything model may be a necessary stance for personal survival in a work world that is simultaneously predictable and chaotic.

4. *Moving beyond Members' Personal Versions*. In addition to surveying freelance composers' perceptions of work at different points in their career lines, I also developed independent sources of information on the total array of events in this occupational community. While W. I. Thomas's famous dictum concerning the definition of reality is a useful guide for determining members' interests and versions of what is happening to them and others, it is dangerous to link microlevel participants' views with macrolevel data and independent analysis. It is also risky for the student of Hollywood to assume that persons are their own best theorists. Nor should we assume that by telling us how they make decisions and choices in work situations they save us time in finding out for ourselves. The composers are not my research assistants on the scene when I cannot be there. They are practical actors who have to get on with their business and, only after that, report (reconstruct) what happened to them. To the extent that respondents moving from assignment to assignment focus primarily on issues relating to their particular self-interests while passing over problems confronting the entire occupation, this latter set of issues must be sought out independently by the investigator—whether or not respondents explicitly point them out.

Conceptualizing the interpersonal work life of the freelancing composer as a central node linking complex networks of exchange, information, and evaluation encourages us to move beyond the individual-as-unit research agenda in understanding social organization as symbolic interaction.[15] The aim has been to show how (1) macrolevel interactions and operations are consistently being performed by all participants in their dealings with each other and (2) how those larger-scale features have deeply personal, symbolic consequences for the individuals involved. Thus I have employed an interactionist view of social organization using multiple sources of data collection. The idea has been to approach the turbulance of the source (the film industry) with a corresponding variety in the sensing devices applied to it.[16] I have argued that composers' career concerns and short-run interests are indeed important in their subjective experiences of their turning points, strategic interactions with employers, and work satisfactions. However, there is overwhelming evidence that much of what goes on in Hollywood's film industry persists regardless of how professional composers, film producers, directors, writers, and cinematographers define it, feel about it and about each other. It may be that the comparatively stable distribution of work preserves a social order where its participants are in flux.

Career "status attainment" as a sum total of possessions, attributes, attributed deference (or derogation), is neither firmly frozen nor enduring; it is continually reshaped and reinforced or destroyed in a succession of publicly communicated actions and reactions. What is clear, at least, is that Hollywood is a social market defined by a consistent demand for "qualified" candidates and that freelancers are the promoters or entrepreneurs of their own "qualifications." They compete for the attention of filmmakers, a notoriously nosy, anxious, and interfering "audience" of potential employers. Freelancers are not self-made; their announced qualifications are selectively perceived, defined, and reacted to by significant others. The sources of this demand for symbolic proof of expertise are to be found in specialization and in the underlying tensions that reverberate in a business that is part art and part commerce.

The structure of work among freelancers and filmmakers has an orderly pattern and routinized dynamic. While interests and alliances are typically short-lived and new coalitions are continually being organized for each business enterprise, the distribution of productivity and influence is stable. Freelancers are influenced by the demands of powerful networks of filmmakers but are also able to serve their own ends and to achieve substantial autonomy over the short run as they are asked to do more and "better" work by more and "better" employers. Cumulative advantages for the chosen few lead to a gradual focusing in on the field of choices between preferred freelancers and preferred filmmakers. Their dependency on each other and their resource positions are structurally coincident, and their self-interest and work behavior are willfully matched. This leads to a narrowing of the field of freelancers labeled as "contributors," "hot," "bankable," but above all "qualified" to work by virtue of their conspicuous track record, connections, and calculable accomplishments. I have also provided detailed evidence suggesting that the number of ties which a freelancer maintains reflects his importance in this work system, and that a specialist tied to other active and important specialists is himself more important than one tied to an equal number of specialists on the periphery of the network. The varying access to network "centrality," resources, and alternatives in the film industry constitutes the organized means for building what Simmel called "the inevitably disproportionate distribution of qualifications and positions" in which "there are always more people qualified for superordinate positions than there are such positions."[17]

Notes

1. Carol Lawson, "Behind the Best Sellers: Steve Shagan," *New York Times Book Review,* (December 2, 1979).
2. Paul Baratta, "Bill Conti: He Put the Musical Punch in 'Rocky' and 'F.I.S.T.'," *Songwriter* (August 1978): 24–31.
3. Will Tusher, "Elite Cadre of H'W'D' Stuntmen Get the Bulk of Pic, TV Work," *Variety* (May 24, 1979). The estimates come from stuntman-turned-director Hal Needham, one of the 36 who belong to Stunts Unlimited. Needham says the monopoly and steep distribution is the result of "a field narrowed by expertise, not by discrimination."
4. On the dilemmas of role and career see Everett C. Hughes, *The Sociological Eye* (Chicago: Aldine, Atherton, 1971).
5. Productivity is a *proxy* for structural location in the labor marker of freelancing. Those in the *center* of Hollywood's action appear again and again in movie projects from 1964–65 to 1980–81. Those on the periphery are part of a barren structure of fleeting, nonrecurrent transactions. The center is blocked into networks; and networks differentially distribute attributes associated with rewards and resources. The latter in turn increase the freelancer's *cachet* and visibility in the publicity system linking back on market worth and increased productivity. The cycle is complete. But this success string can be easily broken as projects flop, "hotness" and visibility recedes in the social market of opinion, as kudos dries up, as filmmakers move to other more successful film scorers and market demand sags for particular composers. The model appears self-perpetuating and even optimistic at first glance; the reality is far more precarious and pessimistic, as the interviews with people in Hollywood show.
6. Composer Bill Conti was tightly linked to writer-producer-director Paul Mazursky. He scored a string of his work, including: *Blume in Love* (1973), *Harry and Tonto* (1974), *Next Stop Greenwich Village* (1976), and *An Unmarried Woman* (1978), which Mazursky wrote, directed, and coproduced. In 1976 Conti broke into the inner circles with his *Rocky* score and *Gonna Fly Now* tune; *Rocky* was directed by John Avildsen and produced by heavyweights Irwin Winkler and

Robert Chartoff who were turned down by one of the inner-circle composers and forced to go down the list. Agent Al Bart moved Conti into contention and consideration. The film was a tremendous hit and Conti's career took off. The following credits accumulated very quickly: he worked with Sylvester Stallone, of *Rocky* fame, on the Norman Jewison film *F.I.S.T.* (1978) and the Edward Pressman-coproduced *Paradise Alley* (1978). Then came *The Big Fix* (1979) produced by actor Richard Dreyfuss, *Dreamer* (1979), *Golden Girl* (1979) for Elliot Kastner, and *Rocky II* (1979), the sequel for producers Chartoff and Winkler, this time Stallone directing the project. Along the way, Chartoff and Winkler tapped Conti for their *Uncle Joe Shannon* (1978), with Maynard Ferguson doing the trumpet work. The same year, a busy Conti worked for director John Avildsen on his directed and coproduced project *Slow Dancing in the Big City* (1978). In 1977 and 1982 he directed (musically) the Academy Awards. "Every composer wants that assignment," he said in an interview with *The Hollywood Reporter's* Frank Barron in February 1978, "whether he admits it or not. And all he gets is scale." (Frank Barron, "Bill Conti's turning two more films amid other jobs." *The Hollywood Reporter,* February 21, 1978.) Conti may have been getting scale for the annual show, but his price was going up elsewhere after the success of *Rocky*. Asked by Paul Baratta in 1977 if Conti's fee skyrocketed after that film, Conti's agent, Al Bart, exclaimed, "It sure did. We get our biggest kick out of being able to raise someone's price. Like with Bill, we've more than tripled his price in less than a year. It's a very gratifying business to be in and one that is very unpredictable."

7. There are therefore often more people with credits than there are films. Where producers *recurrently* work together, they are coded as a team, as one "producer." Where they do not, unless otherwise noted, multiple producers working *once* in a given period are treated as single producers. I am therefore likely to overreport producers teams with single film credits. The error is one of inclusion: approximately 1 to 2 percent of the productivity rank by people, as in Tables 10.1 and 10.2 contain this overreporting. Despite the problems with multiple credits and my own caution in using the nonrecurrent category, one conclusion emerges with overwhelming clarity: the proportion of work done by people by volume category remains identical across specialties in these periods: (1) composers, 1964–65 to 1975–76; (2) producers, directors, cinematographers, and screenwriters, 1973–74 to 1977–78, as shown in Table 10.1; (3) the four specialties, 1964–65 to 1977–78, as shown in Table 10.2.

8. The American Film Institute's *American Film* contains materials on various industry participants, including filmmakers, directors, screenwriters, and cinematographers. See "Dialogue on Film: Chartoff-Winkler," *American Film* 2 (1977): 37–52. The trade-book business has also gotten into this act. See Michael Pye and Lynda Myles's uncritical but informative work on the new kids, *The Movie Brats: How the Film Generation Took Over Hollywood* (New York: Holt, Rinehart, & Winston, 1979).

9. J. Derek de Solla Price, *Little Science, Big Science* (New York: Columbia University Press, 1963).

10. In a different context, but one already evoked through the use of Price's important work, Edward Shils has observed of scientific and intellectual occupations: "The work itself becomes a work when it is presented in a conventionally complete form, when it takes a physical form capable of being received, assessed, and acknowledged." Edward Shils, "Intellectuals, Tradition, and the Traditions of

Intellectuals: Some Preliminary Considerations'' *Daedalus* 101 (1972): 21–34. Similarly, it is when a freelancer is recurrently *at work* within the structure of the film industry—that is, when the person becomes subject to the ongoing demands and sanctions of personnel outside his own occupational stratum—that we can appropriately speak of a Hollywood-made *career*.

11. William Froug, *The Screenwriter Looks at the Screenwriter* (New York: Dell, 1972). Some of the major figures in writing circles are interviewed at length in this volume.

12. The concepts of leveling, sharpening, and assimilation suggest that conspicuous productivity and identity promotion are constituted in part through Hollywood gossip and rumor. The "qualified candidate" is an emergent product, transformed over time according to a sequence of transactions, prospective readings, retrospective readings about "what he or she really did" on a project, "what happened" to the film, and so forth. When freelancers and filmmakers seek the "underlying patterns" to film work, they employ these procedures to explain a mass of hunches, wishes, "data," and assessments about who is talented enough to work on their films. The practical uses of leveling, sharpening, and assimilation are found in Aaron V. Cicourel, *The Social Organization of Juvenile Justice* (New York: Wiley, 1968), esp. pp. 332–36. See also Gordon W. Allport and Leo J. Postman, *The Psychology of Rumor* (New York: Henry Holt, 1947).

13. Erving Goffman, *Frame Analysis: An Essay on the Organization of Experience* (New York: Harper Colophon, 1974), p. 1–2.

14. Robert K. Merton, "The Matthew Effect in Science," in *The Sociology of Science: Theoretical and Empirical Investigations*, ed. Norman W. Storer (Chicago: University of Chicago Press, 1973), pp. 432–59. "For unto everyone that hath shall be given and he shall have abundance: but from him that hath not shall be taken away even that which he hath." See also Paul D. Allison and John A. Stewart, "Productivity Differences among Scientists: Evidence for Accumulative Advantage," *American Sociological Review* 39 (1974): 596–606.

15. These features of social ties are discussed by J. C. Mitchell, "Networks, Norms, and Institutions," in *Network Analysis Studies in Human Interaction*, ed. J. Boissevain and J. C. Mitchell (The Hague: Mouton, 1973), pp. 15–35.

16. Eugene Webb and Karl E. Weick, "Unobtrusive Measures in Organizational Theory: A Reminder," *Administrative Science Quarterly* 24 (1979): 650–59.

17. Kurt H. Wolff (ed.), *The Sociology of Georg Simmel* (Glencoe, Ill.: Free Press, 1950), pp. 300–303.

Index